NORTHERN IRELAND'S

CONTEMPORARY IRISH STUDIES

Series Editor Peter Shirlow (The Queen's University of Belfast)

Also available

James Anderson and James Goodman (eds)
Dis/Agreeing Ireland:
Contexts, Obstacles, Hopes

Edited by Frank Gaffikin and Mike Morrissey
City Visions:
Imagining Place, Enfranchising People

Paul Hainsworth (ed.)
Divided Society:
Ethnic Minorities and Racism in Northen Ireland

Denis O'Hearn
Inside the Celtic Tiger:
Irish Economic Change and the Asian Model

Peter Shirlow and Mark McGovern (eds)
Who are 'the People'?:
Unionism, Protestantism and Loyalism in Northern Ireland

Gerry Smyth
Decolonisation and Criticism:
The Construction of Irish Literature

Gerry Smyth
The Novel and the Nation:
Studies in the New Irish Fiction

NORTHERN IRELAND'S TROUBLES
The Human Costs

Marie-Therese Fay, Mike Morrissey
and Marie Smyth

Pluto Press

LONDON • STERLING, VIRGINIA

in association with

The Cost of the Troubles Study

First published 1999 by Pluto Press
345 Archway Road, London N6 5AA
and 22883 Quicksilver Drive, Sterling, VA 20166–2012, USA

British Library Cataloguing in Publication Data
A catalogue record for this book is available from the British Library

ISBN 0 7453 1379 5 hbk

Library of Congress Cataloging in Publication Data
Fay, Marie-Therese, 1973–
    Northern Ireland's troubles: the human costs/Marie-Therese
Fay, Mike Morrissey, and Marie Smyth.
        p. cm. — (Contemporary Irish studies)
    Includes bibliographical references (p.).
    ISBN 0–7453–1379–5 (hbk.)
    1. Northern Ireland—History. 2. Political violence—Social
aspects—Northern Ireland—History—20th century. 3. Political
violence—Economic aspects—Northern Ireland—History—20th
century. 4. Victims of terrorism—Northern Ireland—History—20th
century. 5. Violent deaths—Northern Ireland—History—20th
century. I. Morrissey, Michael, 1940– II. Smyth, Marie, 1953– III.
Title. IV. Series.
    DA990.U46 F39 1999
    941.6—dc21   98–45434
                                                             CIP

Designed and produced for Pluto Press by
Chase Production Services, Chadlington, OX7 3LN
Typeset from disk by Stanford DTP Services, Northampton
Printed in the EC by TJ International, Padstow

Contents

List of Tables

List of Figures

Acknowledgements

We wish to acknowledge the help of the following people:

Dr John Yarnell, Department of Public Health, Queen's University and the Health Promotion Agency; Dr Debbie Donnelly, NISRA; Wendy Hamilton, General Registry Office; Alison Hamilton, Central Services Agency; Ronnie McMillen, John Park, Social Services Inspectorate; Yvonne Murray, Linenhall Library; Andy White; Conor Barnes; Jonathan Blease; Alan Breen; Survivors of Trauma, Ardoyne; Greencastle Women's Group; Damien Gorman, An Crann/The Tree; Tony McQuillan, Northern Ireland Housing Executive; Staff in the Central Library, Belfast, Queen's University Library; David McKittrick; Professor John Darby; Dr Andrew Finlay, Trinity College Dublin; Dr Maggie Martin, Eastern Connecticut State University; Brandon Hamber, Centre for the Study of Violence and Reconciliation, Cape Town; Patrick Ball of the American Association for the Advancement of Science in Washington, DC for providing some of the international data; The Community Information Technology Unit, Belfast; The Centre for Childcare Research at the Queen's University of Belfast; Dr R. Scullion of the Central Statistics Unit; Arlene Healey from the Young People's Centre; John Park from the Social Services Inspectorate of the Department of Health and Social Services; Dr Brian Tipping, Research Services Ireland; young people from various communities in North and West Belfast, Derry and elsewhere contributed enormously to our understanding of their position; over sixty adult interviewees participated in our enquiries, and many gave us much by way of understanding of parental roles, and their experience. Dr Roger McGinty at INCORE provided feedback on a draft of the book. Our colleagues, Gwen Ford, Sarah Oakes and Mark Mulligan at The Cost of the Troubles Study, and fellow directors of The Cost of the Troubles Study, particularly David Clements, Brendan Bradley, John Millar, Hazel McCready, Sam Malcolmson, Linda Roddy, Mary Donaghy and Shelley Prue have provided assistance, guidance and feedback. Tracy Wong of the Urban Institute assisted with the statistical analysis. Others who offered feedback were Paul Morrissey, Mary Enright, Bel McGuinness, Marguerite Egin, and Dr Yallowly from the

Department of Public Health at the Queen's University of Belfast, who also provided useful suggestions about other research. We thank those who funded the research on which this book is based: the Central Community Relations Unit of the Central Secretariat; Making Belfast Work, North and West teams; the Special Support Programme for Peace and Reconciliation through the Northern Ireland Voluntary Trust; the Joseph Rowntree Charitable Trust; a private donation; Barnardo's Northern Ireland, Save the Children Fund; the Cultural Diversity Group of the Community Relations Council, the Belfast European Partnership Board and the Community Relations Council. Finally, we thank Roger van Zwanenberg and everyone at Pluto Press.

Introduction

The purpose of this book is to describe the human costs of Northern Ireland's Troubles, and to set those human costs in the historical, political, economic and social context of Northern Ireland. The book is organised in two main parts. The first part of the book provides a detailed context, both local and international, for the conflict and its human costs that are analysed in the second part. In this analysis, the demography of deaths in the conflict are discussed, and the geographical distribution of deaths and their relationship to other factors such as deprivation examined. Deaths are also analysed by perpetrating organisation and by the affiliations and other characteristics of those killed. Finally, Chapter 7 examines data on the impact of the Troubles on children and young people, and the conclusions look to the future of Northern Ireland in the light of the human costs incurred over the last 30 years.

The book is written in an atmosphere unprecedented in Northern Ireland. The cease-fires of 1994 ushered in a new sense of energy, possibility and determination for many people involved in understanding, participating or intervening in the Northern Ireland conflict. The declared end of violence on the part of both Loyalist and Republican paramilitaries removed a pressure to which we had become habituated in order to live with the relentless violence of the Troubles since the 1960s.

Yet in that new atmosphere, it became painfully clear how those cease-fires had come too late for many. The suffering of those who had lost family members, homes, parts of their bodies, peace of mind or the ability to sleep through the night, could begin to be explored. Until then, it was as if we dared not realise the extent of the damage in case we had to live with more of it.

A mother of five children in Beirut, cited by Raija-Leena Punamaki (1988: p. 4), said:

> Let's talk about psychology when the war is over. When the war is over, I will dream all those dreams I cannot afford to now... If I were to sit down and think of my emotional state, I would break down. You Europeans, you can have the luxury of analysing your feelings; we plainly have to endure.

1

For the first time in our adult lives in Northern Ireland, after the 1994 cease-fires, it seemed possible to turn our attention to exploring the issue of loss, and the suffering that many people had endured. An earlier study (Smyth and Hayes, 1994) shocked the researchers into the realisation that the depth and scale of suffering might well be greater than anyone imagined. Yet at the time the study was conducted, the violence was continuing. Under such conditions, the conduct of such research was very challenging, and the discourse about suffering and loss was highly polarised – and remains so. The suffering of one group may be dismissed and disqualified by referring to the suffering of another group on the 'other side', or to wrongs that have been done by the faction associated with those who had suffered. In that pre-cease-fire atmosphere – and indeed subsequently – there can be competition between groups and individuals for the position of 'those who had suffered most'. Implicit in this competition is the assumption that those who have lost the most, or had the largest number killed cannot be held morally culpable for any damage done by their side, since any wrongs can be seen as understandable retaliation. Such is the inhuman dynamic of armed conflict.

Repeatedly, those who have been bereaved have called for no retaliation. However, the voices of those who have lost most do not carry sufficient authority, and often go unheeded. Those who have been bereaved and injured, as we demonstrate in this book, are predominantly civilians, unconnected with paramilitary groups or security forces. They have often been randomly targeted. The loss and injuries inflicted are 'nothing personal' – it could happen to anyone. Therefore, the bereaved and injured have no basis on which they may influence the political process. They have no political clout, they do not have the capacity to wreck the prospects for peace, nor do they have the power to command the ears of politicians.

They are not a coherent group of people, they do not agree among themselves, they have been hurt by various people – Republican, Loyalist and security forces. They do not all want or feel comfortable with the same things, or with each other.

It was in that atmosphere, and with these concerns that a group of people with direct personal experience of loss in the troubles were invited by one of the researchers to meet in Belfast in order to explore some of these issues. The group that began to meet were diverse – people bereaved by Republicans, Loyalists, the security forces; disabled police officers. It was out of these meetings that The Cost of the Troubles Study – a Belfast-based recognised charity that researches and documents the impact of the Troubles on the population of Northern Ireland and beyond – was formed.

The Cost of the Troubles Study is a limited company, the directors of which are people bereaved and injured in the Troubles, working in partnership with researchers. The approach is participative action research, in which those with expertise based on personal experience participate in the management, design, data collection and analysis of the research. We wish to avoid the kind of alienation which can happen when researchers see people as containers of data, from which the data can be extracted and appropriated without further reference to those from whom they are extracted. The value of this collaboration between researchers and local experts must be judged on its fertility and this book is part of the produce of that partnership.

Our goal is to establish quality, well documented and scientific research on which work aimed at addressing the impact of the Troubles on the population can be based. To begin with, the project compiled an independent and cross-checked database of deaths in the Troubles since 1969, and much of the analysis presented in this book is based on that data. The project has also conducted 65 in-depth interviews with people across Northern Ireland, and these interviews have been audio-taped, transcribed and coded in NUD.IST.[1] A survey of 3,000 people across Northern Ireland has also been conducted, and both of these exercises will be written up for subsequent publication. A small project with children and young people has led to two publications, one by the young people and the second by one of the researchers (see Cost of the Troubles Study, 1998; Smyth, 1998).

A further goal is to produce materials that are accessible to the general public. For this reason, we have produced one exhibition on the effects of the Troubles on children and young people, and the young people have also produced a book on the same subject. We are committed to giving talks about our findings in local areas, and are exploring new ways in which we can present our work in clear, non-jargonised language, and in attractive and accessible forms. Our audience is the general public, as well as policy makers and other researchers.

A review of the late John Whyte's (1991) book, *Interpreting Northern Ireland*, leads to the observation that the conclusions of much of the scholarship on Northern Ireland are closely correlated with the background of those who reach the conclusions. There are few scholars from the Protestant tradition who reach conclusions that challenge the Unionist perspective, and few from the Catholic tradition whose conclusions would challenge the Irish Nationalist perspective. Impartiality is a stance that is perhaps unattainable in Northern Ireland. Are any of us above the situation? We are influenced – even if it is only to react against – our socialisation into a divided society. Researchers from outside Northern Ireland bring other influences to bear: the impact of the British media on international views on Northern Ireland; the impact of the Irish-American vote on perceptions of the conflict here. Research strategies that address rather than ignore this situation are necessary to the advancement of our understanding of the conflict itself.

By enlarging our research team to include those with personal expertise from both of the main traditions in Northern Ireland, we have attempted to move beyond the usual constraints and limits exposed on research by the background of the researchers. Conversely, we have tried to avoid the tendency that can emerge in 'mixed' groups to steer away from the most divisive issues. We remain concerned about the impact of the composition of the staff and research team on the research analysis, and it seems to us that we must continue to worry about and monitor these issues. Our goal is synthesis and inclusion, rather than some 'balance'. As we work, we become aware of other significant differences between us.

The analysis we produce made each us uncomfortable in various ways, and challenged assumptions we each had about the nature of the conflict, and the justifications we had used for our political conclusions. We remain committed to the integrity of the data, and have avoided the tendency to 'weed out', omit or explain away the data that challenged our views or beliefs. We have tried to face those discomforts, and we present in this book data and analysis that is uncomfortable in different ways for those in all political standpoints.

In this changing political atmosphere, we have anxieties about the use to which our research will be put, and the actions that it may be used to justify. Nonetheless, we are convinced that reliable and comprehensive audit of the damage done, with all its contradictions, can play a useful role in 'complicating' a picture that is all too often seen in simple, polarised, black and white terms. What emerges from our analysis is that no faction or political grouping in Northern Ireland has a monopoly on suffering, nor indeed has any grouping exclusive title to the most overcrowded piece of turf – the moral high ground. Our objective in the long run is to contribute to the synthetic picture of what has happened, a picture that can contain contradictions and paradoxes, and one that can include and connect seemingly opposing accounts.

The differences between us shape our perceptions for reasons that emerge from our analysis of the data. In Chapter 6, we present an analysis of the data on deaths by gender, where it becomes clear that males and females have materially different experiences of the Troubles. In Chapters 5 and 6, we present case studies of selected postal districts which illustrate that our experience of the Troubles is shaped by where we live. Yet we discuss the Troubles as if our experience can be or should be undifferentiated, and we attribute failure to see another's point of view to narrow-mindedness, when there are real material differences that have shaped our perceptions and lead us to conflicting views. An understanding of these multiple and various realities of the Troubles will, we hope, lead to an improvement in our capacity to recognise and accept realities other than the one we live in. Ultimately, our goal must be to create a common account of the Troubles which includes all accounts in a larger, complex and perhaps contradictory picture. We hope that our work will make a positive contribution to that end.

Many of us, including those working as researchers or providing services to vulnerable people, have operated during the last three decades by not mentioning the Troubles. When the Troubles come to your door in the form of bereavement or other forms of loss, this is a luxury you no longer have. Our work on the data on deaths has changed us. Screening through hundreds and thousands of lines of data, the thought that every line of data used to be a human being with a future, a home, a family, makes work on the data emotionally demanding. It is particularly hard when one comes across data on the death of a child, or the death of someone we know. We are convinced that it is important to maintain this relationship with the data, and that it is crucial that we avoid seeing the data we present in this book as simply sets of numbers. We work closely with the relatives and neighbours of many of those whose deaths are included in this analysis. This keeps us focused on the real priorities.

If we are to build a peaceful society, the hurts of the past cannot be swept under the carpet. If we are to have a society based on justice, then those who have suffered must be a central concern. If we are to have a society based on humanitarianism, then we must go out of our way to comfort, support and listen to those who have lost most. If we are to move beyond the divisions of the present, then we must learn to listen to those who have been hurt in the name of politics or causes we support. And when we are listening, we must learn to allow our hearts to soften in compassion. Commitment is also necessary in order to make good what can be made good, and ease the pain of what cannot. This work is also a way of ensuring that we never forget why peace – if we achieve it – is so precious.

Just after we completed the first draft of this book, a bomb exploded in Omagh on 15 August 1998, killing 29 people. It was the largest number of people killed in a single incident in Northern Ireland. In the tragic aftermath of that event, it seems clearer than ever that the will of the people is for an end to violence. People have suffered enough. The cruelty of that bomb seems to have reaffirmed the will for peace. To add 29 and two unborn babies' names to our database in a single sitting was hard to do. To realise the long and painful road that faces the family, neighbours and friends of those killed and injured is to realise that it can never truly be over. Our hope is that no more people have to embark on that road.

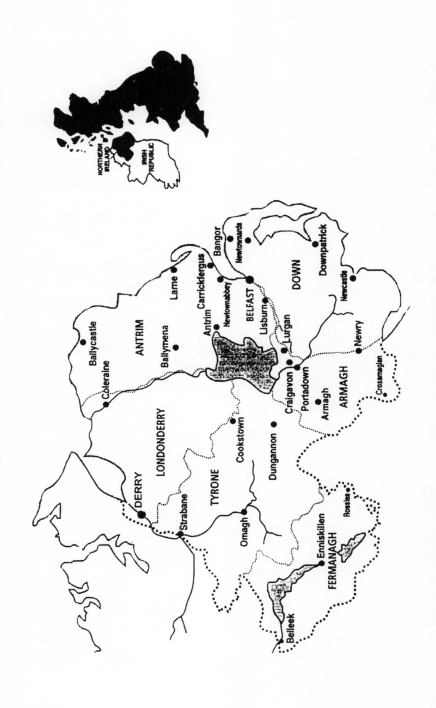

CONTEXT

Outlines of Protagonists

Nationalist paramilitaries are revolutionaries dedicated to the overthrow of British rule in Ireland and the establishment of an independent Irish nation state throughout the island. They see themselves as conducting a 'long war' of attrition against the British State and regard British security forces as legitimate targets in a war of national liberation. (McGarry and O'Leary, 1993)

Provisional Irish Republican Army (Provisional IRA)

The split in the Republican movement in 1970 into two competing factions, the Official and Provisional IRA, had profound consequences for Northern Ireland. The largest and more militarist faction was the Provisional IRA. Their birth was a direct response to the sectarian violence that erupted in Belfast and Derry in 1969. The Provisionals quickly built on the strength of the local defence committees, which were established in the Catholic ghettos of West Belfast in August 1969 to protect Catholic areas from Loyalist attacks. The Provisional IRA soon became recognised as defenders of the Catholic people and attracted large numbers of young Catholic volunteers to their ranks. Their analysis of the conflict in Ireland was simple. British presence in Ireland was the root cause of all conflict on the island. Only a British withdrawal would address the problem. What the IRA analysis failed to acknowledge was the existence of a Protestant community in Northern Ireland that is vehemently opposed to Irish unification.

By 1970 the Provisionals were fighting a war with the British Army. They firmly believed that the British would weaken under a sustained bombing and shooting campaign. A shortage of arms and ammunition was soon addressed with help from Dublin and the United States. By mid-1970 their strength was estimated at around 1,500 activists (Flackes and Elliott, 1994). The structure of the organisation duplicated the military organisation of the old IRA of the 1920s through the use of battalions, commanders and brigade staff. The large number of volunteers was reflected in the increase of violence in 1971. In the six months between January and July the IRA was responsible for most of the 304 explosions (ibid.) and the deaths of 32 people. Internment in August 1971 was designed to capture activists and known sympathisers of the IRA. The government believed that violence would be greatly reduced if the most experienced members of the IRA were arrested and jailed. The outcome was very different. Instead of weakening the organisation and its support base, internment alienated huge sections of the Catholic population throughout Northern Ireland, increased support for the IRA and thereby increased the violence. In the remaining five months of 1971, 152 people lost their lives in the violence.

By 1972, the IRA had assembled a wide diversity of weapons, and events such as the shooting dead of 13 unarmed civilians on Bloody Sunday in Derry by the Parachute regiment of the British Army strengthened their support base. In June 1972 the IRA declared a cease-fire and its leaders were flown to London for talks with the British government. These talks proved unproductive and the cease-fire collapsed. The IRA moved their bombing campaign to Great Britain, killing and maiming people in the pub bombings in Birmingham. By the late 1970s security force pressure on the IRA forced them to undergo large-scale reorganisation. Active Service Units were introduced which consisted of small teams of only two or three members. There was very little exchange between ASUs, thus making the organisation less permeable to infiltration by informers. The brigade quartermaster tightly controlled access to weapons. ASUs varied widely in size and operational remit and information about them is hard to verify.

By 1980 the army had estimated IRA strength as 500 operatives throughout Northern Ireland. The deaths of ten men on hunger strike in 1981 again brought increased support and sympathy for the IRA cause from United States, Europe and Libya. It was suggested the IRA were raising over £6 million a year, with £1 million per year coming from the United States (ibid.). The bombing campaigns in the United Kingdom increased and in 1984 the IRA bombed the Grand Hotel in Brighton almost killing the British Prime Minister Margaret Thatcher and members of her Cabinet. The Enniskillen bombing in 1987 killed eleven civilians. The following day the IRA expressed their 'deep regret' for the bomb, but the outrage both nationally and internationally gave the Republicans cause for serious reconsideration of IRA strategy. Throughout the later 1980s the organisation made a series of major mistakes that cost the lives of more civilians. When the IRA declared a cease-fire in 1994, the organisation had been responsible for 1,684 deaths, 58 per cent of all those killed due to the Troubles in Northern Ireland (McGarry and O'Leary, 1993).

> They have killed and injured more people than any other agency and imposed immense economic damage on the region, launched bombing campaigns in the United Kingdom and Europe, assassinated key members of the British elite and came close twice to killing the British Prime Minister and Cabinet. Their power persuaded the British authorities to negotiate with them in 1972 and 1975. Active membership at the beginning of the 1990s was estimated at between 500 and 2,000 but they enjoy wider if passive and minority support within the Nationalist community. (McGarry and O'Leary, 1993: p. 24)

The IRA has also been involved in regulating deviant behaviour and drug trafficking in local communities, in the context of poor relationships between the RUC and local Catholic communities, and a consequent lack of local policing. Some local communities looked to the IRA to control anti-social behaviour, but their use of physical force in the form of punishment beatings and shootings also led to a strong reaction within sections of local communities and in the wider society about their activities in this field. Repeated calls for an end to punishment beatings and allegations that they constitute a breach of the IRA cease-fire have been directed at Sinn Féin in the talks process.

Controversy has also surrounded the nature of the link between the IRA and Sinn Féin. Some Unionists have argued that membership of Sinn Féin is synonymous with IRA membership, concluding that Sinn Féin is not seriously engaged in democratic politics. Whilst the relationship between the two organisations is necessarily close, it seems clear that a separation exists between the two.

Over the period of the Troubles the nature of IRA violence and the targets of that violence have changed. In the early and mid-1970s bombing of city centres was the predominant feature of IRA violence. This was accompanied by high levels of street violence. By the 1980s the killing of local security forces was a focus of their activity, and by the late 1980s, for example, they targeted construction companies undertaking work for the security forces. By the early 1990s, the IRA were placing large bombs to damage commercial centres, and when the peace process began, IRA violence seemed to be turned on or off according to the progress of the talks.

Official Irish Republican Army (Official IRA)

In the Republican movement in 1969 there was strong support for a shift in emphasis to political action mainly because of the lack of support for the border campaign in 1956–62. By political action the leadership of the Official IRA meant having candidates elected to Parliaments in London, Belfast and Dublin on a leftist, broadly Marxist, policy. At the Sinn Féin Ard Fheis (Annual Conference) in 1970 those who advocated this new approach failed to get the majority support and a split occurred. The Official IRA also waged armed struggle against the British state in competition with the Provisional IRA. Each side claimed to be the true inheritor of 1916 and the Official IRA claimed to be able to hold 70 per cent of the total IRA volunteers when the Provisional IRA broke away. Under the leadership of Cathal Goulding, the Officials argued that its attacks were purely defensive. After the split, the tension between Officials and Provisionals was intense. Between 1970 and 1971, feuds between the two groups took the form of gun battles on the streets of Belfast. In 1970 it was estimated that the Official IRA had 600 members in Northern Ireland, but the Provisionals very quickly became the larger of the two factions.

Whereas the policy of internment strengthened the support base of the Provisional IRA, it undoubtedly weakened the Official IRA. Many of its key members were arrested.

> Internment created extra problems for Official IRA because it stirred up hostility towards the British authorities and the NI Government on a massive scale. It was an emotion more geared to IRA strategy than the politically orientated approach of Cathal Goulding. (Flackes and Elliott, 1994, p. 251)

In the early 1970s, Official IRA violence was mainly directed at the security forces. In May 1972 the organisation declared a cease-fire, with its leader Goulding arguing that paramilitary activity was dividing the working class and that class politics between Catholics and Protestants on issues such as housing and employment should be jointly developed. In 1975 the Official IRA again became involved in violence when a bitter feud broke out between them and the newly formed Irish Republican Socialist Party. Since then the Officials have gradually ceased to be a significant paramilitary organisation. It has been claimed that in the early 1980s they were still involved in killings, armed robberies and intimidation, and contrary to other beliefs were still very well armed (Browne, 1982). The relationship between the Official IRA and the Workers' Party has been one of controversy in the Republic of Ireland. In the 1980s and 1990s, government Ministers and other party leaders in the Republic have consistently argued that almost all of the Official IRA members were members of the Workers' Party. This controversy was thought by many commentators to have caused the split in the Workers' Party in 1992, which led to the formation of the Democratic Left.

Irish National Liberation Army (INLA)

From 1975 to 1987 the IRA faced one minor rival within the Nationalist camp – the Irish National Liberation Army. The INLA is the military wing of the Irish Republican Socialist Party. This is another breakaway faction of the Official IRA. Indeed many of the INLA members were former Official IRA members who were disillusioned at the direction of the Official IRA and left the organisation. INLA members thus tended to be older and more experienced. Claiming to be a Marxist-style liberation army, the INLA maintains that class unity could only come about after the national struggle had been won. The stated aim of the organisation is to end the British political, economic and military presence in the island of Ireland. Many of its attacks have been directed at the security forces. The main strongholds of the INLA have been in Belfast and South Derry. The organisation soon gained a reputation for its extreme ruthlessness. In 1979 it admitted responsibility for the assassination of Conservative MP Airey Neave, Shadow Secretary of State for Northern Ireland. In 1981 it killed more people than the IRA. Throughout its very bloody history, INLA activity has involved attacks directed against Loyalist paramilitaries and internal feuding.

In 1982 it was said to be responsible for nearly 30 deaths in Northern Ireland. One of its most extreme acts of violence was the bombing of the Dropping Well pub in Ballykelly, County Derry on 6 December 1982. Seventeen people were killed in this attack which was the second highest death toll in any incident during the Troubles. The supergrass system in the 1980s weakened the INLA. On the evidence of one informer, 27 people were arrested and, although 25 were later released, the security forces gathered a great deal of intelligence information on the organisation. The INLA has been a faction-ridden organisation. In 1987 it almost destroyed itself in a very bitter and bloody feud with a breakaway group calling itself the Irish People's Liberation Organisation (IPLO). Twelve people died in this feud and two priests eventually acted as mediators in order to stop the killings. The end of the feud signalled a period of low-level activity for the INLA but by the late 1980s it had reorganised and was estimated to have roughly 50 active members.

Irish People's Liberation Organisation (IPLO)

The Irish People's Liberation Organisation was a breakaway faction of the INLA. This group had tried unsuccessfully to disband the INLA-IRSP (Irish Republican Socialist Party). Their main strength had been in the Divis area of Belfast. In its short history the IPLO was involved in sectarian killings, the most notable being the killing of George Seawright, a prominent Loyalist. In the 1980s it was accused of being heavily involved in drug dealing. In 1992 a bitter feud developed within the IPLO between members who considered themselves 'Army Council' and the 'Belfast Brigade'. Jimmy Brown, leader of the IPLO since 1987, was the first victim of this feud. Three other members were also shot dead. At the end of that year, the IRA was alleged to have used some 100 of its own members to disperse the IPLO on the grounds that it was involved in drug dealing. Within a week, both factions of the IPLO announced their disbandment.

The Real Irish Republican Army (Real IRA)

The Real IRA is a Republican paramilitary splinter group that broke away from the IRA in November 1997. It was formed out of an IRA Convention in Gweedore, Co. Donegal. The Convention was called by IRA dissidents unhappy with the peace process and the decision of Sinn Féin to sign up to the Mitchell Principles on democracy and non-violence. At this Gweedore Convention the majority voted to continue the peace process but a minority of extremists rejected this majority decision and walked out to form the Real IRA. The Real IRA has no electoral mandate nor is it likely to seek one, since it opposes the electoral approach adopted by Sinn Féin. It is estimated that the Real IRA has little popular support, and what support it had was damaged by the bomb in Omagh.

At the Gweedore debate, a leading dissident was forced to resign his position on the twelve-person Army Executive. This man is now a key figure in the Real IRA. He was formerly the Provisional IRA's quartermaster general, in charge of weapons, explosives and ammunition, much of which was imported from Libya in the 1980s. This man is thought to have formed the Real IRA along the lines of Provisional IRA, in that it has an Army Executive and an Army Council. Other influential Provisional IRA figures who have rejected the Republican peace strategy have joined the Real IRA. These men were reputedly top bomb makers in the Provisional IRA and therefore the Real IRA has substantial bomb making capability. The Real IRA's main strength is in the Republic of Ireland. Security sources in the Republic estimate that the group has over 30 experienced former Provisional IRA members, some of whom are from the border areas in the North, especially south Armagh. The group has sought to recruit among university students in Dublin and working-class youths in areas such as Dundalk and Newry. Estimates of total membership vary widely from about 70 to 175, with many analysts believing the figure to be about 100 (Boyne, 1998).

In the context of overwhelming support for peace witnessed by the May 1998 referendums in Northern Ireland and the Republic of Ireland, the Real IRA continued with the armed struggle to force a British withdrawal and Irish re-unification. The Real IRA adopted some of the tactics of the Provisional IRA in that it has sought to attack the North's economic infrastructure. By setting off bombs in town centres, it has tried to inflict casualties on the security forces in Northern Ireland. The Real IRA has sought to fund its campaigns by armed robbery and has also attempted to plant incendiary and car bombs in the United Kingdom.

The first action of the Real IRA, in September 1997, was a bomb attack in Markethill, Co. Armagh. In January 1988 the RUC intercepted a 500 lb bomb in Banbridge, Co. Down. The Real IRA succeeded in bombing Banbridge in July 1997, injuring 35 people and causing £10 million worth of damage to the town. In May 1997, one of its members, Ronan McLoichlainn, was shot dead by Gardai during an attempted robbery. The group also engaged in a gun attack on Lurgan police station in August 1997 although it is thought they have limited access to firearms.

In the longer term, the Real IRA seek, through the use of violence, to force a British withdrawal from Ireland. In the shorter term their aim seems to be to put Sinn Féin under pressure in the peace process. Real IRA operations have been timed to undermine specific moves in the peace process. Their intent is to prove that Sinn Féin cannot deliver peace or the goal of Irish re-unification in the peace process. Some also believe that the Real IRA aim to provoke a Loyalist backlash. Had the Omagh bombing caused only Protestant deaths, the Loyalist paramilitaries could have retaliated with a massacre of innocent Catholics and the Provisional IRA would have been put under enormous pressure to break their cease-fire and retaliate. This would have left the peace process in ruins and would have ensured a return to violence.

On 15 August 1998, a car bomb exploded in the market town of Omagh, killing 28 civilians immediately – one died later of injuries – and injuring more than 200. It was the worst single atrocity in the 30 years of violence in Northern Ireland. The Real IRA (Oglaigh na hEireann) admitted responsibility.

The world-wide revulsion at the Omagh bomb forced the Real IRA to call a cessation of operations in September 1998. The Provisional IRA warned them to disband immediately and the Dublin and London governments announced tough new security measures to permit the summary imprisonment of members of dissident groups, such as the Real IRA, on the evidence of a senior police officer.

LOYALIST PARAMILITARIES

Loyalist paramilitaries are dedicated to maintaining Northern Ireland's status as part of the United Kingdom. They see themselves as counter-revolutionaries. Unlike Republican paramilitary groupings that are perceived as well disciplined and having a hierarchy of authority, Loyalist paramilitaries have been seen as more faction-alised and there have been many splits among the various groups. According to David McKittrick, 'a glossary of Loyalist paramilitary organisations compiled in mid 1970 listed no fewer than 35 groups' (McKittrick, 1989). Although many were small and fictional, up to a dozen groups were well structured and highly trained with access to weapons.

Ulster Defence Association (UDA)/Ulster Freedom Fighters (UFF)

The Ulster Defence Association was throughout the Troubles, the largest Protestant paramilitary organisation, and remained legal until 1992. At its peak the UDA had an estimated 40,000 members. The organisation has been viewed as an umbrella for Loyalist vigilante groups (Flackes and Elliott, 1994). Membership has come mainly from working-class Protestants. Just as the IRA were seen as defenders of Catholics, the UDA were viewed as protectors of the Loyalist community. Its initial objective was the mobilisation of large numbers of Loyalists in opposition to any form of Irish unification. In the early 1970s, with the high levels of Republican violence in Belfast, the UDA began to forge links with the more violent Loyalist paramilitary group, the Ulster Volunteer Force (UVF). In the summer of 1972 it took part in a massive street demonstration in Belfast, with thousands of UDA men, many wearing masks and combat jackets, marching through the city centre.

In the Ulster Workers' Council Strike in 1974 the UDA was heavily involved in mounting road-blocks and intimidating people who refused to stay home from work. By the mid-1970s it emerged that the Ulster Freedom Fighters (UFF) were indeed the military wing of the UDA. From that period the UFF began their campaign of killings, bomb attacks and racketeering. In 1979, eleven men were given heavy prison sentences for their involvement in acquiring arms and ammunition for the UFF. The relationship between the UDA and the UFF has always been uncertain. Many within the UDA argued for the organisation to remain solely political rather than develop as a paramilitary organisation. For example, the UDA refused to support the 'Day of Action' or Third Force organised by the Reverend Ian Paisley in 1981. In the mid and later 1980s, according to security forces, it was involved in sectarian killings. Security forces also believed the UDA had access to large quantities of weapons and ammunition and it was feared there would be a major confrontation between the Provisional IRA and Loyalists. Alongside the paramilitary activities, the UDA has tried to highlight its political dimension. It has been involved in talks with the constitutional Nationalist party the SDLP and has had a delegation visit the United States to have talks with leading politicians. In 1987 it published a document called 'Common Sense' which supported the idea of an Assembly and Executive elected by Proportional Representation, with an all-party coalition, a Bill of Rights and a written constitution.

By 1990 the UDA leadership consisted of an inner circle of young men with an average age of 30 who appeared motivated by military rather than political strategy. This move towards militarism and consequent increase in violence meant 40 people died at the hands of Loyalist gunmen in 1991. By 1991 it was estimated that together the UVF and UFF had 70 to 90 gunmen on the streets. In 1992 the UFF carried out a gun attack on a Catholic bookmakers shop on the Ormeau Road in Belfast. Five Catholics died in the attack, including a 15-year-old schoolboy. The UFF claimed this attack was carried out in retaliation for the IRA attack in Teebane in which eight Protestants were killed. Of the 38 Loyalist killings in 1992, the UFF was probably responsible for at least 21 of those deaths. In response to the increase in this violence Sir Patrick Mayhew, Northern Ireland Secretary of State, banned the UDA claiming it was 'actively and primarily engaged in terrorism'.

Ulster Volunteer Force (UVF)

The Ulster Volunteer Force emerged as a small and highly secretive paramilitary group in the 1960s. The name has derived from the mass movement of Protestants against Home Rule in 1912. This new-style UVF completely rejected the liberal policies and practices of the Stormont government under Terence O'Neill. The UVF was organised along military lines and attracted ex-British soldiers to its ranks. This paramilitary group was very strong in the Shankill area of Belfast, Co. Armagh and East Antrim. Established in 1966 as a sectarian organisation, it was soon outlawed. It claimed to target the IRA, but by the 1970s the UVF was very much involved in the sectarian killings of Catholics. In 1971, 26 UVF men were given a total of 700 years' imprisonment including eight life sentences. In 1974, the British government lifted the proscription on the UVF in an attempt to encourage its members to move into political activity rather than paramilitarism. The UVF was soon illegal again after the group admitted being involved in the violence of 3 October 1975, when twelve people died and many more were injured, many of whom were Catholics. The organisation was weakened in the 1980s, when many members were arrested and imprisoned and weapons and ammunition seized by the security forces. Informers within the UVF were blamed for these arrests.

Between 1990 and 1994, Loyalist violence had increased to a scale never witnessed before in Northern Ireland. The UVF was responsible for over 11 killings in 1992 carried out by an estimated 90 gunmen in the UVF and UFF. Many in Nationalist and Republican circles had long claimed that both of these Loyalist paramilitary groups worked jointly in the assassination of Catholics. This claim was substantiated in 1991 when the formation of the Combined Loyalist Military Command was announced. The groups began to jointly co-ordinate strategies in response to IRA activities and this new Military Command signified that membership of these two main Loyalist paramilitary organisations was interchangeable, if not intermixed.

There have also been persistent allegations by Nationalists of collusion between Loyalist paramilitaries and the security forces in the killing of Republicans. These allegations were investigated by the Stevens Inquiry, and in 1989 28 UDR men were arrested by the RUC on instruction from the Inquiry team. The Inquiry subsequently reprimanded 18 and cautioned one of the 20 RUC officers it investigated.

SECURITY FORCES

The security forces in Northern Ireland comprise the armed police force, the Royal Ulster Constabulary (RUC) and the British Army, which includes the local Northern Ireland regiment, the Royal Irish Regiment. At the outbreak of the Troubles in 1969 the Ulster Special Constabulary, known as the B-Specials, supported the back-up for the RUC. They were disbanded in 1969. By 1989 there were 9658 members of the British Army in NI, 6343 members of the UDR and 12,889 members of the RUC, making a total security force membership of close to 29,000 (McGarry and O'Leary, 1993).

The Royal Ulster Constabulary (RUC)

The RUC is the regular police force in Northern Ireland. It is over-whelmingly recruited from the Protestant population (92.8 per cent). The RUC was established in 1922 with the birth of the new Northern Ireland, and it was intended that Catholics would make up a third of the force. This intention was never realised. In 1922 Catholics made up about one-sixth of the force and this number continually fell as the years went on. In 1969 it was revealed that Catholics accounted for only 11 per cent of the force. The RUC also attracted recruits from the B-Specials, which was an all-Protestant force. The RUC, unlike regular police forces elsewhere in the United Kingdom, was always armed and its members were trained with sub-machine guns and rifles. It was perceived in the Nationalist community as a paramilitary force, which was under the political control of the Stormont government.

When the RUC and the B-Specials attempted to deal with the civil rights movement in 1968, through banning demonstrations and by forceful and violent confrontation with marchers, serious rioting erupted in Northern Ireland. The British government set up the Cameron Commission and Scarman Tribunal to deal with the causes of these disturbances. Both of these bodies agreed that the RUC had made mistakes and reform was needed to render the police force more impartial and immune to overt political control. In 1970 the force consisted of 3500 men and women. As the violence escalated and spread across the Province, the demands on the police increased and their resources were stretched. The British Army was deployed in Northern Ireland to relieve the RUC and in the early 1970s the RUC took a subordinate role. They were mainly excluded from Catholic areas and it was the army that patrolled these areas.

In 1975, the British government changed their military security strategy. The government decided to overlook the political dimension of the conflict and treat the 'Northern Ireland' problem as one of law and order. Three new policies were initiated. Full responsibility for law and order was given back to the RUC, backed up by the local regiment of the British Army, the Ulster Defence Regiment, later the Royal Irish Regiment. This policy became known as Ulsterisation. Internment without trial was phased out and increasing reliance was placed on the trial of suspected paramilitaries as criminals in special non-jury courts. Since 1976, the police and army have worked more closely together on the implementation of these new policies. Ulsterisation meant expanding and rearming the RUC. The force was increased to 7289 in 1979 and 10,296 in 1984 (Irish Information Partnership, 1989). Nationalist confidence in the RUC did not improve over 30 years of violence; in fact it continues to deteriorate as the conflict continues. The RUC have been dogged in recent years with allegations of shoot-to-kill policies and reckless use of plastic bullets. In the 30 years of the Troubles the RUC have lost 303 members to violence (Fay et al., 1997).

The Ulster Defence Regiment (UDR)

The Ulster Defence Regiment was a local, mainly part-time force. It was a replacement for Protestant USC (Ulster Special Constabulary) or B-Specials. As with the B-Specials, the UDR remained a Protestant force. The percentage of Catholic soldiers was so low it is difficult to find figures. In the 1980s the UDR provided support for the RUC and thus had similar problems being accepted by the Catholic community. Its soldiers were prime targets for the IRA, and 197 members and 47 former members have been killed by the Republican paramilitaries. There were persistent allegations of collusion between the UDR and Loyalist paramilitaries and the reputation of the regiment was badly damaged when two UDR soldiers were convicted of killing three members of the Miami Showband in 1975. In 1989 the Stevens Inquiry was established to investigate the allegations of collusion. Twenty-eight members of the regiment were arrested by the RUC and ten members were charged as a result of this Inquiry. There was evidence that UDR soldiers had been involved in killings and had passed security files on Republicans to Loyalist paramilitaries. The outcome of the Stevens Inquiry was a huge blow to the force and the government announced in 1991 that the UDR and the Royal Irish Regiment (RIR) were to be merged. At the beginning of 1993 there were 5700 members of the RIR in Northern Ireland.

The British Army

In 1969 after two days of heavy rioting between Catholics and the police in Belfast and Derry, the British government finally sent in the British Army to take control of the deteriorating situation and prevent the spread of serious sectarian confrontations. Initially the Catholic community saw the army as an impartial peacekeeping force and openly welcomed them. This confidence soon disappeared as the army displayed military style tactics to curb civil disobedience. The Catholic community and especially the Republican paramilitaries now treated the army as defenders of the status quo and the conflict between the army and the Nationalist community soon developed. The British Army now became targets of IRA attacks. Internment solidified the rift between the army and the Catholic community. From 1971 until the fall of the Unionist government and the imposition of Direct Rule in 1972, the army was in charge of security and the RUC took a secondary role. It was the army who policed Republican areas, arrested suspected Republican supporters and sympathisers and searched houses on a regular basis. During the period of internment the army were accused of some of the most serious abuses of human rights, most notably the systematic torture and physical ill treatment of internees. In January 1972, the Parachute Regiment of the British Army shot dead 13 unarmed Catholic civilians in Derry – a fourteenth died later in hospital – after a civil rights demonstration. The army was accused of recklessly shooting at the crowd and killing innocent people. Bloody Sunday, as it became known, was a key event in the decision by the British government to suspend Stormont.

After the fall of Stormont, the army took charge of the security strategy. The Special Powers Act and the Prevention of Terrorism Act gave wide powers of arrest, search, detention and questioning. In an attempt to defeat the IRA the army developed other strategies. These included *agents provocateurs*, undercover techniques, assassination squads and new methods of surveillance, using special equipment and intelligence and information gathering (Hillyard, 1983). In 1972 there were over 21,000 troops stationed in Northern Ireland. The advent of the new policy of Ulsterisation, described above, meant reductions in the number of British troops. The army began to adopt a much lower profile and worked in a supportive role to the police. By 1982 the number of troops on the streets was reduced by over 10,000. With the cease-fires in 1994 the number of troops has been further reduced. The British Army have lost 511 members to the conflict in Northern Ireland.

The conflict has also meant the involvement of other security agencies such as MI5, MI6 and the Special Air Service (SAS). The SAS has carried out operations in Northern Ireland since the 1970s when the SAS-trained Military Reconnaissance Force gathered undercover information on the IRA in West Belfast. The role of MI5 was formally acknowledged by the government in 1988 when they took control of anti-IRA intelligence gathering in Great Britain. MI5 was already responsible for monitoring Loyalist paramilitary movements in Great Britain. With as many as five agencies working in this field there has often been confusion and mistakes have been made. Many shipments of arms and ammunition successfully reached the IRA because of blunders by the security agencies.

A Chronology of Key Events

1921	First Parliament in Northern Ireland opened by George V
1922	Widespread violence in Northern Ireland killed 232 people and injured 1,000
1925	Irish Free State government confirmed the border in the 1920 Act
1932	New Stormont Parliament Buildings opened by Prince of Wales
1956	IRA launched Border campaign
1962	IRA called off its campaign
1963	Terence O'Neill became Prime Minister of Northern Ireland
1965	Sean Lemass visited Stormont for talks, the first Taoiseach of the Republic of Ireland to do so
1966	The Ulster Volunteer Force declared illegal
1967	Northern Ireland Civil Rights Association formed

> We wanted a broad-based movement. We wanted to bring in everybody that actually thought about the whole issue of civil rights. What we were asking, very consciously asking for was reform of Northen Ireland ... What we were challenging was things that were happening inside the State ... which should not have been happening. (Ann Hope, former secretary of the NICRA)

1968

24 August	First civil rights march in Northern Ireland from Coalisland to Dungannon

> Over 2000 people took part in the first march organised by the NICRA. This was a protest at discrimination against the Catholic population in Northern Ireland.

15 October	Nationalist Party withdrew from role as official Stormont opposition

17 November   Nationalist Party adopted a policy of civil disobedience

22 November   O'Neill announced a five-point reform plan

28 November   Electoral Law Act abolished university representation and the business vote in Stormont elections

9 December   Terence O'Neill's 'Ulster at the Crossroads' speech gained 150,000 letters of support

1969

4 January   People's Democracy (PD) march to Derry attacked at Burntollet Bridge. Rioting in Derry resulted in the establishment of a local citizens' army and no-go areas

12 March   Announcement that the RUC were to carry arms on daytime duties in border areas

30 March   Castlereagh electricity sub-station damaged in explosion by Loyalist extremists

18 April   Bernadette Devlin (Unity) won Mid-Ulster by-election to become the youngest Member of Parliament ever elected

25 April   Explosion in Annalong by Loyalist extremists hit Belfast water supply. Five hundred British troops sent to Northern Ireland

28 April   Terence O'Neill resigned as Prime Minister

22 May   British Prime Minister Harold Wilson announced 'one man, one vote' franchise for 1971 in Commons

December   Birth of Provisional IRA

At an IRA Convention in December 1969 a group of dissidents from within the organisation argued that the IRA had lost all credibility because of its failure to protect Catholic areas of Belfast from sectarian attacks. This group of dissidents formed the Provisional IRA and in the summer of 1970 it began its bombing campaign.

1970

11 January   Sinn Féin Ard Fheis failed to amend policy on abstentionism and split in Officials and Provisionals

1 April   Ulster Defence Regiment became operational

The Ulster Defence Regiment replaced the all-Protestant B-Specials. The new regiment had almost 40,000 members over its 22 years of existence, but attracted very few Catholics to its ranks. It was envisaged that the UDR would assist the regular army by guarding the key locations and checkpoints.

17 April	Reverend Ian Paisley won South Antrim by-election
21 April	Alliance Party of Northern Ireland formed
15 September	One-hundredth explosion in 1970 occurred
30 December	Cost of disturbance in 1969–70 estimated at £3.5 million

1971

10 March   Three British soldiers found dead at Ligoneil. Provisional IRA were blamed for the killings

12 March   Four thousand shipyard workers marched in Belfast seeking internment of Provisional IRA leaders

9 August   Internment dawn swoop lifted over 300 people. Violence in Belfast and Derry

In the early hours of 9 August 1971 the army and police engaged in a series of dawn swoops and arrested 342 people. Within two days 100 people were released. In the first six months of internment over 2400 people were arrrested. The inhumane treatment and torture of internees was a controversial feature of internment.

11 August   According to Flackes and Elliott (1994) 7000 'refugees' moved to the Republic of Ireland for safety

17 October   Rent and rates strike in protest at internment

4 December   Bomb left at McGurk's Bar by the UVF killing 15 people

The UVF attacked McGurk's bar on North Queen Street, Belfast on 4 December 1971. Fifteen people were killed and many were injured. It was the most horrific incident of the unrest. One of the first bodies to be removed from the rubble was McGurk's wife. Their 11-year-old daughter was also killed in the explosion. A 14-year-old boy who was playing snooker upstairs at the time explained

> Everything went dark and I remember being under the rubble. My back was scorched by the fire and I have stitches in my leg. (Seamus Kane interviewed in *Belfast Telegraph*, 6 December 1971)

John McGurk, the owner's son was upstairs at the time the bomb exploded. He told reporters

> I was ten years old and I was playing in the sitting room of our house ... we lived above the bar ... all I seem to

remember it was like being spun in the air and not knowing what was happening and just this terrible whoosh and wind and obviously I was plummeting through the air. (John McGurk, interviewed in *Belfast Telegraph*, 6 December 1971)

1972

30 January — **Thirteen men shot dead in Derry by the army (Bloody Sunday), and one died later of wounds**

Thirteen people were shot dead by British soldiers on the streets of Derry, when rioting broke out after a civil rights march held in defiance of a Government ban. The Army alleged the dead were snipers firing at the troops but local people contended that the soldiers had panicked and fired wildly.

They came in and they came in firing, the people, there was no provocation ... it was lead bullets they fired ... they seemed to fire in all directions ... people ran in all directions and they opened fire. Most people had their backs to them when they opened fire at the time. (Fr Edward Daly, eye witness on Bloody Sunday)

The 15,000 people who were marching yesterday were not 15,000 violent men. They were 15,000 citizens out to express that very point, while doing so they were gunned down. (John Hume, SDLP)

I believe that day was very significant in the incidents that occured afterwards. I think it was badly handled by everyone. Me, the platoon sergeants, the individuals soldiers and our superiors. (Parachute Regiment Company Sergeant Major)

22 February — **Seven people killed by bomb planted by the IRA at Aldershot military barracks in England**

4 March — **Abercorn restaurant in the centre of Belfast bombed: two killed, 130 injured**

24 March — **British government announced Direct Rule in Northern Ireland**

The Government in London is obliged to take over for the time being full responsibility for the conduct of affairs in Northern Ireland. (British Prime Minister, Edward Heath)

7 July — **Secretary of State met Provisional IRA for secret talks in London.**

An IRA cease-fire in June 1972 led to the secret meeting between leading members of the IRA and the Secretary of State in London. At this meeting the IRA demanded a British withdrawal from Ireland within three years. The Secretary of State could not agree to this and talks broke down. Two days later the IRA ended their cease-fire.

21 July **Nine people killed and 22 IRA bombs exploded in Belfast (Bloody Friday)**

The IRA detonated 20 bombs in Belfast City centre, eleven were killed and 100 seriously injured. Dorothy Parker who lost her son in one of the bomb explosions gave this account:

> I ran up the road and when I got to the corner and looked up I could just see everything was burning and I tramped over the glass and burning net. I said 'it's my children, I can't find them ...' somebody said 'I've got Karen', that's my little girl. And I said 'but I still haven't got Stephen'.

31 July **Army entered West Belfast in 'Operation Motorman', which was designed to bring to an end the 'no-go areas' in the Nationalist community**

1 December **Two killed and 80 injured in Dublin when two bombs exploded in the Dáil (Irish Parliament)**

1973

1 January **Northern Ireland joined the European Community as part of the United Kingdom**

21 November **Agreement reached on setting up Power Sharing Executive to administer Northern Ireland**

> Today is a very historic occasion when the Secretary of State at Westminster was able to announce a completely new concept of political operations in Northern Ireland. (Gerry Fitt MP, Deputy Chief Executive of the Power Sharing Executive)

6–9 December **Sunningdale Conference**

A 20 point communiqué had been agreed between the parties at the Conference. The key aspect of agreement was the creation of a Council of Ireland which would comprise a Council of Ministers, with executive and harmonising functions and a consultative assembly with advisory and review functions. The Council of Ministers would have seven representatives of the Dublin government and the Northern Ireland Executive. The consultative assembly would have 30 members of the Ulster Assembly and 30 members of the Dáil.

Reactions to the Sunningdale Agreement were positive from a Nationalist perspective but very negative and hostile from many in Loyalist circles.

If the institutions are made to work and the people give them full support ... Most people in Northern Ireland will agree that this was an equitable settlement, a partnership in the north between equals and a partnership between north and south. The whole agreement is having the backing of the British Government, the Irish Government and of the parties forming the Northen Executive then I think that is a formula for lasting peace. (John Hume, Deputy leader of the SDLP)

A United Ulster Unionist Council was formed in opposition to the Sunningdale Agreement. There was a unanimous declaration to make the Executive unworkable and to bring an end to power sharing.

We now have a foreign government having a right to be consulted on the political, the security, the judicial – every aspect of life. (Rev. Harold Allen, Presbyterian Church and Government Committee)

1974

14 May	Loyalist Ulster Workers' Council threatened power cuts in protest at Sunningdale Agreement
15 May	Power cuts forced the closure of several factories and many workers go on strike

On the first morning of the strike most of the Northern Ireland workforce turned up for work. The UDA and the UVF issued a statement ordering Loyalists to stop work immediately. Widespread intimidation followed so that by Friday of the first week of the strike the stoppage was all but complete.

17 May	Twenty-two killed in Dublin when car bombs exploded without warning and five were killed in a car bomb in Monaghan in the Irish Republic. Three more died later from their injuries
28 May	Power Sharing Executive collapsed and Direct Rule of Northern Ireland from Westminster is resumed
29 May	Ulster Workers' Council called off strike
5 October	Five people, four off-duty soldiers and one civilian, killed and 54 injured when bombs exploded without warning in a pub in Guildford, Surrey
6 November	Thirty-three Republican prisoners escaped from Long Kesh prison (later the Maze). Thirty-two were recaptured

21 November Nineteen killed and 182 injured when IRA bombs exploded in Birmingham pub

5 December Westminster Parliament extended the new Prevention of Terrorism Act to Northern Ireland

10 December At Feakle, Co. Clare, a group of Protestant churchmen met Sinn Féin and the IRA

22 December IRA announced cease-fire from 22 December 1974–16 January 1975

1975

31 July Three members of Miami Showband killed and one seriously injured in UVF gun attack. Two UVF men also died in the attack

2 October In a series of UVF attacks, twelve people were killed, including three women and four UVF men, and 46 were injured

The UVF claimed that it carried out the attacks because of a lack of effective counter-paramilitary action following recent IRA bombings.

1976

4 January Five Catholics killed in two separate shooting incidents in South Armagh and in Ballydugan, County Down

5 January Ten Protestant workers shot dead at Kingmills, near Bessbrook, County Armagh. Republican Action Force claimed responsibility

21 January Government claimed 25,000 homes damaged in violence

28 October Máire Drumm, Vice President of Sinn Féin shot dead by Loyalists in Belfast's Mater Hospital, where she was a patient

October Republican prisoners began the Blanket Protest

The Blanket Protest was a protest against the removal of special category status. Prisoners destroyed the furniture in their cells and the prison authorities restricted them to a mattress and three blankets each. John Deery, a blanket protestor at the time said:

> I decided to go on the blanket in the first place because I refuse to accept ... the criminalistion policy. I am a political prisoner and demand to be treated as such.

In 1978 the prisoners began a no-wash protest which later escalated into a dirty protest when prisoners resorted to pouring their urine out of the cells and smearing the cell walls with their excrement. By 1980 almost half of the Republican prisoners in the Maze were involved in the dirty protest.

1 December   Fair Employment Act introduced making it an offence to discriminate in employment on religious or political grounds

1977

11 March   Twenty-six UVF men sentenced to a total of 700 years' imprisonment

21 June   Unemployment in Northern Ireland reaches 60,000, the highest June total in 37 years

27 July   Four killed in Belfast as a result of the feud between the Provisional IRA and the Official IRA

10 October   Betty Williams and Mairead Maguire, founders of the Peace People, are awarded the 1976 Nobel Peace Prize

21 December   Five hotels throughout Northern Ireland damaged by IRA firebombs

1978

17 February   Twelve people killed and 23 injured when La Mon House Hotel destroyed by IRA firebombs

2 August   Government announced 2000 jobs in the De Lorean sports car factory in West Belfast

8 October   Sixty-nine RUC officers injured in disturbances associated with a march to celebrate the anniversary of the 5 October civil rights march – 67 of the police were injured by Loyalists who held a counter-demonstration, and the remaining two were injured by those associated with the march

1979

20 February   Eleven men known as Shankill Butchers sentenced to life imprisonment for 19 killings

30 March   Conservative Northern Ireland spokesman Airey Neave killed in bomb explosion at House of Commons car park. INLA claimed responsibility

17 April   Four RUC men killed by Provisional IRA at Bessbrook, Co. Armagh

27 August	IRA bombers killed 18 soldiers at Warrenpoint, Co. Down. Lord Mountbatten killed by IRA. Three others died with him
28 November	John Hume became leader of SDLP (Social Democratic and Labour Party)
16 December	Four soldiers killed by Provisional IRA landmine in County Tyrone and another by a booby-trap bomb in South Armagh

1980

19 June	European Commission of Human Rights rejected case of protesting H-Block prisoners, finding that the debasement arising out of the 'dirty protest' was self inflicted. The Commission criticised British government for inflexibility
26 June	Dr Miriam Daly, prominent Republican member of National Block/Armagh Committee, shot dead at her home in Andersonstown, Belfast
6 August	Extra government spending of £48 million in NI announced after Irish Congress of Trades Unions delegation met Thatcher to protest at 14.7 per cent unemployment
8 August	Three killed and 18 injured in widespread violence on anniversary of internment
27 October	Seven H-Block prisoners began hunger strike in support of the right to wear their own clothing
	On this day, seven prisoners refused food. As the hunger strike continued three women from Armagh jail joined and a fortnight later a further 23 prisoners in the Maze joined the hunger strike. The National H-Block Committee continued to campaign with protest marches all over the island.
18 December	H-Block hunger strike called off with one Provisional IRA prisoner critically ill
	With one prisoner close to death and believing that the government was prepared to make a deal, the hunger strike was called off. When the government document arrived, it failed to meet the demands of the prisoners. Now that the strike had been called off the prisoners had lost their bargaining power. The hunger strike had been a failure.

1981

16 January	Bernadette McAliskey and husband shot and seriously wounded at their home near Coalisland.

21 January	Two leading Unionists, Sir Norman Stronge and son James, shot dead by Provisional IRA
1 March	New H-Block hunger strike in support of political status for prisoners
5 March	Death of Frank Maguire, Independent Member of Parliament for Fermanagh–South Tyrone
9 April	Bobby Sands, one of the Republican prisoners on hunger strike, won Fermanagh–South Tyrone by-election.
5 May	Bobby Sands died on the 66th day of hunger strike

> There can be no question of political status for someone who is serving a sentence for crime. Crime is crime is crime. It is not political, it is crime. (Prime Minister Margaret Thatcher)

> In the course of the hunger strike protest, ten men died, seven from the IRA and three from the INLA. Bobby Sands was the first to die after 66 days of fasting. Over 100,000 people attended Bobby Sands' funeral. That was almost one-fifth of the Catholic population in Northern Ireland. The others who died were: Francis Hughes (12 May), Raymond McCreesh (21 May), Patsy O'Hara (21 May), Joe McDonnell (8 July), Martin Hurson (13 July) Kevin Lynch (1 August), Kieran Doherty (2 August), Thomas McIlwee (8 August) and Michael Devine (20 August).

19 May	Five soldiers killed in bomb in Bessbrook, County Armagh
21 May	Raymond McCreesh died on hunger strike

> Raymond would never have been in prison had it not been for our political troubles here. He is not a criminal. He'd never have been in prison … were it not for the political turmoil and the civil unrest which erupted here following the denial of our basic civil rights to our people. (Fr Brian McCreesh, brother of hunger striker Raymond McCreesh)

11 June	Two H-Block prisoners elected to Dáil Eireann
20 August	Owen Carron won Fermanagh–South Tyrone by-election
23 August	Sinn Féin announce that it will fight in any future Northern Ireland or Westminster election
2 September	Ian Paisley called for a Third Force to be established on lines of B-Specials

7 September	Two RUC officers killed in Pomeroy, County Tyrone
13 September	James Prior became Secretary of State for Northern Ireland
3 October	Hunger strike called off
6 October	Secretary of State Prior announced that all prisoners would have the right to wear their own clothes
8 October	Independent Councillor Lawrence Kennedy shot dead in Ardoyne
10 October	Provisional IRA nail-bomb in Chelsea Barracks, London killed one woman and injured 23 soldiers and 17 civilians
14 November	Reverend Robert Bradford, Ulster Unionist MP, assassinated by Provisional IRA in Finaghy, Belfast. Another man also died in the attack
3 December	Paisley claimed Third Force had between 15,000 and 20,000 members

1982

16 March	Eleven-year-old boy killed and 34 people injured in bomb explosion in County Down. No warning given
25 March	Three British soldiers killed in West Belfast
28 March	RUC Inspector shot dead in Derry Londonderry by the Provisional IRA
1 April	Two plain-clothes soldiers killed in Derry Londonderry by the Provisional IRA
20 April	Two killed, twelve injured and £1 million worth of damage caused by Provisional IRA bomb attack in Belfast, Derry Londonderry, Armagh, Strabane, Ballymena, Bessbrook and Magherafelt
13 May	European Parliament called for ban on use of plastic bullets throughout European Community
18 June	Former RUC Inspector shot dead at his home in Newry, County Down
25 June	Devolution Bill for Northern Ireland amended in the British House of Commons to ensure 'cross-community support' before transfer of powers
20 July	IRA bomb in London killed eight soldiers and injured 51 people, three of whom died later

25 August	SDLP decide to contest Northern Ireland Assembly elections but not to take their seats
28 August	IRA suffered its biggest setback through the seizure of arms and explosives
20 October	Sinn Féin contest Assembly elections on an abstentionist ticket

This was the first election to be fought by Sinn Féin. The Party secured 10.1 per cent of the vote and gained five of the 78 seats. The SDLP won 18.8 per cent of the vote and 14 seats. The results of this election caused concern in government circles that Sinn Féin could be poised to displace the SDLP as the main political voice of Nationalism in Northern Ireland.

27 October	Three RUC officers killed in an explosion in Lurgan, County Armagh
11 November	Three Provisional IRA volunteers shot dead by the RUC after allegedly driving through a checkpoint in Lurgan, County Armagh
16 November	Lenny Murphy, leader of the Shankill Butchers, shot dead. Two RUC constables shot dead in Markethill, County Armagh
6 December	Seventeen people, including eleven soldiers, died in an INLA bomb in Ballykelly, County Derry Londonderry

1983

6 January	Two RUC officers shot dead in Rostrevor, County Down
11 April	Fourteen UVF men jailed on evidence of supergrass
24 May	A 1000 lb bomb exploded outside Andersonstown police station, Belfast, and caused £1 million worth of damage
30 May	New Ireland Forum comprising main constitutional Nationalist parties in Ireland met in Dublin to pursue structures and processes to achieve a new Ireland
5 August	After a 120-day trial of 38 people implicated by IRA supergrass Christopher Black, Mr Justice Kelly jailed 22 with sentences totalling more than 4000 years

25 September	Thirty-eight IRA prisoners escaped from the Maze; 19 were recaptured within a few days, the others got away
4 November	Provisional IRA bomb at the Ulster Polytechnic killed an RUC Inspector and injured 33 other people
4 December	SAS undercover soldiers shot dead two Provisional IRA members in Coalisland, County Tyrone
17 December	Five people killed and 80 injured in IRA bomb at Harrods, London

1984

14 March	Sinn Féin president Gerry Adams shot and wounded in Belfast
3 May	New Ireland Forum Report, sponsored by the Irish government is published, and reflected Nationalist and Catholic opinion in Ireland

The Forum Report adopted a traditionally Nationalist approach, stating that Britain was ultimately responsible for Partition by 'refusing to accept the democratically expressed wishes of the Irish people and by establishing an artificial political majority in the north'. In the report the parties agreed that a unitary 32-county state was their first choice in any new constitution. They did put forward other options such as joint authority and a federal arrangement. The British government expressed the view that it found the Forum's account of the British position difficult to accept and in November 1984 British Prime Minister Margaret Thatcher publicly rejected the three options of the Forum Report.

18 May	Two RUC officers are killed and another seriously injured in Provisional IRA explosion in South Armagh
28 September	Seven tons of arms and ammunition intended for the IRA was seized off the Irish coast. Biggest arms capture since 1973
1 November	Kilbrandon Report published. Written by an unofficial committee set up by the British Irish Association, the majority report suggested that a five-member executive, including an Irish government minister run Northern Ireland.
6 December	SAS shot dead two Provisional IRA members in Derry Londonderry

24 December	Court of appeal quashed the convictions of 14 men jailed on evidence of UVF supergrass Joseph Bennett

1985

28 February	Nine RUC members killed in IRA mortar attack in Newry, County Down
15 May	Sinn Féin took 59 seats in District Council elections
20 May	Four RUC officers killed by an IRA bomb in Killeen, County Armagh
15 November	Prime Minister Margaret Thatcher and Taoiseach Garret Fitzgerald signed the Anglo–Irish Agreement (AIA) at Hillsborough

It was by a long way the most far-reaching political development in Northern Ireland since 1920. The Anglo–Irish Agreement was presented by both leaders as a foundation stone on which a lasting settlement could be built. It brought a close working relationship between the British and Irish governments on Northern Ireland. The Agreement was also an attempt to halt the electoral rise of Sinn Féin. The most radical and controversial feature of the Anglo–Irish Agreement was the creation of an intergovernmental conference headed by the British Secretary of State for Northern Ireland and the Irish Foreign Minister. This Conference was to meet regularly to discuss matters of common concern to both governments. The Civil Service was to be made up of civil servants from both the North and South of Ireland.

The Agreement was welcomed by Nationalists but seen as treachery from the Unionist population who felt betrayed that the government of the Republic of Ireland was given a role in the internal affairs of Northern Ireland.

23 November	Massive Loyalist demonstrations against the AIA in Belfast City centre

One hundred thousand Unionists gathered at the City Hall in Belfast to voice their anger at the Anglo–Irish Agreement. In December 1985 all 15 Unionist MPs resigned from their Westminster seats and forced by-elections throughout Northern Ireland.

1986

3 March	Unionist 'Day of Action' against the AIA disrupted public services, transport, halted most of industry and led to extensive power cuts

This Day of Action closed down much of Northern Ireland's industry and commerce. That night rioting erupted in Loyalist areas. The Anglo–Irish Agreement and the Unionist stance on it created a political stalemate in Northern Ireland for the next five years with Unionists refusing to negotiate with Nationalists in Councils throughout the country.

23 June   Northern Ireland Assembly dissolved; 22 Assembly members refused to leave the chamber and were physically removed by the RUC

13 July   Chief Constable Sir John Hermon suspended two senior officers after investigations into alleged 'shoot-to-kill' policy in 1982. This decision caused violence to erupt and 128 police and 66 civilians were injured

18 July   Orange Order held inquiry into rioting in Portadown and blamed the RUC

1987

8 May   SAS shot dead eight IRA men in Loughgall, Co. Armagh. One civilian passer-by was also killed

Eight IRA activists were shot dead by the SAS during an attack on Loughgall RUC station. The SAS had prior knowledge of the attack and were prepared for it. This ambush in effect wiped out the IRA's East Tyrone brigade.

8 November   Eleven killed and 63 injured when an IRA bomb exploded at a Remembrance Day service in Enniskillen

Eleven people including six pensioners and three married couples were killed when a no-warning bomb exploded before a Remembrance Day Service was due to begin in Enniskillen. The building collapsed under a 30 lb bomb burying women and children under a heap of rubble. The following day the IRA expressed 'deep regret' for the bombing. This bombing was condemned world-wide and the words of one survivor Gordon Wilson touched the hearts of people who heard him describe the last moments he had with his daughter:

'Daddy, I love you very much.' These were the exact words she spoke to me and those were the last words I heard her say ... I have lost my daughter but I bear no ill will, I bear no grudge.

British Prime Minister Margaret Thatcher claimed:

It was so cruel and so callous that the people who did it can have nothing of human thoughtfulness or kindness or sensitivity at all. It was utterly barbaric.

22 December	UDA leader John McMichael killed by IRA booby-trap car bomb

1988

11 January	SDLP leader John Hume and Sinn Féin leader Gerry Adams met for talks in Belfast
6 March	IRA volunteers Mairead Farrell, Sean Savage and Daniel McCann shot dead by SAS in Gibraltar
16 March	Loyalist Michael Stone attacked the funeral of those shot at Gibraltar with grenades and a pistol at Milltown Cemetery, Belfast. Three people were killed and several injured
19 March	Two Army Corporals killed by mob at West Belfast funeral of one of those killed at Milltown
15 June	Six soldiers killed by bomb at Lisburn, County Antrim
4 July	Twenty RUC officers are subjected to disciplinary proceedings as a result of the Stalker/Sampson investigations into an alleged shoot-to-kill policy
20 August	Eight British soldiers killed by bomb attack on their bus near Ballygawley, County Tyrone
30 August	Three Provisional IRA members shot dead by the SAS in County Tyrone
2 September	SDLP and Sinn Féin talks collapsed

1989

12 February	Prominent Nationalist solicitor, Pat Finucane, shot dead by Loyalist gunmen
14 March	Stevens Inquiry reprimanded 18 and cautioned one of the 20 RUC officers it investigated
6 August	Northern Ireland allocated £535 million sterling from European Community
22 September	Eleven soldiers killed and one died later of injuries as a result of an IRA bomb at Royal Marines School of Music in Kent, England
8 October	Twenty-eight UDR officers arrested by RUC on instruction from the Stevens Inquiry team
19 October	Guildford Four, convicted of bombing, released by Court of Appeal in England

1990

9 April	Four UDR officers killed in IRA landmine in Downpatrick, County Down
22 May	Bank of Ireland said the annual cost of the Troubles to British and Irish governments was £410 million
9 October	Two Provisional IRA volunteers shot dead by the British Army in Loughgall, County Tyrone. Three others were arrested
24 October	Five British soldiers killed at Coshquin, near Derry, Londonderry, and one British soldier and a civilian killed in Newry, County Down
27 November	John Major replaced Margaret Thatcher as British Prime Minister
23 December	Provisional IRA declare a three-day cease-fire, first in 15 years

1991

30 April	Bilateral talks between Secretary of State for Northern Ireland Peter Brooke and the constitutional parties
3 July	Peter Brooke ended the talks
24 November	Explosion in Crumlin Road Prison killed two Loyalist prisoners and injured several others

1992

4 January	An 800 lb IRA bomb exploded in Belfast city centre and caused extensive damage
5 January	A 500 lb IRA bomb exploded in Belfast city centre
17 January	IRA explosion killed nine Protestant workers in Teebane, County Tyrone
4 February	Three men shot dead at Sinn Féin office on Falls Road by an off-duty RUC officer who later shot himself
5 February	Five Catholics killed by Loyalist gunmen at Catholic bookmaker's shop
15 February	A 250 lb IRA bomb exploded in Belfast city centre
16 February	Four IRA men shot dead by undercover soldiers at Coalisland
17 February	Albert Reynolds replaced Charles Haughey as Taoiseach in the Irish Republic

5 March	A 1000 lb bomb exploded in Lurgan devastating the town
24 March	A 500 lb bomb exploded in Donegall Pass, Belfast
10 April	Joe Hendron SDLP defeated Sinn Féin President Gerry Adams in General Election for Westminster seat in West Belfast constituency
1 June	Derry City Council elected a DUP (Democratic Unionist Party) Mayor for the first time, on a power-sharing basis.
21 October	A 200 lb bomb destroyed the main street in Bangor, County Down
13 November	Massive bomb devastated commercial centre of Coleraine, County Derry Londonderry
1 December	Bomb in centre of Belfast injured 27 people

1993

20 March	IRA bomb in Warrington, England, killed two children and launched 'Peace Initiative 93'
25 March	UFF killed four Catholic workmen at Castlerock, County Derry Londonderry
11 April	John Hume, SDLP and Gerry Adams, Sinn Féin renewed talks
24 April	The Bishopsgate bomb in London caused £350 million worth of damage. Hume and Adams issued joint statement on their talks
20 May	A 1000 lb bomb exploded in Glengall Street, Belfast and caused £6.5 million worth of damage
22 May	A 1000 lb IRA bomb exploded in Portadown, County Armagh and in Magherafelt, County Derry Londonderry a 1500 lb bomb exploded
10 June	Jean Kennedy-Smith, sister of former United States President John F. Kennedy, confirmed as US Ambassador to the Republic of Ireland
11 August	Women members of the RUC to be armed for the first time
23 October	IRA bomb in fish shop on Shankill Road killed nine civilians and injured 58 others. One of the bombers was also killed
26 October	UFF killed two Catholic workmen and injured five others in West Belfast

28 October   UVF killed two Catholic brothers in Waringstown, Down

30 October   Six Catholics and one Protestant civilian killed and 13 injured in Rising Sun Bar at Greysteel, County Derry Londonderry by UFF

11 December Two RUC officers shot dead by the IRA in Fivemiletown, County Tyrone

15 December Downing Street Declaration published by the British and Irish governments

The Downing Street Declaration stated that Britain had no selfish strategic or economic interest in Northern Ireland. The document outlined that agreement on a political settlement had to be based on 'the right of the people on parts of the island to exercise the right of self determination on the basis of consent … north and south to bring about a united Ireland, if that is their will'.

1994

29 January   United States President Bill Clinton authorised a 'limited duration' visa for Gerry Adams to enter the USA

10 February INLA leader Dominic McGlinchey shot dead in Drogheda, in the Irish Republic

30 March   IRA announced a three-day cease-fire to facilitate talks between Britain and the Republican leadership

1 April   Women members of the RUC issued with guns

6 April   Margaret Wright from Belfast was beaten and shot dead in a Loyalist band hall. She was mistaken for a Catholic

12 April   UVF member Ian Hamilton shot dead by the organisation for his part in Margaret Wright's killing

26 August   An influential delegation of Irish Americans led by Congressman Bruce Morrison arrived in Belfast

31 August   IRA announced a complete cessation of all military operations

A statement issued by the IRA announced an unconditional cease-fire would come into effect from midnight on 31 August 1994. All IRA units were ordered to cease military activities and operations. The statement claimed Northern Ireland was now at an historical crossroads and 'an opportunity to secure a just and lasting settlement had been created'.

Responding to the IRA cease-fire Sinn Féin President Gerry Adams said: 'I want to see a permanent peace. I want others to acknowledge the enormity of the historical opportunity the IRA has presented to us all.'

6 September   Albert Reynolds, John Hume and Gerry Adams met and shook hands in Dublin

21 September   European Commission increased its contribution to the International Fund for Ireland to £47 million

13 October   Combined Loyalist Military Command announced a cessation of violence and apologised to the families of all innocent victims killed in the conflict

When the Combined Loyalist Military Command announced their cease-fire they warned it would be completely dependent upon the continued cessation of all Nationalist/Republican violence. 'The sole responsibility for a return to war rests with them.' The announcement declared that the Union was safe and they offered 'abject and true remorse to innocent victims'.

24 October   Troops stopped patrolling the streets in Derry Londonderry for the first time in 25 years

10 November   IRA killed postal worker Frank Kerr but the IRA leadership claimed the action was not sanctioned by the IRA leadership

17 October   Albert Reynolds resigned as Taoiseach following the controversy surrounding his appointment of Harry Whelan to President of the Irish Supreme Court

7 December   The European Commission agreed £230 million for Northern Ireland over next three years

9 December   British civil servants met Sinn Féin for the first formal meeting at Stormont

14 December   British Prime Minister John Major announced a £73 million investment package for Northern Ireland

15 December   Fine Gael leader John Bruton was elected Taoiseach

1995

12 January   Troops in Belfast ended daytime patrols

15 January   The government ban on contacts between ministers and Sinn Féin, Ulster Democratic Party and Progressive Unionist Party was lifted

18 January   Irish government released nine Republican prisoners

22 February	Irish and British governments released the documents 'Frameworks for the Future'
7 March	Secretary of State Patrick Mayhew announced a three-point plan on decommissioning of paramilitary weapons
9 March	Gerry Adams was invited to the White House for St Patrick's Day
30 March	Fair Employment Commission published report that stated that 62.7 per cent of the workforce in Northern Ireland was Protestant and 37.3 per cent Catholic
11 April	The Irish government released seven IRA prisoners
10 May	A Sinn Féin delegation led by Martin McGuinness met Northern Ireland Office Minister Paul Ancram
17 May	Unemployment figure for April was 11.8 per cent, the lowest in 13 years
1 June	SDLP councillor Alisdair McDonnell was elected Deputy Lord Mayor, the first Nationalist councillor to hold the Office
12 June	Anti-paramilitary laws are renewed at Westminster despite paramilitary cease-fires
3 July	Lee Clegg, a British soldier convicted of the killings of Martin Peake and Karen Riley, two Catholic teenage joy-riders, was released after four years in custody. This led to widespread rioting in Nationalist areas
9 July	Stand-off between RUC and Orangemen after they were prevented from marching down Nationalist Garvaghy Road in Portadown, County Armagh
10–11 July	Stand-off continued until compromise was reached and 500 Orangemen were allowed to walk the road unaccompanied by Loyalist bands
28 August	James Molyneaux announced his resignation from the leadership of the Ulster Unionist Party
8 September	David Trimble was elected leader of the Ulster Unionist Party
18 September	At a Liberal Democrat Conference in Glasgow Sinn Féin and the Ulster Democratic Party shared a platform for the first time

21 September	John Major claimed there must be a decommissioning of arms before Sinn Féin can enter all-party talks
17 November	A total of 83 prisoners were released from jails in Northern Ireland as part of the confidence-building measures
30 November	American President Bill Clinton became the first ever serving President to visit Northern Ireland
6 December	PUP (Progressive Unionist Party) member Lindsay Robb was convicted with two others of attempting to obtain guns for the UVF
15 December	Members of the international body set up to examine decommissioning of paramilitary weapons arrived in Belfast
18 December	Former IRA prisoner Fra Collins was shot dead in north Belfast. Reports suggested it was drug related

1996

5 January	RUC Chief Constable believed the IRA was responsible for six allegedly drugs-related killings since the cease-fire under the guise of Direct Action Against Drugs (DAAD)
24 January	Ulster Unionist Party member Ken Maginnis and Sinn Féin member Pat McGeown took part in a radio discussion in Belfast
30 January	Gino Gallagher, alleged leader of the INLA, was shot dead in Belfast
9 February	The IRA ended their cease-fire when a bomb exploded in Canary Wharf in London which killed two men and injured more than 100 others
12 February	Women Together held a peace rally in Belfast which was attended by several thousand people
18 February	An IRA bomb in central London left one dead and six injured
21 March	The British government announced the Northern Ireland Forum for Political Dialogue Elections to be held on 30 May 1996
22 March	INLA announced an end to its cease-fire
17 April	IRA bomb exploded in Earls Court, London

24 April	Two IRA bombs exploded in Hammersmith, London and caused minor damage
31 May	Forum election results were as follows: UUP (Ulster Unionist Party) 24.2 per cent (30 seats), DUP 18.8 per cent (24 seats), SDLP 21.4 per cent (21 seats), Sinn Féin 15.5 per cent (17 seats)
7 June	Garda Jerry McCabe shot dead in County Limerick
15 June	IRA claimed responsibility for the killing of Jerry McCabe
15 June	IRA detonated a bomb in Manchester, which injured 200 and caused £100 million worth of damage
6–11 July	Drumcree stand-off, but after three days of Loyalist rioting across Northern Ireland the RUC allowed the parade to proceed down the Garvaghy Road, Portadown, County Armagh
8 July	Catholic taxi driver Michael McGoldrick shot dead by Loyalists
13 July	Dermot McShane killed by an armoured car during riots in Derry Londonderry
13 July	IRA splinter group bombed a hotel in Enniskillen
7 October	Two IRA bombs in Thiepval Barracks, Lisburn, British Army Headquarters in Northern Ireland, injured 31 people, one of whom, a British soldier, died later

1997

30 January	Independent Review of Parades launched
2 February	25 anniversary of Bloody Sunday marked by a weekend of events and a commemorative march in Derry Londonderry
1 May	Labour Party won British General Election in a landslide victory ensuring Labour Prime Minister Tony Blair's overwhelming majority in the House of Commons
6 June	New government formed as a Coalition after elections in the Republic of Ireland
6 July	Riots broke out on the Garvaghy Road due to contested Orange Order parade
20 July	IRA restored cease-fire

15 September	Unionist parties boycotted first day of multi-party talks in Belfast
20 October	Unionist walked out of multi-party talks at Parliament Buildings, Belfast
November	A minority of dissidents walked out of an IRA convention in Donegal in opposition to the IRA participation in the peace process and the cessation of violence. They formed the Real IRA and vowed to continue military opposition to British rule
27 December	Loyalist Volunteer Force leader Billy Wright killed in the Maze Prison by INLA prisoners
31 December	Eddie Treanor, a Catholic civilian from North Belfast, was shot dead by Loyalists in retaliation for the killing of Billy Wright

1998

7 January	Secretary of State Mo Mowlam met Loyalist prisoners inside the Maze in an attempt to keep Loyalist parties in the talks
10 January	RUC intercepted a 500 lb Real IRA bomb in Banbridge, County Down
23 February	Sinn Féin were excluded from multi-party talks because of ongoing Republican violence. UDP was readmitted to talks following their eight-week suspension
3 March	Two friends, a Catholic and a Protestant, killed in Poyntzpass as they sat together in a local pub
10 April	Good Friday Agreement

> Northern Ireland embarked on a new political era today as the talks stood on the brink of an historic agreement after negotiations at Stormont. (*Belfast Telegraph*, 10 April 1998)

The Agreement proposes change in the Irish and British Constitutions to enshrine the principle of consent and support for Northern Ireland's place in the Union while also recognising the identity and aspirations of Nationalists. It is the people of Northern Ireland who will decide democratically their future. The Agreement creates new institutions; a Northern Ireland Assembly and a North/South council known as the Council of Ireland to encourage joint actions and co-operation.

> We owe it to all those who have suffered and died over the past three decades to grasp this opportunity to build

a society that will stand as a living testimony to the victims of our Troubles. (Monica McWilliams, leader of the Women's Coalition)

12 July Loyalists mounted protests all over Northern Ireland as a result of the Parades Commission decision not to allow the Orange march down the Garvaghy Road in Portadown. Three young brothers aged 10, 9 and 8 were killed when their home was petrol-bombed by Loyalists in Ballymoney, County Antrim, in the aftermath of the Drumcree stand-off

15 August Real IRA set off a car bomb in Omagh that killed 29 civilians and injured over 200 people. It was the single worst atrocity in Northern Ireland since the Troubles began

This was an attack upon the whole community – Nationalist, Unionist and neither. It was perpetrated by a small group of dissidents who do not represent anyone, anywhere. Their very barbarity is a reflection of their utter isolation from any strand of recognisable opinion in Irish politics. What I saw in the Royal Hospital on Sunday night in Belfast will stay with me all my life. We sat together in a room – myself, the hospital staff, the families of the victims, talking between the tears. (Prime Minister Tony Blair)

I renew my pledge to stand with the people of Northern Ireland against the perpetrators of violence, they will find no friends here. (United States President Bill Clinton)

The people of Northern Ireland can unite around this tragedy to express not just their grief but also the determination that this atrocity will not deflect from the way forward. (David Trimble, First Minister Designate)

I am totally horrified by this atrocity. I condemn it without any equivocation whatever. (Sinn Féin President Gerry Adams)

She was the kindest girl you could get and would do anything for you. She was more than delighted to get a job in the Oxfam shop. We reared an angel to 15 and now she has been taken away from us. (Godfrey Wilson, father of Lorraine (15) who was killed in the bomb explosion)

> We will drown them in peace. There's no doubt about that. I can see this groundswell. (Laurence Rush who lost his wife Elizabeth in the bomb explosion)

> I believe time will show this was the decisive act in unleashing a fierce determination from the people of Omagh to stand together as a community. (Reverend Ian Mairs as he buried Ann McCoombe)

> The terrible act of killing carried out in Omagh on Saturday would only have the effect to bring peace-loving and god-loving people together once again to show that this crime was utterly evil and totally unacceptable. (Father James Grimes)

22 August   INLA announce cease-fire

The INLA ended its campaign of terror with an apology for the killing of innocent victims:

> We acknowledge and admit our faults and grievous errors in our prosecution of the war. Innocent people were killed and injured and at times our actions as a liberation army fell short of what they should have been. (INLA Statement)

3 September   United States President Bill Clinton made his second visit to Northern Ireland in three years

8 September   Real IRA announce cease-fire

1 Northern Ireland, a State in Conflict

The history of Northern Ireland has been dominated by three principal problems which have changed extraordinary little throughout the entire period of its existence. These are, first, the problem of the triangular relationship with the rest of the United Kingdom and the rest of Ireland; second, the problem of the deep and continuing internal division of the population; finally the problem not only of developing a viable economy in such a small area, but of securing for the people public services and standards of welfare comparable with those in Britain. (Lyons, 1971: p. 695)

The vast literature on the Northern Ireland conflict is uneven in coverage and concentrates extensively on its politics. Politics, however, are just one aspect of Northern Ireland's difficulties; its long-term economic decline is another, that has not attracted the same deal of attention. It is thus important to present the context of the Troubles in terms of both the political and economic development of the region.

One could locate the interests and tensions that led to the formation of the Northern Ireland state deep in the recesses of Irish, European and British history. That history reveals Ireland as a land under successive conquest whereas in the interests of brevity, this account begins, rather arbitrarily with the Act of Union in 1801, under which Britain governed all 32 counties of the island of Ireland. Resistance to British rule was by then well formed. According to Bew et al. (1995), 1918–19 is a significant starting point in any discussion of the formation of the Northern Ireland state. In the 1916 Easter Rising, local armed groups, the forebears of the modern Irish Republican Army (IRA), took up arms against the British in an insurrection. The subsequent British execution of the leaders of that insurrection dramatically changed the political landscape. Prior to this, Sinn Féin, the political party espousing independence, was not a strong political force. In the subsequent general election of 1918, they swept to an astounding victory across Ireland. The newly elected Sinn Féin MPs refused to recognise the British government, or take their seats in the Westminster Parliament: instead they swore allegiance to an Irish Republic. British forces were seen as an occupying army against whom the IRA was to wage war. From 1919 to 1921, the Anglo–Irish War was fought between Britain and the IRA. By July 1921 a truce was agreed and Britain and the Republicans entered into negotiations.

Bew et al. (1995) suggest that three events in that period 1918–19 amounted to a crisis that set the parameters for the formation of both Northern Ireland and an Irish state. First, the IRA broke the British political and military domination of Ireland. In response, a shift took place in political relations within the establishment Unionist bloc. Finally, the British government devised a series of new Irish strategies, aimed at coping with the new situation and ensuring an outcome that would do least damage to British interests (Bew et al., 1995: p. 21).

The Government of Ireland Act introduced in 1920 divided the island of Ireland, establishing two new governments, one in the new Irish Free State, one in the new state of Northern Ireland. This new state comprised six of the nine counties of the province of Ulster, predominantly Unionist and Protestant in composition. The southern part of the island, the new Irish Free State, consisted of the remaining 26 counties. The manner of drawing the boundary of Northern Ireland resolved to some extent the problem of the resistance among Northern Protestants and Unionists to severing the link with Britain, and ensured a Protestant and Unionist majority within the new northern state. The 1920 Act had been essentially constructed to solve the Irish problem as it was stated in 1914, not 1920. By then, there were bitter divisions in the north over Home Rule, with Unionists resisting such a move, perceiving it as a treachery and a dilution of the Union.

Following the introduction of the new Act, enormous difficulties were encountered in establishing a political and administrative system for the six counties. In the period 1920–22 violent sectarian attacks on the Catholic community in Belfast resulted in 455 people being killed and an estimated 1776 wounded (Foster, 1988: p. 526). Ulster Unionists, who were now reluctantly in power in the north, did not have 'a political philosophy to help them take responsibility they never accepted or wanted' (Buckland, 1981: p. 23). The legacy of those early months of the Northern Ireland state was to leave indelible marks on political life. The new Parliament of Northern Ireland was described by its first Prime Minister Sir James Craig, later Lord Craigavon, as 'a Protestant Parliament for a Protestant people'. Majority rule, the party system and the electoral arrangements ensured permanent power for the Ulster Unionist Party. Security of the new state was a high priority, perceiving as it did a threat in the substantial Catholic minority. This minority had Irish Nationalist aspirations, and allegiances that lay elsewhere, and they challenged the legitimacy of the state from the outset. Law and order, defence of the state was a crucial issue, and was therefore underpinned by emergency legislation that lasted the life of the devolved parliament. Under this legislation, the Stormont government was empowered to take whatever measures it considered necessary to deal with insurgents and threats to security, including interning people without trial. The police force and the armed reserve force were militarised and almost exclusively Protestant.

Commentators such as Johnson (1981) and Bew et al. (1979) suggest that the rationale for partition lay in the uneven development of the economy of Ireland. The way devolution operated in Northern Ireland restricted opportunities for regional development in one crucial and fatal way: it facilitated the working out of sectarian rivalries.

Northern Ireland was born in the midst of the economic boom that immediately succeeded the First World War. By 1919, wage rates has surpassed their pre-war levels. Moreover, as a result of successful industrial action, weekly hours in shipbuilding and engineering had been reduced to an average of 44 – regarded as a significant assertion of trade union power (Morrissey, 1982: p. 67). It appeared to have a strong industrial base and a prosperous working class with wage rates and terms of employment comparable to any British region.

At that time, it was not perceived to be a region with acute economic problems. The North East of Ireland had successfully industrialised in the middle nineteenth century in a pattern similar to British regions. This pattern, known as regional sectoral specialisation (see Byrne, 1978), consisted of a concentration in key industrial sectors in which particular regions had comparative advantage. This concentration in Northern Ireland took the form of shipbuilding and textiles (originally cotton, to be replaced by linen), both of which generated complementary engineering industries. The comparative advantage of linen initially consisted of access to home-grown flax although, later, when Northern Ireland accounted for nearly all linen production in Britain, flax had to be imported from Belgium and Russia. The comparative advantage in shipbuilding was based on high rates of labour productivity and the irrelevance of distance to markets. At one of only two British Trade Union Congresses held in Ireland (Belfast, 1893) the delegate from the Belfast Trades Council lauded the industry, high wage levels and good housing in Belfast which attracted shipyard workers from less fortunate British cities (Byrne, 1978). It should be remembered, however, that agriculture remained the biggest employer of labour accounting for about 25 per cent of total employment between the wars compared to 6 per cent in Britain (Probert, 1978: p. 51). Nevertheless, the predominant unit of production in agriculture was the small family farm. Those who worked there were generally exempt from National Insurance and therefore were not registered among the unemployed.

During the Home Rule crisis, the Unionist argument was first to oppose it for the entire island and then to keep Ulster within the Union. The arguments were both political/religious and economic. With respect to the last, the fear was that even a partial separation from Britain would irrevocably damage industries fully integrated into the British industrial system. The Unionist case was that the area was economically self-sufficient with the biggest shipyards and biggest linen producers in the British Isles. When economic crisis occurred in the 1920s and 1930s, however, it was precisely the dominant industries of the nineteenth century that suffered irreversible decline. The very narrowness of its industrial base made Northern Ireland vulnerable to the structural changes of the inter-war period. Although the development of regional sectoral specialisation had served the region well, it also meant that the region was affected by economic change in four respects:

- first, it was sensitive to structural shifts in demand – typified by the shift in demand towards cotton and away from linen;
- second, it was affected by structural shifts in supply – particularly the rise in international competition in shipbuilding;
- third, one of its key sources of employment, the linen industry, competed on the basis of low costs (largely through paying low wages to women) and thus was sensitive to cost factors – as happened with rising prices of flax in the 1920s;
- finally, its industries were export oriented and therefore depended on Britain maintaining its share of global trade – this steadily declined after 1914.

In the 1920s, all of these factors were subject to adverse developments, so the region suffered disproportionately. Moreover, because of the narrow industrial base, employment decline in a single industry had a substantial effect on the numbers unemployed – unemployment was 'supercyclical'. In addition, it was not until the late 1950s that the region succeeded in attracting a sufficient number of replacement industries to counter the downward trend. Capital's slowness to react to economic change can probably be explained by the fact that the 'family firm was the typical unit of production in the province and the local economy remained largely unaffected by the rise of monopoly capital in the rest of the United Kingdom' (Probert, 1978). It had neither the resources nor adaptability to shift production into the new industries being developed in the 1930s. Thus:

> A long period of industrial expansion, stimulated towards the end of the First World War and the ensuing boom, came to an abrupt halt in 1921. Employment in shipbuilding that stood at 15,000 in 1913 and rose to 29,000 in 1919, fell to just over 7000 in 1924 and 2000 in 1933. (Haughton, 1987: p. 41)

The impact of such changes on unemployment was considerable. Official unemployment rose from 6.6 per cent in 1919 to 22.9 per cent in 1922 and the unemployment rate ranged between 13 per cent and 24 per cent through most of the 1920s. The full figures for the period are presented in Table 1.1.

Table 1.1 Average Unemployment, 1922–29

Year	No. of Insured Persons	Unemployment Rate
1922	260,993	22.9
1923	261,267	17.9
1924	258,160	16.6
1925	265,919	24.2
1926	263,500	23.3
1927	254,000	13.1
1928	251,000	17.2
1929	258,400	15.1

Source: Morrissey (1982)

The administration of the Stormont Parliament has been the constant subject of controversy. A first-past-the-post electoral system ensured strong one-party government, and thus from 1929 to 1969 inclusive, 37.5 per cent of all seats went to the Ulster Unionist Party (Darby, 1976, p. 117). Allegations of gerrymandering of local government electoral boundaries and systematic economic discrimination against the Catholic minority were constant, and the extent of discrimination continues to be alleged by Northern Catholics and contested by some Northern Unionists. Discrimination against Catholics in local government employment and the provision of services which excluded and marginalised Catholics was similarly alleged and contested.

Nor did the impact of the Second World War and the post-war boom affect the relative position of Northern Ireland's unemployment. Isles and Cuthbert (1957) record that for every year between 1939 and 1954, the region's unemployment rate was around three times that in Britain (Isles and Cuthbert, 1957: p. 18). The picture for the 1930s is presented in Table 1.2.

Table 1.2 Unemployment Rates, Great Britain and N. Ireland, 1931–39

Year	Great Britain		Northern Ireland	
	Males	Females	Males	Females
1931	22.4	17.7	30.3	24.8
1933	23.0	11.2	31.4	18.9
1935	17.5	9.4	27.8	21.9
1937	11.9	7.5	26.1	19.5
1939	10.7	9.4	24.8	20.3

Source: Isles and Cuthbert (1957: p. 37)

Unemployment rates in Northern Ireland were consistently higher over the period. Moreover, the difference increased. In 1931, unemployment rates in Northern Ireland were about a third higher for males and two-fifths higher for females. By 1939, unemployment rates in the region were more than twice as high as in Britain. Admittedly, a closer comparison could be drawn with weak British regions, but Northern Ireland's rates steadily drew away from those in Britain and the trend increased in the post-war period. Only the return of mass unemployment in Britain in the 1980s produced a relative convergence of unemployment rates.

Equally, there were significant differences between male and female unemployment over the period. In 1931, female unemployment rates were about 80 per cent of males in both Britain and Northern Ireland. Between 1933 and 1937 female unemployment rates in Britain were averaged at just over 50 per cent of the male rate. The relevant comparative figure for Northern Ireland was just over 70 per cent – reflecting the impact of the decline in linen employment.

Corresponding to the rest of the UK, unemployment rates in Northern Ireland fell after the Second World War. The region's unemployment remained substantially more serious than even in depressed British regions (see Table 1.3). By 1946, Britain had a rate of unemployment far below that defined as full employment in the Beveridge Report. At that time, only Northern Ireland and

Wales had unemployment rates above the Beveridge threshold. Eight years later, the worst British regional unemployment was represented by Scotland's 2.4 per cent while Northern Ireland's rate was nearly six times the British average. Full employment was not a readily achievable target in Northern Ireland.

Table 1.3 Rates of Unemployment (Selected Regions) 1946–54

	1946 (July)	1948 (June)	1950 (June)	1952 (June)	1954 (June)
Northern (England)	5.0	3.0	2.6	2.3	2.0
Scotland	4.5	3.0	2.7	3.2	2.4
Wales	8.5	5.5	3.4	2.6	2.1
N. Ireland	8.8	6.5	5.5	10.6	6.3
Britain	2.5	2.0	1.4	2.1	1.1

Source: Isles and Cuthbert (1957: p. 18)

The problem was that the regional economy was still heavily dependent on traditional manufacturing and had not experienced the rapid industrial restructuring seen in Britain during the 1930s. It was thus in no position to take advantage of the buoyant demand conditions prevailing after the immediate post-war difficulties. The annual percentage growth of manufacturing net output in Northern Ireland grew by only 0.6 per cent between 1951 and 1954 and 1.7 per cent between 1954 and 1958. The comparable rates for Scotland (1.2 per cent and 3.1 per cent) and Wales (6.3 per cent and 3.0 per cent) were considerably higher (Harris, 1991: p. 16). Moreover, traditional industries like linen had extensive local linkages. A high proportion of linen production was sold to other firms for further processing before export. Even in 1963, over 40 per cent of the demand for textile output came from within the textile industry. Thus, the structural decline of the linen industry had extensive effects on employment. O'Dowd et al. (1981) note that between 1960 and 1973, 27,000 (mostly female) jobs were lost in the traditional textile industry (O'Dowd et al., 1981: p. 53).

Harris (1991) describes the comparative position of the region thus:

> the average unemployment rate between 1949–59 was 7.4 per cent compared to 3.0 per cent for Scotland (which had the next highest regional rate) and 1.7 per cent for the UK;
> net outward migration of the labour force was 7.2 per cent between 1951–61, while in Scotland it was 5.7 per cent (and –0.5 per cent for the UK);

earnings in industry were 83 per cent of the UK for non-manual
workers in 1951 and 80 per cent for manual workers (the comparable
figures for Scotland were 93 per cent and 95 per cent);
  the average growth in manufacturing net capital stock (plant and
machinery) over the 1948–58 period was 0.3 per cent per annum (which
compares with 5.5 per cent p.a. growth in the UK). (Harris, 1991: p. 16)

By the 1950s, it was clear that Northern Ireland relied on industries
that were in long-term, in some cases terminal, decline. The rate
of indigenous industry formation was too low to tackle the scale
of unemployment. Accordingly, the view was taken by government
that only a policy of attracting inward investment would introduce
new products and new technologies while broadening the narrow
industrial base.

The limits on the development of this policy were essentially
political. Because of the electoral dominance of the Unionist Party,
shifts in leadership and policy directions occurred through internal
'coups' when it became apparent that a particular leader was
especially unpopular. The Prime Minister, Lord Brookeborough,
had been in office since 1943. He was a traditional, rather than
modernising Unionist, although he had steered through Stormont
the legislation to implement a welfare state and had intervened to
replace Andrews partly because of public concern with the high levels
of unemployment during the Second World War. His successor's
autobiography (O'Neill, 1972) suggests that he regarded planning
as a 'socialist menace'. In 1963, Brookeborough was faced with a
backbench revolt over the issue of unemployment and resigned.
He was replaced by the previous Minister of Finance, Terence
O'Neill who moved Brian Faulkner into the Finance Ministry. Both
were associated with a vigorous campaign to reconstruct the region's
industrial base.

Moreover, in late 1960s, a world-wide movement for civil rights
committed to non-violent action to secure rights to votes, jobs and
services, drew massive support from Catholics in Northern Ireland.
Civil rights demonstrations drew a hostile response from the state.
The eruption of violence on the streets, and the wholescale
movement of population in urban areas into separate communities
of Protestant and Catholic, led to the formation of local vigilantes
that in turn ultimately contributed to the resurgence of paramilitaries in local communities. The intensity of sectarian violence
resulted in the deployment of the British Army on the streets in
Northern Ireland. The British Army was deployed in Northern
Ireland from 1969, initially to defend vulnerable communities,
and they were initially welcomed by the Catholic community, who

saw themselves as defenceless against the power of the Stormont state. This however, was only a brief interlude.

In 1968 and 1969, tensions within the Republican movement over the issue of electoral absentionism led to a split in Sinn Féin and the IRA and the formation of the Provisional IRA, who 'became the most formidable organisation of its kind in the western world' (Taylor, 1997: p. 1). The IRA was reorganising, and began a declared war on the British troops and the Ulster Constabulary. After the beginning of the IRA campaign, in 1971, under emergency legislation, the Stormont government instituted a policy of internment without trial. Prison camps were established and filled with largely Catholic inmates. Perhaps of all government actions, these two together – the introduction of internment, and the later killing by the British Army of 14 Catholics on a civil rights demonstration in January 1972 (Bloody Sunday) – consolidated support for the IRA in Catholic communities. Soon, the British Army, together with the local police force became symbols of oppression in the Catholic community as they pursued a counter-insurgency strategy that involved suspension of the normal rule of law, the institution of non-jury courts, and saturation policing and surveillance in pursuit of the IRA. The fight for Irish independence was to become inextricably intertwined with the struggle of the Catholic minority for civil rights, and their complaints about harassment and ill-treatment at the hands of the security forces.

Northern Ireland was set on a path of escalating violence which peaked in the 1970s but which was to continue almost unabated until 1994. Meanwhile, the Stormont government struggled to manage the situation. Terence O'Neill's 'Ulster at the Crossroads' speech in December 1968 was followed by the arming of the police in March 1969, but O'Neill was perceived to be 'soft' and resigned in April 1969. In May 1969 Harold Wilson, then British Prime Minister, introduced electoral reform for Westminster elections and this was followed by the disbandment of the reserve police force, the Special Constabulary, known as the 'B-Specials', and their replacement on 1 January 1970 with the Ulster Defence Regiment, a local regiment of the British Army. Following the split in Sinn Féin in September 1970, an IRA bombing campaign was mounted. The introduction by the Stormont government of internment on 9 August 1971 led to civil disobedience largely in the Catholic community, and to street violence. The pattern for residential segregation was set by the population movements of August 1971, when 7000 refugees were said to have moved to the Republic of Ireland.

The 1970s also saw a reorganisation of the paramilitary organisations on the Protestant side, some of which remained legal for periods of time. The Ulster Volunteer Force and the Ulster Defence Association and various other military wings began a paramilitary campaign which randomly targeted Catholic civilians for assassination and which was intended as retaliation for the IRA's campaign. 1971 saw the beginning of the Loyalist bombing campaign, when a bomb left at McGurk's Bar in Belfast by the Ulster Volunteer Force killed 15 people. After January 1972 when the British Army fired on a civil rights march on Bloody Sunday, feelings in the Republic ran high. The British Embassy in Dublin was burned down three days later. The IRA intensified their operations culminating in a devastating bomb attack in Belfast in July 1972 in which nine people were killed. The IRA bombing campaign also moved to England when on 22 February 1972 seven people were killed by a bomb at Aldershot military barracks. The violence – bombing, shooting, riots – continued in Northern Ireland.

International attention was on Northern Ireland, and the continuing IRA violence, together with the crisis within the Stormont government meant that the violence could no longer be dismissed as an internal Northern Irish affair. The British government prorogued the Stormont Parliament and announced Direct Rule in Northern Ireland.

The 1970s can be seen as a period of political stalemate. The Sunningdale Agreement in 1973 was an attempt at establishing a Power Sharing Executive and a Council of Ireland. The Power Sharing Executive lasted only six months, however, and collapsed under the pressure of the Ulster Workers' Council strike of 1974. Between 1976 and 1981 Britain, first under a Labour administration and then under Margaret Thatcher, introduced policies that redefined the conflict in Northern Ireland as a problem with criminal activity, not a political struggle. Roy Mason, Secretary of State for Northern Ireland, instituted a policy of 'Ulsterisation' whereby British troops were replaced by members of the (largely Protestant) Northern Ireland regiment of the British Army, the UDR, later the Royal Irish Regiment. This had the effect of localising the conflict, and in retrospect, it also probably contributed to an increase in sectarian hatred. The local (Protestant) regiment and police force were being attacked and killed by the local (Catholic) IRA. In the minds of the IRA they were attacking the British state, in the experience of the Protestant community, it was they and their sons who were being killed.

Meanwhile, Westminster rule in Northern Ireland responded to the problems of the ailing economy by greater public expenditure. This was perhaps most noticeable in the allowances made by the Labour government (1974–79), for the special circumstances of Northern Ireland. While imposing greater fiscal restraint in Britain by 1976, the government treated Northern Ireland's expenditure with a greater latitude. For example, in 1977 Selective Financial Assistance for industry was improved alongside other reliefs and concessions. The impact was evident in the number of job promotions, which in 1976 had dropped to a low point of 3678, but which by 1978 had climbed to over twice that level.

This Labour approach was characterised by some commentators as combining a tough military offensive against the IRA with a tender 'hearts and minds' campaign based on greater support for social and economic improvement. The interventionism adopted was also in response to pressure from organisations such as trade unions as well as sections within the local Civil Service. For example, the Quigley Report (1976), which argued for greater public sector-led development, helped to generate a climate sympathetic to greater state expenditure.

So, while up to 1970, public sector expansion in Northern Ireland was roughly proportionate to that in Britain, 'since 1970 about 50,000 jobs have been created in the public sector over and above what would have been expected given national trends' (Canning et al., 1987: p. 223). Though the absolute accuracy of this estimate may be disputed, the period did see a substantial increase in public service employment, which offered new labour market opportunities for women, and absorbed some of the surplus labour of declining industries.

The 1970s and early 1980s policy innovations of criminalisation, and 'normalisation' – presenting the conflict as a crisis in law and order created by criminals, rather than a political conflict – added a further dimension to the conflict itself. After the introduction of direct rule, the abolition of internment and special category status for prisoners ended the distinction between political and ordinary crime. The removal of the recognition of politically motivated offences and the redefinition of prisoners convicted henceforth as criminal met with strong resistance from both Loyalist and Republican paramilitaries. Some collaboration occurred between them to resist this development. Up until then, prisoners were allowed to wear their own clothes, and to associate freely with each other, and they used this situation to live under a military command structure that was recognised by the prison authorities. It was

Republican prisoners who challenged the British government – now Conservative under Margaret Thatcher – on the issue of the political status of prisoners. In the 1980s Republican prisoners undertook prison protest involving the refusal to wear prison uniform. This meant that they were locked in their cells, and required to use buckets instead of toilets, and their access to washing facilities was also restricted, since they were dressed only in blankets. The protest escalated in the absence of concessions and prisoners refused to wash, and began to smear faeces on the walls of their cells. Again no concessions meant the announcement of a hunger strike to the death against political status and criminalisation. The first hunger strike was called off, since rumours of concessions were taken seriously. It restarted when no concessions materialised. The leader of the hunger strike, Bobby Sands, stood in a by-election for the British Parliament whilst on hunger strike and was elected as a Member of the Westminster Parliament. On the second hunger strike led by Sands, Margaret Thatcher refused to concede and ten hunger strikers including Sands died. World media attention was relatively critical of the British government, and quietly, in the aftermath, without apparently conceding anything, the prison authorities ostensibly met the prisoners' demands (McGarry and O'Leary, 1993).

The hunger strikes radicalised the Northern situation and specifically led to a change of strategy within Sinn Féin. With the success of hunger strike candidates in elections both in the North and South, Sinn Féin adopted a new approach that became known as the 'armalite and ballot box' – the pursuit of electoral mandates simultaneously with paramilitary action. They were now to contest elections within the state of Northern Ireland, which meant competition against the constitutional Nationalist party, the SDLP, for the share of the Nationalist vote. Sands' victory in the election of 1981 had strengthened the argument within the Republican movement about ending their electoral abstentionism, and members of Sinn Féin (the political wing of the IRA) entered electoral politics. Sinn Féin began to stand in opposition to the Social Democratic and Labour Party (constitutional Irish Nationalists) in Nationalist areas. This began a trend where Sinn Féin were elected in a growing number of Catholic constituencies. Sinn Féin's share of the Catholic vote, with the exception of the 1987–92 period, rose steadily. By 1997, in a population that was then 43 per cent Catholic: 47 per cent Protestant, Sinn Féin polled 16 per cent of the electorate. This compared to the 22 per cent polled by the SDLP (constitutional Nationalists), 33 per cent by the Ulster Unionist

Party and 14 per cent polled by the Democratic Unionist Party, a militant Loyalist party. The change in voting patterns was driven, not only by political events, but also by demographic change: a rise in the Catholic population and a corresponding decline in the Protestant population began to be evident in electoral terms.

By the mid-1980s, the failure of sporadic attempts by the British at achieving an internal settlement led to a change in thinking in London. Gradually, by 1985–87, Britain had come to accept the Irish government must play a central role in the management of the conflict in the North. The Anglo–Irish Agreement, signed in November 1985, provided the acceptance that the northern problem was a joint one. It gave the Irish government a consultative role in the running of the north for the first time, thus marking a significant shift in British thinking and policy. For British policy makers, the Anglo–Irish Agreement was an attempt to 'stem and reverse the growth of Sinn Féin, to stabilise support for the SDLP; and to encourage positive attitudes towards devolutionists within the UUP at the expense of both extremists within the DUP and integrationists within the UUP' (McGarry and O'Leary, 1993b: p. 258). The Agreement was vehemently opposed by the two main Unionist parties within Northern Ireland and by Sinn Féin. Unionist opposition was most visible in a massive demonstration on 23 November 1985, which brought Belfast city centre to a standstill. It was estimated that between 50,000 and 100,000 people turned out to voice their opposition to the Agreement. Just as Prime Minister Margaret Thatcher stood firm against the hunger strikers in 1981, she withstood Unionist opposition to the Anglo–Irish Agreement. Unionists had to accept that, unlike the Sunningdale Agreement which fell under their opposition, the Anglo–Irish Agreement was here to stay.

In the 1990s, it emerged that the British government had maintained secret contact with the IRA from the early 1970s. Similarly, it emerged that the SDLP had been talking secretly to Sinn Féin and openly talking to them since the late 1980s.

In January 1990, Peter Brooke, Secretary of State for Northern Ireland, began a series of 'talks about talks' with the constitutional parties in Northern Ireland and the Irish government. Sinn Féin was to be excluded until they renounced political violence. Formal discussions were to start on 30 April 1991. The agreed formulae for talks consisted of three strands. The first was the internal relationship between the parties; the second was the all-Ireland relationship and the third the relationship between Britain and Ireland. As with previous attempts the talks were ended in July 1991 when the parties failed to reach any agreement. Arguably, the position of the British government, who were dependent on the Ulster Unionist votes at Westminster for their survival as a government, was crucial.

Between 1991 and 1993 attempts at resuscitating these talks failed; 'false dawns are as common as political murders in Northern Ireland' (McGarry and O'Leary, 1993a: p. 1). For the next two years, both governments persisted in holding lateral and bilateral talks with the parties, with the role of the United States becoming more important for the Nationalist parties. The result was the Downing Street Declaration in 1993. By then, the beginnings of what came to be known as the 'peace process' was under way, leading to the Loyalist and Republican cease-fires of August 1994.

On 31 August 1994 the IRA announced 'a complete cessation of military operations'. 'We believe that an opportunity to create a just and lasting peace has been created. ... a solution will only be found as a result of inclusive negotiations' (IRA Statement: August, 1994). On 13 October 1994, the Combined Loyalist Military Command announced their cease-fire but warned it would be completely dependent on the continuation of the IRA cease-fire. Northern Ireland was to experience peace and an end to 25 years of violence that had seen the loss of 3535 lives. In February 1995, the two governments released the Framework Documents, which again were based on the three-stranded approach. With breakdowns in both cease-fires the following year, the peace process always remained fragile. From the cease-fires of 1994 until 9 April 1998, a further 69 people lost their lives to violence. Both cease-fires were subsequently reinstated, but all political negotiations proved difficult to establish, with major distrust and disagreements between the parties involved.

After the British Labour victory in the general election of 1997, the peace process had new life, and the landslide that elected the new British government meant that they were not dependent on Ulster Unionist votes in Westminster. The traditional stand of the Unionists of refusing to engage in talks with Sinn Féin because of their paramilitary links still caused difficulty for the talks process, in which the perennial issue of the decommissioning of weapons by paramilitary groups led to recurring impasses. The Loyalist parties with paramilitary links to the Progressive Unionist Party and the Ulster Democratic Party agreed to participate, and eventually the Ulster Unionists agreed to 'confront Sinn Féin' by actually attending talks. The more radical Democratic Unionist Party refused to participate, and boycotted the talks, refusing to 'negotiate with terrorists'. The newly elected British Labour government demonstrated a more energetic commitment to the talks process, and the United States government supported the process by providing a chairperson, Senator George Mitchell, to oversee the process. Senator Mitchell was to preside over almost two years of negotiation.

What made these peace talks different from all other attempts at conflict resolution was the fact that all parties were invited to participate alongside the two sovereign governments. Two parties, the Democratic Unionist Party and the United Kingdom Unionist Party, refused to participate. Crucially, however, the political wings of the paramilitary groupings were at the talks table. With a deadline for agreement set for 9 April 1998, both the British and Irish premiers joined in the negotiations as the deadline grew closer. On Good Friday, 17 April, the parties and the two governments finally reached agreement. The agreement, subject to referenda in both Northern Ireland and the Republic of Ireland, involved constitutional change in the Republic of Ireland to withdraw the territorial claim to Northern Ireland, cross-border bodies with executive powers, a Northern Ireland assembly with power sharing and the early release of paramilitary prisoners.

INTERPRETATIONS OF THE NORTHERN IRELAND CONFLICT

In his 1983 inaugural lecture, John Whyte claimed that in proportion to the population, there might well be as much research available on Northern Ireland as on any other part of the world. While there may be hundreds of books and articles written on the conflict, there is little consensus amongst the numerous interpretations of the violence which has affected Northern Ireland. Both Whyte (1991) and later Cradden (1993) provide comprehensive surveys of the range of theorisation about Northern Ireland.

Reformability

Amongst writers who perceive a problem within Northern Ireland's political formations – and not all do – a key question that has been addressed by many writers is whether the Northern Ireland state is reformable. Analyses are divided on this issue. Some, mainly liberals, social democrats and some Marxists, believe that since 1972 the Northern Ireland state has either fundamentally reformed or conditions for successful reform have been improved. Others, those who espouse more Republican analyses, see Northern Ireland as irreformable whilst it remains a separate political unit. These latter analyses argue that the imperialist project within Northern Ireland is repressive in nature, rendering reform unfeasible, and British withdrawal the only viable solution to the conflict (O'Dowd et al., 1981: p. 53).

Traditional Irish Nationalist Perspectives

The traditional Nationalist/anti-imperialist interpretation of the Northern Ireland situation can be summarised in two main propositions. First, the people of Ireland form one nation, and second the responsibility for Irish division lies solely with Britain. O'Hegarty (1952), Gwynn (1950), Gallagher (1957) and Greaves (1972) are exponents of this view. Greaves (1972) believes there is a clash of interests between English capitalism and Irish democracy. 'This is expressed in the economic, political, constitutional, legal and cultural conflict' (Greaves, 1972: p. 5). The only solution to the conflict, therefore, has to lie in a united Ireland. Gallagher (1957) argues that neither Nationalists nor Unionists originally wanted partition, but rather British politicians, for party advantage, engineered partition. Farrell (1976) suggests that British imperialism, having failed to sustain control over the island of Ireland, clung to the more industrialised north east of Ireland in order to satisfy essentially economic goals by the profit to be made in the north-east's shipbuilding, engineering and textile industries. The formation and structure of the state all connected to the struggle against imperialism in Ireland.

Revisionism

With the onset of violence in 1969, came the beginnings of revisionism, and the concomitant challenge to traditional Nationalist interpretations. Throughout the 1970s and 1980s it became increasingly difficult to argue that Britain alone was responsible for and supportive of Protestant opposition to Irish unity. This shift in thinking is represented in the works of Garret Fitzgerald (1972) and Conor Cruise O'Brien (1972). They both propose that the British role in Ireland is not the crucial problem, but rather Protestant fears about their position in a united Ireland. O'Brien

(1972) argues that the problem is not 'how to get unity, but how to share an island in conditions of peace and reasonable fairness' (O'Brien, 1972: p. 297). O'Halloran's (1987) analysis of the period 1922–37 similarly argues the inability of Nationalists in the Southern state to address the problem of reconciling Irish unity with the absolute refusal of Unionists to countenance such a prospect.

Although recent writings have concentrated on the revisionist attitudes, the traditional Nationalist argument has been kept alive by works such as Collins (1985), Wilson (1985) and Adams (1986, 1988) who continue to argue that British rule in Northern Ireland is still the core of the problem. For Adams (1988) the principal argument is that 'Ireland has a right to self determination and that the British presence prevents the Irish people from exercising that right' (Adams, 1988: p. 26). John Whyte (1991) points out that criticism of British policy is not confined to Nationalist writers. Kenny (1986), Murphy (1978) and O'Malley (1983) also criticise British policy and the conditional nature of their claim to the North. O'Malley suggests that 'none of the parties to the conflict trust Britain ... because she will not declare herself and no one knows where she stands' (O'Malley, 1983: p. 254). This argument seems to be borne out when one examines documents such as the Sunningdale Agreement (1973), the Anglo–Irish Agreement (1985), the Downing Street Declaration (1993) and the Framework Documents (1995), in all of which Britain fails to outline its long-term objectives. Arguably, this ambiguity in the British position, which has been a constant feature since 1972, has played a crucial part in fanning the flames of conflict.

Traditional Unionist Perspectives

The traditional Unionist viewpoint takes a rather different stand to that of traditional Nationalism. The traditional Unionist argument insists the problem lies with the refusal of Nationalists to recognise two distinct peoples and cultures in Ireland: Nationalist and Unionist, and with Nationalist attempts to destroy the state of Northern Ireland and replace it with a united Ireland. Unionists argue that, within Northern Ireland, they should be given the same right to self-determination that Nationalists espouse for themselves in the context of the entire island of Ireland. Shearman (1942), Heslinga (1962), Gibbon (1975), Miller (1978) and Patterson (1980) make substantial contributions to documenting this view, and to the literature on Unionism. Heslinga (1962) provides a counterpart to Gallagher (1957), in that he points to the many differences between the North and South of Ireland, religion in particular, to support the view that partition was the natural result of these divisions. Others, such as McCartney et al. (1981), Paisley et al. (1982) and Kennedy (1989), refer to the threat from the Republic of Ireland to explain the motivation of Northern Protestants in wanting to remain a separate political unit.

The Threat from the Republic of Ireland

The threat (or perceived threat) to Northern Unionists from the Republic of Ireland can be categorised in three areas: religion, economics and nationality.

Religion
Unionists have serious objections to the power and position of the Catholic Church, which is enshrined in the 1937 Constitution in the Irish Free State, and accompanied by the enactment of laws which enforce exclusively Catholic values in education and family life, namely laws on divorce, on contraception and censorship.

Economics
At the establishment of the state of Northern Ireland in 1921, the industrial north-east of Ireland was flourishing, and the link with Britain was certainly more economically advantageous at that time than a link with the agricultural South. In the interim, the decline or disappearance of many of the industries which formed the industrial base of Northern Ireland has shifted the argument, so that now the argument for the union with Britain is based on the need of subvention for the ailing Northern economy from an economic power. Membership of the European Union, and the availability of variable amounts of special aid from that source, has not substantially altered this argument.

Nationality
The right to be British is central in the Unionist argument. Paisley et al. (1982) explain, 'a large section of the community in Ulster has strong and positive loyalties. They do not wish to abandon their allegiances or change their nationality' (p. 52). There are over a million Protestants in the North who regard themselves as British subjects and owe their allegiance to the English Crown. The territorial claim over Northern Ireland set out in Articles 2 and 3

of the Constitution of the Republic of Ireland, which claim the whole of Ireland as national territory, infuriates the Unionists. 'The Northern Unionists object not only to the fundamental nature of the claim to the territory of Northern Ireland, but to the pseudo-legality which it affords to the Provisional IRA's campaign of violence in the North' (McCartney et al., 1981: p. 2). Unionists are infuriated. 'The claim to sovereignty ... provides an ideological umbrella which gave shelter to several campaigns of paramilitary outrages against the people of Northern Ireland, directed and organised from within the Republic' (Paisley et al., 1982: p. 41).

Contested Explanations of the Conflict

Just as traditional Nationalists find it difficult to blame all the problems of the North on Britain, it has become more difficult for traditional Unionists to see the problem as just the demand for Irish unity from the Southern state. The criticisms and allegations of the Unionist regime from 1921 to 1969 have to be addressed. Cormack and Osborne (1983) argue that while Protestants were faced with a Southern state that was Catholic in culture and institutions, and while Catholics refused to accept the validity of the state in Northern Ireland, the social and economic exclusion experienced by Catholics was more than just a defensive reaction on the part of Protestants. This is recognised by a number of authors (Stewart (1977), Bew et al. (1979), Buckland (1979) and Farrell (1983)). The opening of archives in the 1970s provided evidence that some discrimination was systematic and deliberate. Bew et al. (1979) describe a division in the Unionist Party between the populists who were discriminatory and the anti-populists who were more impartial. According to John Whyte (1991) there are now serious disagreements on the extent of the discrimination. 'At one extreme can be found authors such as Rowthorn and Wayne (1988, pp. 28–38) who depict it as pervasive. At the other extreme are authors such as Paisley, Robinson and Taylor (1982, pp. 63–68) who claim that nothing was wrong at all' (Whyte, 1991: p. 167).

The role of the Irish government is still not above criticism. O'Malley (1983), Cox (1985) and Garvin (1988) examine public opinion in the South to unity, and the ambivalence of political attitude to that prospect. Garvin believes unity 'would have devastating and possibly destabilising effects on the Republic' (Garvin, 1988: p. 109). If this is the case, it is difficult to explain Irish government resistance to changes to the territorial claim in their Constitution. The answer must be that even if the bulk of public opinion in the South is indifferent on the issue of unity, there are still a significant number who have strong pro-unity sentiments. The territorial claim in the Constitution is also viewed by many as a vital bargaining tool in any settlement. This latter view angers Unionists in the North and exacerbates their fear that the Republic's territorial claim is a stepping stone towards unity. O'Malley suggests that peace on the island cannot be achieved until the Republic 'confronts its own reality and steps away from the dream of unification' (O'Malley, 1993: p. 357). Clearly, Protestant resistance to unification would not disappear if Britain withdrew, and in practice the government in the Republic gives low priority to achieving unification, nor is there any public pressure to increase that priority, as is illustrated by the results of many opinion polls.

Although we have already mentioned the work of Farrell (1976, 1983) and Bew et al. (1979) in the traditional Nationalist and Unionist interpretations, these authors, together with Greaves (1972) and McCann (1974), provide major contributions to the literature on Marxist interpretations of the Northern Ireland problem. McCann and Farrell both take similar positions; that Northern Ireland was governed by a capitalist class who kept the working class divided, using mechanisms such as sectarianism and differential discrimination. O'Dowd et al. (1981) argue that the Northern state was additionally sustained by division and supremacy. While Partition with its concomitant economic aspects almost guaranteed the island would be politically divided, sectarianism determined the form the state would take. O'Dowd et al. (1981) depart from other Marxist analyses in their emphasis on the tenacity and autonomy of Protestant working-class identity, which they argue other Marxists have underestimated. According to John Whyte (1991), O'Dowd et al. (1981) go beyond simple class analysis. They reject the concept of sectarian superstructure resting on a class base, arguing that class and sectarianism are inextricably intermingled (O'Dowd et al., 1981: p. 187).

Martin (1982) analyses the views of both the traditional and revisionist Marxist analyses. Like O'Dowd et al. (1981) he argues that the greatest weakness of traditional Marxists is their failure to grasp the autonomy of working-class Protestantism. Revisionists, on the other hand, highlight the progressive role of the British state at the expense of attending to its reactionary role in Northern Ireland. Bew (1979) argues 'the Northern Ireland State is not inherently reactionary – the problem lies not in its existence but in the specific forms' (Bew et al., 1979: p. 144). Bew et al. (1979)

and Probert (1978) are less concerned with the national question and imperialism, focusing instead on the Protestant position and on Protestant working-class identity.

Rose (1971) is critical of Marxist analysts' concentration on economic factors. He believes the conflict is so intractable precisely because is not economic. Economic conflicts, he argues, are for the most part resolvable. The Northern Ireland conflict's components of religion and identity render it much harder to solve, he concludes. Other writers such as Burton (1978) accuse Marxist writers on Northern Ireland of 'sacrificing the complexity of the problem ... to maintain the plausibility of a theoretical position' (Burton, 1978: p. 157).

Over and above Nationalist, Unionist and Marxist interpretations of the Northern Ireland conflict, some writers have sought to provide a perspective on the range of approaches. O'Leary (1985) discusses the distinction between endogenous and exogenous explanations of the conflict. Traditional Nationalist, Unionist and Marxist literature offer exogenous explanations believing the problem to be the responsibility of some external force – the British, Irish or the capitalist. O'Leary points to another approach, which relies on endogenous explanations. Authors using this approach view the problem as primarily internal to Northern Ireland. Authors of this school, according to O'Leary, include Rose (1971), O'Brien (1972) and Darby (1976). This endogenous approach is apparent in documents such as the New Ireland Forum Report (1984) and the Kilbrandon Report (1984). This approach is exemplified by the New Ireland Forum Report's statement that 'the conflict between Nationalist and Unionist identities has been concentrated within the narrow ground of Northern Ireland'. Similarly, Boyle and Hadden conceptualise Northern Ireland as 'a divided society in which two separate communities are locked in political conflict' (Boyle and Hadden, 1985: p. 53).

On the other hand, O'Malley (1983), Guelke (1988) and Wright (1987) put considerable stress on external factors. O'Malley discusses the three important relationships that now make up Strands 1, 2 and 3 of the Agreement of April 1998. These are: the external relations between Britain and Ireland; the internal relations between Catholics and Protestants within Northern Ireland; and the relations between the two parts of Ireland. Guelke (1988) believes the conflict cannot be expressed simply as an artefact of either British imperialism or Irish irredentism. 'Internationalisation has made the conflict more intractable' (Guelke, 1988: p. 205). Wright (1987) addresses the interaction of the internal and external factors, comparing Northern Ireland with other societies with similar experiences of conflict, such as Lebanon and French Algeria. Wright conceptualises the population of Northern Ireland as split into the dominant population (the Unionists) who are citizens of the metropolis, and a dominated population (the Nationalists). The internal conflict he suggests is shaped very significantly by the fact that Northern Ireland is a frontier region and the internal conflict is exacerbated by the pull of rival outside powers. Life on the frontier that composes Northern Ireland has, according to Wright, revolved around the ability of the Unionists to dominate the Nationalists.

At the time of negotiating the Good Friday Agreement in Northern Ireland, internal conflict interpretations informed the understanding of the dynamics of negotiations. Relations between the two communities are at the core of any substantive agreement. The traditional Nationalist and Unionist interpretations inform the understanding of the perspectives that each of the parties bring to such negotiations. Understanding the crucial roles of the British and Irish governments, and that of the government of the United States is informed by exogenous and international comparative accounts. Only in the synthetic analysis which employs insights from these various approaches can a dynamic and complex under-standing of Northern Ireland be constructed.

2 Understanding Political Violence in Northern Ireland

The Troubles in Northern Ireland have attracted a great deal of research interest producing hundreds of books and thousands of articles on the Northern Ireland conflict. The following chapter is an attempt to review some of the literature on violence and deaths in Northern Ireland. It will be reviewed in two parts. First, a number of studies conducted at various times in the 20 years of violence, which have used various death and injury statistics to examine the geographical location and other aspects of deaths in the Troubles. These will be reviewed under 'Analysing Statistics on Deaths in Northern Ireland's Conflict'. Second, there has been a great deal of research on the Republican movement, especially the Provisional IRA with works such as *Provos* (Taylor, 1997) and *The Provisional IRA* (Bishop and Mallie, 1987). There is relatively little research on Loyalist paramilitaries, with only one book on the UVF (Cusack and McDonald, 1997) and a more general work on Loyalist paramilitaries (Bruce, 1992). These works will be reviewed under the heading 'Agents of the Conflict'.

ANALYSING STATISTICS ON DEATHS IN NORTHERN IRELAND'S CONFLICT

Schellenberg's (1977) study of geography and violence involved the analysis of 34 regions under the old County Boroughs of Belfast and Derry Londonderry. Correlation and regression analysis were used to study the relationship between the death rate and eleven other variables, several of which were demographic and included population change, population size and probably the most important, the Catholic share of the total population. Schellenberg concludes that just two out of these eleven variables could explain the high proportion of the inter-regional variation in deaths. These variables were population density and the size of the Catholic proportion of the local population. Both of these were positively correlated with violence. His results indicated that the larger the Catholic share of the population in a region, the higher the death rate.

Darby and Williamson's (1978) study of violence in Northern Ireland included a map that illustrates the uneven distribution of violence across Northern Ireland. They point out the lack of official statistics on the distribution of violence, and in order to analyse the distribution of violence, conducted a census of violent incidents during a 14-day period at the beginning of October each year from 1969 to 1975. They used Deutsch and Magowan and a content analysis of the *Irish Times* as data sources. Whilst they lay no claims to the conclusiveness of the exercise, they point out a number of 'interesting themes ... the most remarkable feature is the concentration of violence in the urban areas of Belfast and Derry Londonderry' (Darby and Williamson, 1978: p. 13) and found that 72 per cent of deaths and 91 per cent of injuries resulting from civil disorder took place in these areas. They also found that 55 per cent of bombs, 33 per cent of gun battles and 83 per cent of armed raids occurred in these two locations, and that rural violence was concentrated in border regions and in the so-called 'murder triangle' around Craigavon. They conclude by remarking on the very localised nature of the violence, and the lack of variation in its pattern of distribution from year to year.

In *Social Violence in Northern Ireland*, Mitchell (1979) cited the causes of violence in Northern Ireland as colonialism, sectarianism and class politics. Using official statistics, he found that the majority of victims up to 1977 were innocent third parties, with Republican paramilitaries, Loyalist paramilitaries and the security forces the three main groups responsible for the violence. He found that two-thirds of all fatalities between 1971 and 1976 occurred in Belfast and Derry Londonderry. Mitchell identified three different levels in the spatial distribution of deaths: first, in Belfast, the city of Derry Londonderry and Co. Armagh there had been high levels of violence; second, western counties such as Fermanagh, Tyrone and Derry Londonderry had experienced intermediate levels of violence; and third, Down, Antrim and suburban Belfast had been the least affected. These findings were consistent with Schellenberg (1977), finding that 'the death rate in areas with Catholic majorities is six times as great as in areas which are over 80 per cent Protestant and is twice as great as in areas with large Catholic minorities' (Mitchell 1979: pp. 179–200). By way of explanation, both Schellenberg (1977) and Mitchell pointed out that support for the government is lowest in Catholic areas, and the violent challenge against the status quo has typically come from the Catholic community.

Murray and Boal (1979) investigated the killings of civilians in their homes, what was then known as the 'doorstep killings', as most of the victims were shot on answering the door. There has been a concentration of these killings, nowadays referred to as random sectarian killings, in north Belfast. Murray and Boal (1979) analysed the sectarian geography within an area, together with the situation of small Catholic and Protestant housing areas which have been difficult to defend and easy to attack from the outside. Since killers can also return to the safety of their own neighbourhoods close by, small ghetto areas provide easy targets, whilst the adjacent larger ghettos provide the best security. The authors describe the change in the sectarian geography of north Belfast since 1969 and explain that Catholic expansion has resulted in Protestants feeling threatened and resentful at their loss of territory.

Murray (1982) dealt further with this concept. He distinguished three facets of the violence – the guerrilla war, the economic campaign and the sectarian conflict. He pointed out that by 1977, most of the violence in Belfast was sectarian in nature. In Derry Londonderry, sectarian violence was relatively low, with most of the violence falling into the other two categories of the guerrilla war and the economic campaign. These two forms of violence also predominated in the violence of the border areas. He estimated that up to 1977, either guerrilla war or the economic campaign – both of which have been exclusively fought by paramilitaries from the Catholic community – caused 53 per cent of deaths. Poole (1983), re-working Murray's data, showed that, because of the concentration of sectarian deaths in Belfast, deaths outside of Belfast due to Republican paramilitaries were much higher than the corresponding figure for the Province as a whole. The proportion of sectarian deaths outside Belfast by Catholic perpetrators was higher than it was in Belfast. Poole suggested 'the effect of these two factors produces an estimate that between 75 per cent and 80 per cent of all deaths attributable to the Troubles outside the Belfast region have their origin in the Catholic community' (Poole, 1983: p. 163).

Murray also dealt at length with Schellenberg's (1977) findings. His own analysis covered a more detailed 322 areas based on Northern Ireland wards. He found the correlation between violence and ethnicity was not as strong as Schellenberg's work suggests. His analysis deviated from Schellenberg's in two principal ways. First, Murray argued that there were many parts of Northern Ireland where Catholics were in the majority, yet there was little political violence. Second, if Belfast was treated as a single entity, at the time of writing it had a clear Catholic minority, yet there was a high level of political violence. This second point tended to ignore the marked residential segregation which arguably made it difficult to justify looking at Belfast as a single entity, since in certain substantial areas of Belfast, Catholics did form the majority. Murray established a more complex set of hypotheses than those of Schellenberg (1977) or Mitchell (1979). He set up four further conditions which influence the level of violence: the presence of historical precedents; a tradition of violence; a high level of alienation of Catholics from Protestant society; and an environment which both provides the target and security for the perpetrators. Murray pointed out that the 'difference between Catholic majority areas and Catholic minority areas is more salient in affecting the location of violence' (Murray, 1982: p. 165). According to Poole (1983), the implication of Murray's work was that the amount and type of violence in a geographical area depended on the identity and nature of the ethnic majority in that area. 'The level of violence at any one location is thus dependent on the ethnic composition at a whole series of spatial scale levels involving that location' (Murray, 1982: p. 166).

Poole (1983) provided a detailed analysis and literature review on the demography of political violence. In discussing the quantitative analysis of the geographical location of political violence undertaken by Schellenberg (1977), Mitchell (1979), Murray and Boal (1979) and Murray (1982), he concluded that the double majority model could be used to explain why violence originated in the Catholic community. Catholics were described as the frustrated majority (p. 162), being deprived of political power and having their wishes on the constitutional question constantly blocked. Hence violence was legitimised.

Poole (1983) went on to analyse the level of political violence according to geographical location in Northern Ireland, using government statistics. Urban and rural areas were separately analysed, with 'urban' defined as settlements with a population exceeding 5000 – a definition which included 31 towns and 64.4 per cent of Northern Ireland's total population. The remaining 35.6 per cent was classified as rural and divided into 28 regions of approximately equal population size. Fatal incidents were calculated per 1000 of the population for both urban and rural areas. This analysis of urban violence revealed geographical unevenness in two distinct senses. First, it emerged that some towns have experienced high rates of violence, whilst others had low rates. Second, there was variation due to regionalisation in areas with both high and low levels of violence. Poole's data revealed a clear clustering of high violence towns in County Armagh and immediate vicinity. This county also contained five of the eight towns with the highest rate of violence according to Poole's analysis. Derry Londonderry and Strabane formed a cluster in the north-west, leaving Belfast isolated as the urban area with the highest rate of violence in the east.

Poole searched for an environmental effect to explain the different spatial distribution of towns with high and low levels of violence. In his earlier work (1983), he found a positive correlation between the level of violence and the size of the Catholic ghetto population. By Catholic ghetto population he meant 'the number of Catholics living in urban neighbourhood which were at least 90 per cent Catholic in 1971' (Poole 1983: p. 175).

In 'The Spatial Distribution of Political Violence in Northern Ireland: An Update to 1993', Poole revised his earlier analysis on location and death. He was one of the first authors to conduct a detailed, in-depth geographical analysis of political violence in Northern Ireland. It is the only work of its kind to provide analysis from 1969 and 1993 and identify any variation over time in the spatial pattern of violence. In this later paper he tested this hypothesis in a more complex way and made some changes to his earlier methods. In his earlier study (1983), urban neighbourhoods were identified as geographical sub-areas, each averaging 200 households. For the later analysis, smaller areas of 100 households were examined. In the later study he also adjusted his methods to compensate for low response rates to the question on religious affiliation. With these adjustments, his later study replicated his earlier findings of a strong correlation between the rate of urban political violence and the presence of a Catholic ghetto population.

Poole demonstrated that towns in Northern Ireland varied massively in the degree of their levels of political violence. His data clearly revealed a distinct group of towns with a high rate of violence and another distinct group with a low rate of violence. Poole compared location and death rates within four short periods from 1969 to 1993. Four towns – Armagh, Belfast, Derry Londonderry and Newry – all ranked in the top seven for each of the four periods. He concluded that what emerges 'is the dominant temporal characteristic of this urban violence and the remarkable stability of its spatial pattern over the whole period' (Poole, 1993: p. 36).

Rural violence, Poole found, was less uniformly geographically distributed than its urban counterpart, and had a wider range between maximum and minimum levels of violence. Five of the 28 rural regions he examined formed a belt along the border in south

Ulster and together contained 53 per cent of all rural deaths from 1969 to 1993. As with the urban regions, these six most violent rural regions were all ranked in the top seven areas with highest violence in both 1969–73 and 1985–93 and they constituted the top six in 1974–76, confirming Poole's assertion about the stability of these patterns over time. Poole concluded that the geography of urban and rural violence suggested there is 'a process of localised social reproduction involving both political violence itself and the environment which may be hypothesised to influence it' (Poole, 1993: p. 42).

O'Duffy and O'Leary (1990) examined long-term trends and aggregates of the statistics on deaths, and commented on a number of features of these. They pointed to the extremely high death rate at the beginning of the Troubles, with over a quarter of all deaths at that time (1989) occurring in the first four years since 1969, and identified a 'dramatic fall off in deaths' since the early 1970s. They isolated an increase in the death rate after the signing of the Anglo–Irish Agreement in the short term, but not sufficient to reverse the longer-term downward trend. They posited three explanations for the downward trend: first, the decrease in the number of sectarian killings of Catholic civilians carried out by Loyalist paramilitaries; second, the reorganisation of Nationalist paramilitaries into 'active service units' and the resultant reduction in the death toll due to Nationalist paramilitaries; and third the increase in the effectiveness of surveillance by the security forces which may have also acted to reduce the level of violence. They pointed to the reduction in the number of deaths among British Army personnel and a concomitant rise in the death rate of local security forces as a result of the British government security policy of 'Ulsterisation' whereby local security forces were deployed to gradually replace British troops. They also alluded to possible changes in targeting strategy on the part of Nationalist paramilitaries which may have accompanied this policy.

The overall breakdown of people killed in the Troubles in the period studied was also analysed. They wrote, 'Surprisingly, in the light of British public perceptions, the largest single category of victims has been Catholic civilians (32.5 per cent) who just shade the security forces (31.2 per cent).' They pointed out, given the smaller size of the Catholic population in Northern Ireland, that, 'Catholic civilians (896 deaths) have suffered both *absolutely* and *relatively* more than Protestant civilians (575 deaths)' (O'Duffy and O'Leary, 1990: p. 322); emphasis in original. They offered four explanations for this: first, the targeting of Catholic civilians by

Loyalist paramilitaries; second, that local security forces were predominantly Protestant, and simple comparison of Catholic–Protestant deaths obscures the true Protestant death rate; third, the high number of Catholic civilians killed by Nationalist paramilitaries, whether by accident or by 'disciplining' (*sic*) their own community; and fourth, Catholic civilians were more likely to be killed by the security forces due to high levels of security forces presence in Catholic areas. They concluded that Nationalist paramilitary violence is primarily strategic rather than sectarian, even though 'Protestants understandably *interpret* killings of Protestant members of the security forces as sectarian' (O'Duffy and O'Leary, 1990: p. 324). They also pointed to the lower number of deaths amongst paramilitaries than amongst civilians, or amongst security forces, although they also pointed to the higher death rate amongst Nationalist paramilitaries – which was four times that of Loyalist paramilitaries.

O'Duffy and O'Leary (1990) also examined responsibility for deaths in the Troubles. They pointed out that:

> contrary to what Irish-American Nationalist propagandists imply ... the security forces have been responsible for only 327 deaths or 11.8 per cent of the overall death-toll ... the security forces kill less than half as many people as Loyalist paramilitaries and ... Loyalist paramilitaries kill less than half as many people as Nationalist paramilitaries [who are] ... responsible for more than half of all deaths, partially confirming the British perception that they are the primary antagonists in the conflict ... Loyalist paramilitaries have killed slightly more civilians than Nationalist paramilitaries ... and that both sets of paramilitaries have been responsible for nearly 80 percent of all civilian deaths. (O'Duffy and O'Leary, 1990: pp. 324–5)

They analysed civilian deaths by agency responsible, and pointed out that the security forces kill a civilian one time in two, that is, they are 'efficient and effective' – if not always law abiding – only one time in two:

> This demonstrable level of incompetence, error or malevolence (depending on one's point of view) is made somewhat more palatable by the low overall share of the death-toll attributable to the security forces ... the low ratio of 'appropriate' to 'wrongful' killings – especially disproportionate wrongful killings of Catholics – helps explain why the security forces are poorly regarded by Northern Ireland Catholics. (O'Duffy and O'Leary, 1990: p. 325)

Using a series of pie charts, O'Duffy and O'Leary illustrated how Nationalist paramilitaries:

by far exceed other agents in responsibility for killings ... they kill civilians just over 3 times in 5, a 'kill ratio' which also indicates a high degree of incompetence, error or malevolence with respect to civilians. Although they are more likely to kill their declared targets than the security forces ... the absolute level of civilian deaths which they have caused is very close to the number of civilians killed by Loyalist paramilitaries ... Although Nationalist paramilitary killings are primarily 'non-sectarian' ... they also kill a very high number of Protestant civilians ... Time-series data ... show ... that Nationalists have killed proportionately higher numbers of non-civilians in the last decade. (O'Duffy and O'Leary, 1990: pp. 326–7)

Loyalist paramilitaries, they pointed out:

kill civilians almost exclusively. This feature of their activities has been consistent since their first eruption ... It is also easy to explain. Catholic civilians are easier to identify than Nationalist paramilitaries. They are also softer targets. They are therefore killed in acts of 'representative violence' ... which are meant to deter Catholics from supporting the IRA or other Nationalist organisations ... there have also been a number of psychopathic killings by supposedly politically motivated Loyalists ... the most barbaric of these ... were carried out by the 'Shankill butchers'. (O'Duffy and O'Leary, 1990: p. 328–30)

Here O'Duffy and O'Leary relied on popular definitions of psycho-pathology rather than any official diagnosis of the Shankill butchers, since there is no evidence to suggest that any of the so-called Shankill butchers were, in fact, mentally ill.

O'Duffy and O'Leary went on to examine agents responsible for deaths of the various categories of people with high death rates: Nationalist paramilitaries; members of the security forces; Catholic civilians; Protestant civilians and Loyalist paramilitaries. They pointed out the high level of death inflicted by Nationalist para-militaries on themselves. They explained this with reference to 'internal disciplinary' (*sic*) killing, i.e. the execution of (often merely alleged) informants and wayward (or unreliable) members; 'faction fighting' and, 'in the racist language of the British security forces, "Paddy factors" i.e. bungled actions'. The killers of the security forces, they found, unsurprisingly, were primarily the Nationalist paramilitaries, with 97 per cent of security forces deaths having been caused by them. Catholic civilians were killed by Loyalist para-militaries (over half of Catholic civilian deaths), and by Nationalist paramilitaries (one in five Catholic civilian deaths) – who had killed more Catholic civilians at the point of their analysis than they had killed security forces. Loyalist paramilitaries had been responsible for one in five of the total Protestant civilian deaths, and over half the deaths of Loyalist paramilitaries had been caused by Loyalist paramilitaries.

O'Duffy and O'Leary examined other data available on the effects of the Troubles – injuries sustained due to the 'Troubles'; annual numbers of explosions; number of bombs neutralised; explosives found; number of shooting incidents; number of firearms found; number of armed robberies; and money taken in armed robberies. They concluded that all these data showed the same pattern as the death toll, with high levels of activity in the years 1971–76, and a turning point in 1976–77. They put forward three main reasons for this turning point: improved knowledge and capabilities on the part of the security forces resulted in an increase in their effectiveness in managing the violence, alongside the end of internment and a resultant reduction in Nationalist militancy; Loyalist reductions in assassinations and attacks on Catholic civilians, as a result of the perception of the reduction in the threat to the Union, and decreased opportunity for easy killing of Catholics due to increased housing segregation; and changes in IRA strategy – moving away from bombing urban centres and toward focusing on military targets and the introduction of the cell structure in their organisation.

Using RUC statistics on injuries, they pointed out that over 20,000 people had suffered serious injuries since 1969, with civilians having been worst affected. They commented that the RUC data is 'unhelpful' since it did not differentiate paramilitaries from civilians, it did not record any civilian injuries for 1968–70 and its classification of the cause of injuries was not clear – for example it was not clear whether injuries caused by the security forces were included in the figures.

They commented that the statistics on bomb neutralisation implied a 'deterioration in the capacities of the security forces after 1986'. This, they said, could be due to a range of factors – increased supplies of Semtex, which is harder to detect; reduced use of warnings by Nationalist paramilitaries; or changes in data collection (O'Duffy and O'Leary, 1990: p. 322). They commented that figures on weights of explosives found were of doubtful use, due to variations in the type and weight-to-potency ratio of explosives used. They found that figures on explosives finds did not reflect the overall trends in other figures related to the general level of violence. Figures on 'shooting incidents' and 'shots heard' were also of questionable value as general indicators of the Troubles in their view, in comparison to the figures on firearms found, which more closely reflected the general level of violence. RUC figures on armed robbery were not disaggregated by agent responsible, they pointed out, so it was impossible to distinguish Nationalist from Loyalist paramilitary robberies. They found that the rise in armed robbery in 1986 was much sharper than the increase in the death rate.

O'Duffy and O'Leary went on to examine in detail any changes in these trends which might have been attributable to the Anglo–Irish Agreement (AIA). They concluded that deaths, injuries, shooting incidents, explosions and armed robberies all increased significantly in the three years following the AIA, compared with the previous three years – although they pointed out that these increases may not have been due entirely to the AIA. Other factors such as the INLA feud, the Loughgall killings and the Enniskillen bombing also contributed to the increase in the figures. They used Hartwig and Dearing's (1979) technique to smooth the data. When thus manipulated, the data showed a clear upward trend in violence after the AIA and a downward trend before the AIA.

Their overall conclusion was that the then emerging trends for 1989 indicated a fall in deaths, but this was accompanied by an increase in deaths due to IRA actions outside Northern Ireland. They predicted that the level of violence was likely to fall back to its pre-AIA level.

In later work, O'Leary and McGarry (1993) revisited many of these issues and some new ones. They begin:

> The maps in Figure 1.1 confirm what everybody in Northern Ireland knows: violence does not occur with equal intensity in every area, and there are areas where years go by without the occurrence of a single death. (O'Leary and McGarry, 1993: p. 9)

Using McKeown (1977) and the Irish Information Partnership as data sources, they used a map adapted from McKeown (1989) to plot the spatial distribution of killings in Northern Ireland for the period 1969–89. They commented on the scale of the conflict, arguing that the same ratio of victims to population applied to Great Britain would have produced over 100,000 victims, and in the United States, the same level of conflict would have produced approximately 500,000 victims. They also commented on the role of the media in creating the illusion that the intervals between major incidents in the Troubles have been calm.

> The government and the security forces have obvious incentives to downplay the scale of the conflict and to stress 'normality'; the tourist and economic development agencies are keenly aware that the external

perception of violence affects the success of their endeavours. The police force, the Royal Ulster Constabulary (RUC) emphasises that the number of civilians killed annually as a result of road accidents in the period 1969–1989 usually exceeded the total number of those who died annually because of political violence, or, 'as a result of the security situation' as they prefer to put it. (O'Leary and McGarry, 1993: p. 12)

O'Leary and McGarry argued that road deaths are in addition to deaths from the Troubles, and that the comparison between Troubles-related deaths and road deaths is a distraction. They pointed out that comparisons made between death rates in the Troubles in Northern Ireland and those in situations of urban violence in large cities in United States were similarly misleading, in that they tended to equate deaths from political violence with deaths from criminal violence. They pointed to the fact that there were fewer deaths due to political violence in United States between 1948 and 1977 (434) than in Northern Ireland in 1972 alone. They went on to compare deaths in Northern Ireland with per capita death rates from internal political violence in liberal democracies. They used a 'slightly modified' version of Taylor and Jodice (1983), unfortunately without having specified how the data were modified. The time frame they used for comparative purposes (1948–77), however, does not coincide with the main years of the current conflict in Northern Ireland. Several conflicts which have run more concurrently with the Northern Ireland conflict were not included in the comparative analysis, presumably due to the age of the data they employ. As a result of this analysis, O'Leary and McGarry concluded that the

> per capita death tolls in Northern Ireland and Cyprus during this period exceeded those in 15 of the 30 most internally politically violent states (including Ethiopia, the Philippines, Argentina, Greece, Colombia, India, Iraq, Sri Lanka, and Mozambique). (O'Leary and McGarry, 1993: p. 16)

They went on to argue that Northern Ireland's location within the UK explained how the UK ranked as the 41st most violent state that had been continuously liberal democratic in the 30 years 1948–77. These comparisons, they suggested, meant that 'it is legitimate to classify the Northern Ireland conflict as similar to those which have riven Lebanon, Sri Lanka, and Cyprus' (O'Leary and McGarry, 1993: p. 18). The scale of the Northern Ireland conflict should therefore be seen as very intense, they opined, 'given that it has taken place in the presence of moderately amicable relations between relevant neighbouring states and regional powers, and in the absence of superpower rivalries'. They analysed numbers killed in political violence in Ireland from 1886 to 1990. As a result of this analysis, they concluded that the number killed in Northern Ireland in the last 20 years was proportionately greater than the number killed in the whole of Ireland in each of the extended periods of political violence in the first 60 years of this century. According to O'Leary and McGarry, the number killed in this present conflict was absolutely and proportionately greater than either the Irish War of Independence (1919–21) or the violence surrounding the formation of the Northern Ireland State (1920–22).

The authors revisited the issues raised in O'Duffy and O'Leary (1990) in their discussion of the military agents and their nature. They concluded that the conflict is best understood as two wars – one between the armed and military agents, and one involving the military agents and civilians. They identified four main categories in which deaths between 1969 and 1989 can be located:

1. the paramilitary killings of civilians (44.2 per cent of all deaths),
2. the war between the Nationalist paramilitaries and security forces (34.8 per cent of all deaths),
3. internecine conflict and self killings within paramilitary organisations (6.7 per cent of all deaths) and
4. the killings of Catholic civilians by security forces (5.3 per cent of all deaths). (O'Leary and McGarry, 1993: p. 28)

They identified trends in deaths from 1969 to 1990 which showed that 58 per cent of all deaths occurred in the five years from 1971 to 1976. They explained this with reference to the unrestrained war by the IRA against the British state in 1971, the Loyalist backlash against civil rights demonstrations, the high number of sectarian killings by Loyalist paramilitaries between 1971 and 1976 and the 'repressive and counter productive' policy of internment between 1971 and 1975. Their analysis of the status of victim and responsibility for their death and details on bombings, shootings and injuries replicate material reviewed here earlier (O'Duffy and O'Leary, 1990).

In *The Politics of Antagonism* (1993b) McGarry and O'Leary dealt with the other costs of the war. Violence, they argued, resulted in heavy financial burdens on both the British and Irish governments. Figures from the Irish Information Partnership (1987) showed that between 1969 and 1982 the extra security costs for the Republic of Ireland were estimated at £IR1050 million and £4105 million sterling for Britain in the same period. They outlined the economic costs other than security expenditure, which included the extra expenditure on health and welfare services, housing administration, prison service and the public utilities. Compensation payments for losses and injuries had increased to an average 13,000 cases per annum they pointed out, and the result was that between 1965 and 1985, the British government paid over £570 million in compensation directly related to the conflict. Paramilitary racketeering had also damaged the profitability of private sector organisations, as had the high insurance costs for shop and business owners, according to them.

Rowthorn and Wayne (1988) have described the Northern Ireland economy as a workhouse, because of the very high numbers of people employed in security. They argued that human rights costs have had an extremely negative effect on public trust in political institutions in the British Isles. This has been compounded by the British government's conviction of violations of the European Convention on Human Rights. Other factors, they argued, contributed to damaging the belief in the impartiality of British justice, in Ireland, Britain and internationally. These were the introduction of Diplock Courts; the abandonment of the right of silence in 1988; and delays of several years which were not uncommon on inquests on persons killed by security forces. They pointed to the manner in which broadcasting authorities had been subjected to censorship both internally and externally, when reporting Northern Ireland. McGarry and O'Leary (1993b) argued that journalism on Northern Ireland had been subject to much greater editorial and political interference, leading to tensions and strains between the government and the media. They concluded that their analysis proved that 'Northern Ireland is the most serious source of political conflict and instability in the British Isles' (McGarry and O'Leary, 1993: p. 50).

Some writers, like O'Duffy (1993), have used RUC statistics interchangeably with those from other sources. O'Duffy used RUC data, although there is some variation between his data and RUC published data: O'Duffy's data show 467 deaths in 1972, yet the RUC data show 470 deaths for that year. O'Duffy's main concern was to analyse the death rate in the context of events such as internment, emergency legislation and other security strategies. He pointed to the dramatic increase in the death rate after the introduction of internment without trial on 9 August 1971, to the distribution of responsibility for deaths in the Troubles, and the primary role played by Republican paramilitaries.

Finally, Hewitt (1993) examined the consequences of political violence in five different western societies: Italy, Spain, Germany, Uruguay and Northern Ireland. Hewitt saw political violence as taking three forms: rioting, terrorism and civil war. He claimed that very little attention has been given to the social, political and economic consequences of political violence, and no systematic theory explained the effects of such violence. He constructed a set of hypotheses about the consequences of political violence. These were as follows:

1. the economy will be disrupted in both the short and long term, especially the tourist industry;
2. social activities will decline (use of public transport and cinema attendance were tested as surrogates of social life to determine if there was a decline);
3. the ability of government to enforce its rule will specially affect law and order and public administration will be curtailed; and finally,
4. public opinion, public perception and the role of the media will also be affected.

In the case of Northern Ireland, Hewitt claimed that his hypotheses were proved. Political violence had severely damaged the economy, there had been a widespread breakdown in social order and a severe breakdown in normal policing. Data were produced to show that Northern Ireland had the highest number of victims of violence, highest government expenditure on security and the highest costs of deaths and injuries of any of the regions examined, using RUC statistics, British Army records and newspapers as data sources.

Hewitt classified Northern Ireland as a chronic ethnic conflict that was 'not about civil rights or jobs but about Nationalism' (Hewitt, 1993: p. 24). In the final chapter, he touched briefly on a number of key issues that have merited rather more extensive treatment elsewhere. These included sectarianism, polarisation, discrimination and political socialisation. In his concluding chapter, Hewitt opined that there could be positive consequences to violence, such as increased democracy, although he did not say whether, in his opinion, this had happened in Northern Ireland. He recommended that government strategy in Northern Ireland should be to facilitate negotiation between the important organisations and actors, with government participating as only one of the actors involved.

AGENTS OF THE CONFLICT

Research on the agents and protagonists in the conflict has concentrated much more on Republican activities and analysis. There has been wide-ranging research on the IRA and Sinn Féin yet there is a comparable shortfall in research on the Loyalist paramilitaries. In a review in 1995, Smyth stated that any discussion of the conflict in Northern Ireland must address three questions: why did it start; why did it persist; and what forces led to the current cease-fires? (J. Smyth, 1995). Taylor's *Provos* (1997) addressed these three questions. It recounts the story of the evolution of the Provisional IRA and Sinn Féin over the 30 years of conflict in Northern Ireland charting the rise of the leaders in the Republican movement from gunmen to statesmen. The development of the IRA from an organisation, which in 1969 was threatening to become just a fading memory, to one of the most formidable and sophisticated paramilitary organisations in the western world is explained through the medium of in-depth interviews with members of the Provisional IRA. Taylor questioned their motivations and ambitions in joining a paramilitary organisation asking why would they dedicate and risk their lives for such an organisation and destroy the lives of others. Published after the first cease-fires in 1994, Taylor concluded that there has been a fundamental shift in the thinking of the Republican movement. He explained the reasons behind their decision to put their core aim of a united Ireland on hold for the foreseeable future, in order to enter a process that inevitably will mean compromise for them.

O'Brien's *The Long War* (1993) is another more recent account of the relationship between the IRA and Sinn Féin and their war with Britain. O'Brien dealt in detail with the evolution of the Republican peace strategy since 1987. He analysed the shift from their position in the mid-1980s of the Republican demand for a British withdrawal to their position by the 1990s, of seeking recognition of the principle of self-determination. The exercise of self-determination necessarily includes the Unionist community in Northern Ireland, so had there been a re-thinking on Unionism within the movement as well? O'Brien seemed to think not, suggesting that:

> these shifts in Sinn Féin language were shifts of emphasis, which, despite powerful strands of history and politics, continued to work on

the basis that the 'Britishness' of northern Protestants was not real, that their 'fears' for an independent Ireland were falsely based and could relatively easily be assuaged. (O'Brien, 1993: pp.

273–5) O'Brien stated that, in spite of the revival of support from Republicanism in the North after the hunger strikes, the Republican movement had to accept that they still could not force a British withdrawal. This analysis on the part of Republicanism led to the break with abstentionism in the South. O'Brien argued that the Northern group led by Adams gave significant concessions to the fundamentalists within the organisation in order to minimalise any potential split that the break with abstentionism could have caused. Hard-liners were therefore given key positions on the army council. Wilson (1994) argued that this had two important implications. First, it indicated that the current leaders of the Republican movement were not 'doves' trying to isolate 'hawks' (Wilson, 1994: p. 47). The move from the hard-line position in the 1970s and 1980s to the peace strategy of the 1990s was a tactical recognition of the limitations of the Republican movement, rather then the result of a move to the ethics of non-violence, he argued. Second, the Downing Street Declaration (1993) asked a great deal more of Republicans according to Wilson. Republican failure to secure a British withdrawal meant that, in order to remain part of the political process, Sinn Féin would have to address the sensitive issue of decommissioning. Perhaps the most refreshing aspect of O'Brien's work is the commentary on the political talks held by Mayhew, which O'Brien based on the papers of the participants.

Coogan's *The Troubles* (1995) covered the well-trodden ground of the last 30 years of the conflict in Northern Ireland. He detailed the sins of the Stormont government and the failure of the British government to grasp opportunities presented to them by the Republican movement. He blamed British equivocation for the duration of the conflict. Using his extensive contacts in the political administrations in Dublin and Washington, together with his contacts among Nationalist and Republican politicians in Ireland, Coogan provided a clear picture of events of the peace process from the early 1990s onward. From his position of participant observer, there were many places where Coogan failed to produce any analytic account of the respective strategies of the political parties or what they were variously looking for in a political settlement. While Coogan clearly had high-level contacts in Ireland and the United States, he did not seem to have the same quality of contacts in the British government or with Unionist politicians. This limited his analysis of British and Unionist thinking, and perhaps as a result, key shifts within various Unionist positions are not addressed. Whereas both Taylor (1997) and O'Brien (1993) addressed the shifts and departures within Republicanism, Coogan largely ignored these, concentrating instead on continuities with the movement.

Behind the Lines (1995) is the story of the Loyalist and Republican cease-fires in 1994, written by Brian Rowan, Chief Security correspondent for BBC Northern Ireland. Rowan dealt specifically with the events that led up to both cease-fires, and provided a chronology of events commencing in the late 1980s. Drawing largely on published material, the book set out to explain debates within Loyalism and Republicanism and the factors that contributed to their ending of military campaigns. In this account, Rowan accepted the analysis of the Chief Constable of the RUC, that the Republican cease-fire was based on the knowledge that a continuation of violence would never achieve a British withdrawal. The book details the journey from the long war to the peace strategy, and this is combined with interviews with many of the key players in Republican and Loyalist circles, which were conducted both before and after the cease-fires.

In *Fighting for Ireland*, Smith (1995) provided a perspective on the military strategy of the IRA. Smith's position as a lecturer in the Royal Naval College, Greenwich is indicative. In a very narrow account of the conflict, Smith examined the context and motives for IRA violence, and concluded that the real problem is the refusal of the Irish to behave logically and rationally in relation to the position of Northern Ireland within the United Kingdom. Smith admitted the success of the IRA in the early 1970s, but argued that support for the IRA from within the Catholic community was a result of manipulation by the paramilitary organisation. 'PIRA had skilfully implanted itself within the Catholic Community' (Smith, 1995: p. 102). His tendency towards conspiracy theories, and the one-dimensionality of his analysis allowed him to ignore key events. He dealt with Bloody Sunday in a few lines, and completely ignored shoot-to-kill allegations against the security forces and the subsequent controversy surrounding the Stalker Inquiry. Smith examined the IRA in a one-dimensional and static manner as a purely military organisation unrelated to its social and political context. His solution to the 'Irish problem' was unsurprisingly simple – defeat the IRA.

Bishop and Mallie's (1987) *The Provisional IRA* was one of the first full-length studies to be completed on the Provisional IRA. From the beginning of the Troubles very little was known about the organisation, what were its objectives, how was it structured, who were its leaders and how many people were actually involved. Bishop and Mallie meticulously answered these questions. They described the journey of the IRA, from its birth in 1970, through its bombing campaigns, Bloody Friday, internment, the hunger strikes to the political and electoral development of the Republican movement in the 1980s. The authors provided fascinating interview material, with frank interviews with former and current leaders and activists.

The Enemy Within (Dillon, 1994) dealt with the IRA's military campaign in Britain. In the first comprehensive work in this area, Dillon analysed the IRA bombing campaign in Britain before and after the Second World War, in the context of the Southern government's policy of neutrality. New evidence was presented of political and military mistakes that left many cities in Britain vulnerable to paramilitary attack. With as many as five agencies competing to combat terrorism, the IRA still managed to successfully carry out bombing missions in Britain. Dillon described how mistakes and inter-group rivalry between the government security agencies benefited the IRA. He presented rare information about the IRA active units in Britain, and their operations since 1990. Dillon also discussed such questions as why the British government held secret talks with the IRA and Sinn Féin, just days after the IRA bombed Warrington and killed two children. He concluded by explaining how communications between the British government and Sinn Féin were the foundation stones of the current peace strategy.

INLA: Deadly Divisions (Holland and McDonald, 1994) was the first account of the INLA. It provided a vivid account of the Irish National Liberation Army and its ruthless and violent history. Holland and McDonald used interview material and secret letters smuggled from prison by Gerard Steenson, dubbed 'Dr Death'. With the assassination of Airey Neave, one of Margaret Thatcher's closest political allies and friend, the INLA achieved paramilitary prominence. The authors charted the development of the INLA from 1979, and attempted to explain why this organisation has been faction-ridden and constantly caught up in feuds. They described how, in the first few years of its existence, the INLA was very active, and in 1981 the INLA killed more people than the IRA. Most of its early operations were directed at Loyalist paramilitaries, yet in later years most of the deaths caused by the INLA were due to their own members killing each other. Twelve of its members were killed in the 1987 feud. McDonald and Holland examined the background to this feud which lay in the relationship between the

INLA and the Irish Peoples' Liberation Organisation. A chronology was provided at the end of the book on the activities of the INLA from 1979 to 1992.

Ulster's Uncertain Defenders (1984) by Sarah Nelson is one of most articulate and original pieces of work on Loyalism and the Northern Ireland conflict. This book analyses the political beliefs and expectations which people from a Loyalist tradition derive from their upbringing in Northern Ireland. It examines how Loyalists shaped their reactions to the civil rights movement and the violence of the late 1960s onwards. Nelson details the background and motivations of people who joined action groups in the 1960s and 1970s, including political, paramilitary and community groups. She discusses their activities and attitudes in the period of reform in the early 1970s, which culminated in the fall of the Stormont government, the home of Unionist politics. In this period, she claims, Loyalist upheaval was more mental than physical. 'While Catholics bear the brunt of the physical suffering, their beliefs about themselves, their sense of identity and their conviction that their demands were justified was more often strengthened than weakened by the events triggered by civil rights, while Protestants found their world collapsing around them' (Nelson, 1984: p. 11). In Protestant minds, the introduction of reform meant instability in the very state structure they were defending.

Nelson examines the communal street violence of August 1969, the impact of Direct Rule and the activities and direction of Loyalism after the Ulster Workers' Council (UWC) strike in 1974. Much of the book is based on interview material in a successful attempt to show Loyalists as a much more complex and multifarious group, a goal rarely achieved by other commentators. In the final chapter of the book, Nelson discusses the move into community action and activity by paramilitary organisations, especially the UDA (Ulster Defence Association). Nelson claims that the lesson they learned from the 1974 strike was that real power lay in mobilisation of the grass roots. Their style of political and social protest altered after the strike. 'The strike had thrown political power structure into turmoil' (Nelson, 1984: p. 197). Community movement was viewed as the vehicle to bring in radical change and provided an alternative to the more traditional style of sterile politics previously extant in Northern Ireland. Indeed throughout the unstable period of the 1970s, Nelson argues that grassroots action built Loyalist political confidence by rekindling some sense of political effectiveness and supported the hope that change could occur in the politics of Northern Ireland.

Steve Bruce's *God Save Ulster* (1986) was the first work that provides a real analysis of the religious and political careers of the Reverend Ian Paisley, one of the most charismatic leaders Northern Ireland has ever seen. Moloney and Pollack's (1986) *Paisley* is described by John Whyte (1991) as 'a hostile biography' (Whyte, 1991: p. 107) which highlights Dr Paisley's more controversial aspects. Bruce's access to 'insider' information was much greater than Pollack and Moloney's. Over 20 ministers of the Free Presbyterian Church and leading activists in the Democratic Unionist Party were interviewed by Bruce in an attempt to understand why people support and follow Ian Paisley. Bruce maintains that the key to Paisley's success has been his ability to represent traditional evangelical Protestantism alongside traditional Ulster Unionism. Bruce charts the rise of this leader and examines the synthesis of religion and politics that separated him from other religious and political leaders in Europe. Bruce's view that the conflict in Northern Ireland is religious, with politics and economics as merely contributory factors, leads him to argue that Paisley's political success can therefore 'only be understood if one appreciates the central role which evangelical religion plays in Ulster Unionism' (Bruce, 1986: p. 249). Paisley is a consistent advocate of the view that Protestants should never see their future as one of a choice between either remaining British citizens of Ulster or becoming equal participants with Roman Catholics in a secular Republic of Ireland. Rather, Paisley argues, they should see their future as the choice between the preservation of Ulster or their subordination in a Roman Catholic theocracy. Bruce concludes that Paisley's rise can be seen in two contrasting ways. First, he argues that Paisley's views on the civil rights marchers and later the IRA were proved correct. Paisley has always argued that minor reforms to the state would increase Catholic commitment to a united Ireland. Such views, Bruce feels, were confirmed by the violence of the IRA and subsequently by the electoral rise of Sinn Féin. Critics of Paisley argue that he promoted the approach which saw anything that pleased Catholics as a loss to Protestants. Paisley crystallised the opposition to the civil rights movement and, according to Bruce, many liberal Unionists blame him for the proroguing of Stormont. Bruce believes Paisley's rise can be most clearly attributed to the fact that he was able to express 'the core of unionist ideology and the heart of what it means to be a Protestant' (Bruce, 1986: p. 267).

Bruce's subsequent analysis of Ulster Unionism, *The Edge of the Union* (1994) attempts to get to the heart of the Unionist position by examining two important sections of Ulster Unionism: the

Loyalist paramilitaries and the supporters of the Reverend Ian Paisley. Bruce again argues that the Troubles in Northern Ireland are due to an entrenched ethnic conflict, and that a failure to appreciate the strength of Loyalist identity has impeded real understanding of the Troubles in Northern Ireland. Bruce sets out to discuss and explain the Loyalist view of the world. Loyalist paramilitaries maintain three different faces: the political face, the community action and the marching uniformed body. Bruce goes on to discuss Loyalist attitudes to violence, ethnic cleansing, sectarianism and discrimination. Some of Bruce's opinions in these chapters, especially the Loyalist views on sectarianism and discrimination, seem to contradict some of the other material in the book: 'Unionists do not approve of discrimination. In theory they are very much in favour of treating people fairly' (Bruce, 1994: p. 54). Bruce maintains that Loyalists did not accept the claim of the civil rights movement that Catholics were discriminated against in employment. According to Bruce, Loyalists see the 'fair employment issue as a device to further nationalist interests under the disguise of equitable social policy' (Bruce, 1994: p. 55)

Bruce also discusses the 1990 talks and the Loyalist agenda within them. Bruce submits that in the early 1990s, under the leadership of Molyneaux and Paisley, the Ulster Unionist Party and the Democratic Unionist Party operated as a good cop/bad cop team. However, when predicting a form of settlement that would be a major change to Northern Ireland's position, Bruce guessed that Unionists would fight together for an independent smaller Ulster state with no Dublin involvement. In the four years since the publication of this work, political developments – that have surprised many – have perhaps challenged that analysis.

Bruce's (1992) book, *The Red Hand*, was based on interviews conducted with members of Loyalist paramilitaries. He aimed to analyse the behaviour of Loyalist paramilitaries, yet much of the work is an account of the central personalities within the Loyalist paramilitaries. He examined the origins, structures and fundraising methods of the paramilitaries. Bruce catalogued killings and other attacks carried out by Loyalist paramilitaries without much by way of an analytical account of the thinking or strategy behind these actions.

For the first time during the Loyalist cease-fires in 1994, UVF sources spoke to journalists Jim Cusack and Henry McDonald, and the results have been recorded in the book *The UVF* (1997). This work attempts to examine the reasons why such organisations exist and to analyse the roots of Loyalist violence. The book traces the history of the modern UVF, an even older organisation than the IRA, from the crisis of Home Rule to the battle of the Somme. The purpose of the book according to the authors is to:

> show the other side of the Irish question, to point up how trenchant, ruthless and brutal Protestant resistance towards violent Nationalism's agenda has been in the past and will be in the future. (Cusack and McDonald, 1997: p. 3)

Based on exclusive interviews with members of the UVF, this work describes the history and activities of the organisation. It details UVF operations, with a chapter dedicated to the May 1974 Dublin bombing. The authors also provide material on international arms dealing and secret contacts with the Irish government in the search for peace. The final chapter describes the Loyalist cease-fire and provides information about the difficulties within the UVF, especially the difficult relationship between the Belfast leadership and the Portadown brigade of the organisation. The authors recounted how the killing of Catholic taxi-driver Michael McGoldrick by the Portadown unit in 1996 was a direct challenge to the authority of the UVF leadership. The decision within the leadership to disband the Portadown unit was explained as an attempt to deal with this as an issue of internal discipline. The authors also discuss the internal problems within the Combined Loyalist Military Command, especially after the IRA cease-fire collapsed. They detail how one section of the UDA supported the idea of escalating the level of violence in an attempt to put pressure on the Nationalist community and force the IRA into calling another cease-fire. Such moves were opposed by the UVF and the authors conclude that at the time of finishing the book, it was still not clear if the Loyalist paramilitaries were preparing for peace or for war. Although Protestant paramilitaries such as the UVF and UFF have been responsible for nearly 30 per cent of all deaths in the conflict in Northern Ireland, these groups remain poorly understood and relatively under-researched.

3 Economic and Social Aspects of the Troubles

There have been more than human costs to the Northern Ireland Troubles. Over the past 30 years, there has been frequent debate about the impact on the economy and jobs. It is very difficult to separate out the impact of developments in the international economy, the effects of changes in the British economy, economic problems specific to Northern Ireland and the economic costs of the region's conflict. All were happening simultaneously and interacting with each other. As Bradley comments, 'The published direct analysis of the impact of the Troubles on the whole economy, on sectors or on the public finances in isolation, is seriously flawed and cannot be reliably used to isolate the Troubles from other factors' (Bradley, 1996: pp. 63–4) Moreover, an exclusive focus on the economic costs of the Troubles, as though an entirely autonomous process, ignores the extent to which a long history of social and economic grievance might have contributed to their development. To ignore these factors implies that the Troubles have been nothing more than a Republican conspiracy. Whilst some people remain convinced that this is the case, such a view does not stand up to serious scrutiny. Accordingly, this chapter will explore the social and economic aspects of the Troubles by examining three themes:

- a review of the evidence of the level of discrimination practised in Northern Ireland, particularly in the labour market;
- an assessment of the degree of poverty and deprivation in the region, particularly whether this has been a disproportionately Catholic experience; and
- an account of the development of the economy in the 1970s and 1980s attempting to assess the impact of violence.

LABOUR MARKET DISCRIMINATION: A SOURCE OF CONFLICT?

Although there were frequent charges of labour market discrimination since the establishment of Northern Ireland, there remains, however, little systematic evidence for the situation in the 1930s, particularly since the Census did not contain a religious variable at that time. Basil Brooke, who was to become Prime Minister between 1942 and 1963, was quoted as saying that Loyalists should not employ Catholics because they were '99 per cent disloyal' (quoted in Boyd, 1985: p. 60). Boyd provides a catalogue of similar examples:

> Dawson Bates, Northern Ireland's first Minister of Home Affairs, was horrified when he learned that a young Catholic girl was working on the government switchboard. Edward Archdale, Minister of Agriculture, publicly apologised to Loyalists in his constituency because there were four Catholic civil servants (out of a total of 109) in his department. Sir Joseph Davison, Grand Master of the Orangemen in the 1930s, reminded Protestant employers that it was their duty to employ Protestants in preference to Catholics. (Boyd, 1985: p. 60)

Charges of discrimination in the public sector were frequently made at Stormont, but there was a lack of comprehensive data on the religious affiliation of the unemployed. Nevertheless, few now contest the basic proposition that unemployment has been nearly twice as high amongst Catholics as amongst Protestants and that this has persisted over decades. The 1971 Census offered the first authoritative and comprehensive account of the problem. Protestant male unemployment was 6.6 per cent compared to 17.3 per cent for Catholic males (see Table 3.2). The equivalent rates for women were 3.6 per cent and 7.0 per cent respectively. (Cormack and Osborne 1983). In a year-long cohort survey of male unemployed the following characteristics detailed in Table 3.1 emerged.

Table 3.1 Religious Difference among Males in the Experience of Unemployment

	Protestant	Catholic	Sig.
Frequency of unemployment in previous three years	1.8	2.1	.001
Age first registered as unemployed	22.8	20.6	.001
Number of job submissions	1.15	.84	.001
Found employment in one year	54.5	38.2	.001

Source: Miller and Osborne (1983)

Catholic males suffered more unemployment while having first registered at a younger age. Protestant males seemed to make greater efforts to find work as evidenced by the higher average number of job submissions. At the same time, it may have been that Catholics had a more realistic assessment of their job opportunities. The key difference lay in the success rate in finding employment. Just over half of Protestants found work within the year compared to just over a third of Catholics. Thus, a significantly greater proportion of Catholics were moving into the long-term unemployment category.

Gillespie provides a picture of the religious unemployment differential covering most of the period of the Troubles (Gillespie, 1997: Table 1.2). Moreover, he argues that because of concealed unemployment, the relative positions may actually be worse. Between 1981 and 1991 the number of economically inactive Protestant men (excluding retired and students) rose from 9557 to 19,288, just over 100 per cent. The equivalent figures for Catholic men were 6846 and 17,146, over 250 per cent. Catholic men were thus moving into economic inactivity at a greater rate than Protestants.

Table 3.2 Different Unemployment Rates between Religions, 1971–91

Census	Protestant (a) (%)	Men Catholic (b) (%)	Ratio (a:b)	Protestant (c) (%)	Women Catholic (d) (%)	Ratio (c:d)
1971	6.5	17.3	2.6	3.6	7.0	1.9
1981	12.4	30.2	2.4	9.6	17.1	1.8
1991	12.7	28.4	2.2	8.0	14.5	1.8

What is fiercely disputed is the explanation for this disparity. One view sees it as an inevitable outcome of deliberate Unionist government policy to implement discriminatory employment practices in the public sector and to recommend a similar disposition to its brethren in the business community. From such a perspective, the mechanisms deployed for this purpose included:

- ensuring industry was located in places inaccessible to Catholics;
- refusing to select Catholics who applied for jobs;
- companies establishing reputations as being unreceptive to Catholic recruitment, so that Catholics come to perceive the futility of job applications;
- by-passing public processes of selection, so that informal networks, including the channels of the Orange and Masonic Orders, substitute as recruitment agencies (Rowthorn and Wayne, 1988).

In addition to such factors as the location of jobs and job losses, and the procedures of selection and promotion, another device seen as curtailing Catholic employment was threats and intimidation in the workplace itself (Rolston and Tomlinson, 1989). Thus, discrimination can be overt or covert: it can be intentional or the legacy of policies of the past. Whatever the form it takes, it persists, remaining the most significant determinant of religious distinctions in the labour market.

An alternative perspective explains the differential unemployment rates largely in terms of factors inherent in the Catholic community itself. Included in these are higher population growth rates, lower social status, bigger family size and a disjuncture between its geographical distribution and job location (Compton, 1981). In addition, Catholics are seen to be deficient in education and training. The 1990 Labour Force Survey found that 39 per cent of Protestant males had no educational qualifications compared to 51 per cent of Catholic males. The obvious corollary of such interpretations is that resolution of religious inequalities in the labour market is the responsibility of the community experiencing the disadvantage.

The variation in fertility rates between the two communities is a long-standing issue of contention. The fertility rate in Northern Ireland as a whole is greater than that in Britain, and within Northern Ireland, Catholic fertility rates have traditionally exceeded those of Protestants. Arguing that this inevitably results in high labour market entry and surplus labour supply in the Catholic community, Compton has suggested that these account significantly for the 'extra' unemployment suffered by Catholics (Compton, 1981). Eversley (1989) disputes its importance, pointing out that the inconsistencies of the differential rate historically had no notable impact on the disparities in unemployment:

> The further we go back in the post-war evolution of the Northern Ireland population the smaller the share of Catholics in both the child and the adult working age groups; yet the excess unemployment was always there. (Eversley, 1989: p. 221)

A different emphasis on the fertility factor highlights the link between higher Catholic fertility rates generating Protestant fears of being overwhelmed by its religious and political foes, fears which in turn give rise to prejudice, which itself is the foundation of discriminatory employment practices. But however much this may explain the process, it cannot be used to justify it.

The argument for greater Catholic labour mobility as a means of reducing the unemployment gap is based on the particular geography of jobs in Northern Ireland. It reflects the economic partition of the region between the relatively prosperous east, centred around Belfast, and the depressed west, where Catholics are concentrated. Finding themselves in such a disadvantaged area, Catholics, it is said, should be enterprising enough to move to areas where jobs exist. There are a number of problems with this argument. It fails to distinguish between 'undevelopment' as an inevitable, if unfortunate, outcome of 'natural' market determinants of industrial location, and 'under-development' as a function of deliberate neglect by capital and state. Moreover, it does not explain why even in the prosperous east, the concentrated areas of worst unemployment, like West Belfast, contain predominantly Catholic populations (Gaffikin and Morrissey, 1990).

Another issue raised by those who regard the problem as fundamentally one of supply is that of the 'skills mismatch', whereby Catholic education is said to fail to develop the necessary aptitudes for a technology-intensive economy. Traditional concentration on the arts and humanities displaced the emphasis that should have been attached to engineering and scientific skills. The problem with this diagnosis is that the unemployment differential preceded the more recent period when an increasing bifurcation of the labour market has demanded 'high-tech' skills. Also, despite an increasing convergence in educational attainment between the two communities in recent years, the differential in unemployment remains considerable. Lastly, there is a higher unemployment rate amongst qualified Catholics than amongst their Protestant counterparts.

The inequalities have also been apparent in employment patterns. Successive Fair Employment Agency (FEA) and Fair Employment Commission (FEC) reports (Fair Employment Agency, 1983) have testified to an imbalance in the labour forces, both of whole industrial sectors and particular significant firms. Not only are Catholics under-represented generally but there is also a progressively decreasing representation of Catholics as one progresses up the hierarchy of supervisory and managerial grades. Eversley again disavows the explanation of location:

> Even in the more heavily Catholic areas, Catholics got less than their proportional share of managerial, professional and supervisory positions, men and women alike. In predominantly Protestant areas, their share was even smaller. (Eversley, 1989: p. 228)

Even during the boom years of the 1960s, the differential experience of unemployment did not significantly alter. Certainly, when the Protestant labour market tightened, there were better prospects for Catholics. But this still left them vulnerable if only on the basis of the practice of 'last in first out'. Nor did the advent of transnational capital in the 1950s and 1960s make an appreciable difference. Apparently, despite often bringing in their own senior management, these firms tended to reproduce existing employment patterns. Figures from the 1990 Labour Force Survey (Statistics and Social Division, 1991) suggest that this remains at least partly the case. The larger employers tend to be transnational in character. Yet, the share of male employees who were Catholic was 43 per cent in workplaces with fewer than 25 employed, but 34 per cent in workplaces with 25 or more employed.

The 1990 Labour Force Survey also offered a review of the employment and unemployment patterns between the two communities that had developed during the 1980s. According to its figures, Protestants accounted for 44 per cent and Catholics for 56 per cent of the total unemployed. The rate of unemployment among Catholic males was twice that of Protestant males (22 per cent and 11 per cent, respectively), though the gap for females was less marked (10 per cent and 7 per cent, respectively). The difference in male unemployment rates was greatest in the 25–39 age group (with Catholics at a rate of 21 per cent and Protestants at 9 per cent) and was lowest in the 16–24 age group (with Catholics at 24 per cent and Protestants at 15 per cent).

A comparison of 1989 and 1990 figures shows that of those in employment in 1989, a slightly higher proportion of Protestants (94 per cent) than of Catholics (91 per cent) remained in employment a year later. In addition, of those unemployed in 1989, a significantly higher share of Protestants had found work (35 per cent) compared to Catholics (21 per cent). This is reflected in the data for length of time seeking employment. The percentage of Catholics looking for work after one year or more was 61, whereas the comparable figure for Protestants was 48.

To what extent does the Labour Force Survey bear out the arguments of the main protagonists? Amongst the economically active, while females from both communities had similar levels of qualifications, the share of Catholic males with no qualifications (51 per cent) was considerably higher than the share of Protestant males (39 per cent). This would seem to lend some weight to the argument of those who explain the unemployment disparity in terms of differential educational attainment. On the other hand, the share of Protestants and Catholics attaining higher education qualifications was about the same (12 per cent and 11 per cent, respectively). Yet, arguably, this similarity is not reflected in terms of employment. Another interesting difference is both communities' perception of employment prospects. Of the economically inactive, a higher share of Catholics (16 per cent) than of Protestants (10 per cent) gave the lack of available jobs as the reason for not seeking work.

The 1992 Labour Force Survey confirmed earlier findings. (Policy, Planning and Research Unit, Department of Finance and Personnel, 1993). Even in a more difficult economic climate, 30 per cent of Protestant males who had been unemployed in 1991 had found work compared to only 15 per cent of Catholic males and the male rates of unemployment were 10 per cent (Protestant) and 24 per cent (Catholic). Equally, 37 per cent of Catholics had been out of work for four years or more compared to 20 per cent of Protestants.

The over-representation of Catholics among the unemployed would seem to be multi-causal in terms of the interaction of both supply-side and demand-side factors. The existence of supply-side factors, such as higher fertility or differential educational qualifications, does not invalidate the operation of the many forms of discrimination. Nor does it allow for any complacency about the effectiveness of anti-discrimination legislation.

The situation is complicated by differential employment between the religions in the security forces. The growth of spending on law and order in the 1980s was matched by an increase in security forces personnel particularly in (what was then) the Ulster Defence Regiment and the RUC Reserve. This development presented employment opportunities that were taken up almost entirely by Protestants. The failure of Catholics to pursue these occupations can be explained by: a general opposition to the British state in Northern Ireland; the fear of threats from Republicans who have greater access to Catholic areas; or an alienating and discriminatory culture within the security forces. The British government can be held responsible only for the last. With the first two, the process is one of self-exclusion. (It should also be pointed out that Catholic recruits face greater opportunity costs in joining the security forces: they probably will have to move away from home, forgo usual places of leisure and deal with ostracism from some of their own community as a consequence of 'joining up'.)

The debate around discrimination is also complicated by its entanglement with Nationalist aspirations in Northern Ireland.

Republicans tend to focus on discrimination as part of the legitimation of their campaign. It is thus in their interest to claim that discrimination has been part of state policy and that corrective measures, such as fair employment legislation have failed – this forms part of the irreformability thesis – discrimination, disadvantage and oppression are structural components of the Northern Ireland state. Since political protest in the shape of the civil rights campaign not only failed but was suppressed, violence became the only realistic mechanism for effecting change.

The view taken here is that labour market disadvantage has been a historical characteristic of Catholics in Northern Ireland which does require radical measures of redress. Such patterns of disadvantage have been produced and reproduced for decades and are not easy to ameliorate, and similar patterns of inequality and marginalisation are found in other societies. The British government has taken some steps to improve the situation not only in terms of anti-discrimination legislation but with more general policy measures such as 'targeting social need' and particular programmes like 'Making Belfast Work'. There remain, however, both within Northern Ireland and the United Kingdom and beyond, doubts about the capacity of such measures to reverse decades of relative disadvantage. Affirmative action, anti-discrimination legislation and other measures designed to redress inequality have met with almost universal criticism, which is often justified with reference to the 'failure' of these measures to achieve substantive change. Some of the criticism and reluctance to comply with such measures, however, is undoubtedly based on a reluctance to accept inequality as a problem, and a desire to maintain an unequal status quo. Whilst there is a need to find new ways of tackling inequality, it is also important to recognise that anticipating and neutralising resistance to the achievement of such a goal is a crucial part of any successful strategy. Cyclical downswings in the economy also make progress difficult and unequal access to security employment can create a permanent imbalance.

The differential experience of unemployment and a concern that the situation was a product of public policies and private employment practices have fed Catholic grievances about their place in the Northern Ireland state. As O'Connor suggests:

> Discrimination, fear of physical attack and conviction that the state was 'alien, not ours' are the themes that surface repeatedly when people talk about how they first became aware of being 'Northern Catholics'. (O'Connor, 1993: p. 151)

If this is accepted at face value, it helps explain for some, and justify for others, a campaign of Republican violence of the scale experienced in Northern Ireland. Certainly, the sense of having no stakehold in the political process, and no recognition or effective redress for grievance can be a potent catalyst for violence. From the Loyalist perspective, the Troubles have been a period when the foundations of social, economic and political life have been steadily eroded – when the bulwarks put in place to stem the Republican threat have been steadily removed. With reference to the labour market, they are unimpressed by evidence that Catholics continue to occupy a subordinate position. Instead, they point to the growth of Catholic employment in the public sector and the punitive battery of fair employment legislation – redressing any imbalance reduces Protestant labour market chances. Again, that sense of loss, coupled with political insecurities and a fear that the British government will betray them, is a recipe for backlash. Bradley sums up the fair employment debate as follows:

> The fact that a Catholic male is still almost two and a half times more likely to be unemployed in the North than his non-Catholic counterpart may have come about for a variety of reasons in addition to claims of past or present discrimination, but certainly should direct attention to a serious Northern Problem of complex origins that has been at the heart of the Troubles. (Bradley, 1996: p. 50)

DIFFERENTIAL LEVELS OF POVERTY IN NORTHERN IRELAND

Historically, Northern Ireland has been regarded as one of the poorer regions of the UK. Table 3.3 looks at low-income households as a proportion of all households in selected UK regions. The low-income thresholds are rough equivalents so as to depict the relative position of the selected regions over time. In 1974–75, Northern Ireland had the highest share of households with weekly incomes of less than £40. The situation of such households was exacerbated by also having the highest average number of members. The relative position had actually worsened by 1978–79. During the 1980s, there was substantial improvement for the region so that by 1994–95, both Wales and the North of England had a higher concentration of low-income families. It should be recognised that small sample sizes can contribute to variations in such figures, so that some caution must be exercised in comparison. Nevertheless, were comparison made with depressed conurbations like Merseyside, Northern Ireland's progress on this measure would be more apparent.

Table 3.3 The Proportion of Households on Low Weekly Incomes, Selected Regions

	1974–75	1978–79	1986–87	1994–95
per cent less than	£40.00	£80.00	£125.00	£175.00 (£182.00)
North (of England)	44.0	41.4	43.2	37.9
South West	34.1	32.9	25.2	30.1
South East	34.1	32.9	25.2	27.6
Wales	46.9	43.2	35.3	41.3
N. Ireland	51.5	53.7	42.3	37.0

Sources: Regional Trends (1976, 1981, 1989, 1996)

Note: The figures in brackets represent the real value of £125 in 1974, 1978 and 1994/95. The categories for these years were chosen to correspond with that for 1986–87. The degree of correspondence is least exact for 1978–79. The figure of £125 was chosen because it was closest to the European 'decency threshold' which is defined as 68 per cent of average earnings.

At the same time, studies of income distribution in the region demonstrate that its poorest households have lower average incomes than the UK generally, For example, the average net weekly household income for the lowest decile is £93.02 compared to £100.66 in the UK. The average weekly income of a no-earner couple with children is just 93 per cent of the equivalent household in the UK while a couple of pensioners' income is 76 per cent. At the same time, the average net income of the poorest decile is just 17 per cent of that of the highest decile (Northern Ireland Economic Council, 1998: Tables 4.1 and 4.2). Thus, relative to the UK, all deciles and most household types have lower incomes while the region is also characterised by substantial internal inequalities.

It is sometimes under-appreciated that such income inequalities often correlate with religious status. Differences in levels of unemployment between religions also tend to be translated into differences in poverty levels. In 1985/86 59 per cent of Catholic households had a total annual income of less than £6000 compared to 47 per cent of Protestant households. In the same year 58 per cent of Protestant households were in owner occupation compared to 49 per cent of Catholics (PPRU Monitor, 1993: Tables 5.2 and 6.1). The same report, however, suggests that the rate of improvement on both these variables was greater for Catholic than Protestant households.

Borooah et al. argue that Protestant/Catholic income differences in Northern Ireland are relatively minor compared to the differences within the respective communities (Borooah et al. 1993). Their method was to decompose samples from the Family Expenditure Survey to find the sources of relative disadvantage. Disadvantage may thus arise from different demographic structures, different sources of income and differential incomes even when they arise from the same source. Only the last can be truly labelled discriminatory. Their model of the Northern Ireland population is of substantial economic and social division in which religion is a relatively minor variable. Thus: 'If Catholic families of a particular economic status received the same income as their Protestant counterparts, overall inequality would fall by less than 2 per cent' (Borooah et al. 1993).

The problem with the analysis is whether the decomposition of incomes in this way leads to useful results. In another context, it might be argued that women's average earnings are less than men's because they tend to occupy low-paying jobs in greater relative numbers. The differences between men's and women's earnings when they occupy similar jobs are much less. The problem remains that women are disproportionately 'placed' in such occupations compared to men. Catholics and Protestants on Job Seeker's Allowance are subject to identical entitlement – the difficulty is that proportionately more Catholics are benefit dependent.

Nor have the relative income differences been eroded over time. Table 3.4 compares the average weekly incomes of Catholic and Protestant households in Northern Ireland.

Table 3.4 Average Weekly Household Income by Religion

	1993	1993/94	1994/95	1995/96
Catholic	269.95	279.35	290.46	293.21
Protestant	316.21	304.19	334.77	347.09

Source: Figures provided by NISRA

Over the period assessed, Protestant household incomes increased by around 9½ per cent compared to 8½ for Catholic households. This marginal rate of improvement suggests that it will be a very long time before parity is achieved. Factors such as the greater Catholic exposure to unemployment account for the difference. So long as these kinds of income differentials match the differential rates of unemployment, grievance will continue. In Northern Ireland such grievances have led to violence. At the same time, there should be no illusions about the time scale required to reduce such differences.

THE PERFORMANCE OF THE ECONOMY DURING THE TROUBLES

For much of the post-Second World War period, Northern Ireland's weak economic performance was attributed to its marginal location and restricted domestic markets. This is evident in one of the first comprehensive regional economic surveys, which lamented 'Northern Ireland's geographical situation, together with its smallness as a market for most goods' (Isles and Cuthbert, 1957: p. 316). Similarly, the Hall Report referred to 'Northern Ireland's disadvantages of remoteness, a small domestic market and lack of home supplies of raw materials and fuel' (Hall Report, 1962: p. 4).

In response to these perceived defects, a regional development strategy was adopted in the 1960s to improve physical infrastructure, to enhance the incentives package for industrial development and to sell to potential external investors the particular resources which the local economy could offer – good water supplies and a surplus of labour with a record of low stoppages and accustomed to low pay. The objective was to attract transnational capital, which could help diversify the industrial base away from a dependence on shipbuilding, natural textiles and engineering – a sectoral specialisation which was a legacy of the area's early industrialisation. As such, this strategy was typical of the regional policy approach adopted by depressed regions in Britain since 1945. Northern Ireland caught up with this form of indicative planning in the late 1950s.

In Northern Ireland this development plan met with some success. Up until 1971 around 34,000 jobs were created in the manufacturing sector. As noted by Canning et al.:

> The dominant feature of the period (1961–1971) is the large differential growth in Northern Ireland's manufacturing employment after allowing for its industrial structure. We attribute this primarily to the greatly strengthened regional policies. (Canning et al. 1987: p. 221)

This re-industrialisation process halted and then went into reverse in the 1970s. It would be a mistake, however, to assume that this was entirely a result of the escalation of the political crisis. Certainly, the violent upsurge following internment including the bombing campaign, further population flight, the security forces actively engaged on the streets and increasing sectarian attacks did not make a secure environment either for new investment or existing businesses. Nevertheless, other factors were part of the equation. The impact of two 'oil shocks' on the artificial fibre industry, most of which used a crude oil base, was considerable. Moreover, international mobile capital, upon which the drive to rejuvenate depended, was both more scarce and subject to greater competition, given the whole process of the internationalisation of production and the related reorganisation of the global division of labour. In this changing world economy, Northern Ireland's comparative advantages were being eroded – a situation made worse, rather than caused, by its steadily deepening political crisis (Freeman et al., 1987).

The decline of employment in externally owned plants is presented in Table 3.5.

Table 3.5 Employment in Externally Owned Manufacturing Plants in Northern Ireland

Country of Origin	1973	1986	1990
GB	64,445	22,331	25,259
US	17,344	11,654	9282
Canada	606	808	951
Rep. of Ireland	1379	3012	2718
Rest of EC	2579	2875	3155
Far East	0	13	1496
Other	1208	957	224
Total	87,561	41,650	41,085
% of Total Man. Emp.	52.8	39.5	38.6

Source: NI Economic Council (Nov. 1992, Table 3.2)

Before the first oil shock, externally owned plants accounted for more than 50 per cent of all manufacturing employment. The biggest source of such plants was Britain, accounting for almost three-quarters of all employment (83 per cent of all plants). Despite an overall decline in manufacturing employment over the next 13 years, employment in externally owned plants fell faster to around two-fifths of the total. Employment in British owned plants fell by almost two-thirds of the 1973 figure. In 1973, US and British plants accounted for 94 per cent of all employment in such plants. It was their decline which ended the process of economic diversification through a reliance on external capital investment. Indeed, other sources of external investment marginally increased over the period.

Employment in US plants fell at about half the rate for British plants reflecting different initial investment intentions. In general, British plants took advantage of extremely generous location grants to 'top up' capacity in response to rising global demand. When global demand fell after 1973, such plants were vulnerable to closure – a process exacerbated by their small size relative to other corporate plants. US investment was designed more to put manufacturing capacity close to (and ultimately in) the European market. It was therefore less subject to cyclical shifts in demand.

Westminster Rule in Northern Ireland responded to the problems of the ailing economy with greater public expenditure. So, while up to 1970, public sector expansion in Northern Ireland was about proportionate to that in Britain, 'since 1970 about 50,000 jobs have been created in the public sector over and above what would have been expected given national trends' (Canning et al. 1987: p. 223). Though the absolute accuracy of this estimate may be disputed, the period did see a substantial increase in public service employment, which offered new labour market opportunities for women, and absorbed some of the surplus labour of declining industries.

The decade of the 1970s saw the lowest numbers and rates of unemployment since the creation of the Northern Ireland state. Between 1970 and 1974, the numbers unemployed never rose above 40,000 and in the last year were below 30,000. Following the oil shock, unemployment increased by about 50 per cent to 59,700. This higher figure was still around half the average unemployment for the 1980s (Trewsdale, 1980: p. 17). Moreover, while the proportion of the unemployed in the long-term category remained greater than in Britain (23.9 per cent in 1974 compared to 20.2 per cent), the relative size of this group was also dramatically lower than in the 1980s.

Commenting on Northern Ireland in the 1980s, Gudgin has noted:

> The essence of the economic problem of Northern Ireland is that it is an economy with a rapidly growing labour force tied to a slow growing national economy ... Equally worrying is the fact that recovery in the national economy since 1982 has largely excluded Northern Ireland. (Gudgin, 1989: p. 23)

Also, Northern Ireland was adversely affected by the policy changes implemented in Britain after 1979. First, the Conservative government set about reconstructing key elements of the welfare state and tax system. Social security provisions are applied universally in the UK and so Northern Ireland residents suffered as a result of reforms in that area. The shift in emphasis from direct to indirect taxation disproportionately affects those on low incomes who were well represented in Northern Ireland's population.

Nevertheless, certain policies in Northern Ireland have been operated with greater autonomy. In some of these areas, Northern

Ireland has been relatively protected compared to other areas of the UK. For example, public expenditure, excluding social security, grew in real terms annually by 1.3 per cent between 1982 and 1989 compared to –0.5 per cent in Britain. In 1980/81 public expenditure per head in Northern Ireland was about 33 per cent greater than in Britain. By 1986, this had increased to 42 per cent, a further confirmation of its relative public expenditure advantage (Northern Ireland Economic Council, 1989). The region's fiscal base could not sustain this level of expenditure and so the deficit was made up by a subsidy known as the 'British Subvention'. In 1972 at the beginning of Direct Rule, the subvention was less than £100 million. By 1988/89, it had increased to £1.6 billion–£1.9 billion if the cost of sustaining the British Army and European Community receipts were included.

Even the increased emphasis on law and order spending did not account for the differential. As a result of this 'protection', certain characteristics of Northern Ireland did improve, particularly in relation to poor British regions. The apparent paradox that the citizens of Northern Ireland did, in a sense, benefit from a government generally castigated for its approach to the poor, reflects but one of the ambiguities of the concept of Thatcherism.

To what extent was this insulation from the worst of social expenditure cuts reflected in incomes? Table 3.6 provides information on average weekly household incomes for selected regions.

Table 3.6 Average Weekly Household Incomes (£s), Selected Regions

	1974–75	1978–79	1986–87	1994–95
North (of England)	65.87	102.34	197.60	304.0
South East	74.37	126.67	302.70	435.4
South West	63.39	104.39	250.90	378.9
Wales	60.27	106.44	207.20	282.7
N. Ireland	53.40	92.30	207.80	326.3

Sources: (Regional Trends 1976, 1981, 1989, 1996)

In 1974, average household income in the region was about £7.00 per week below Wales, the poorest British region. In turn, households in Wales were, on average, £14.00 worse off than in the richest British region – the South East. Thus, households in Northern Ireland were, on average, 50 per cent worse off than in the poorest British region compared to its relationship with the richest. In 1979, a similar position prevailed. Northern Ireland households were £10.00 a week worse off than those in the poorest British region – the North. The range for the group of British regions was £22.00, which, in real terms, was about the same as in 1974. Yet, by 1986–87, Northern Ireland had caught up with both the North and Wales. The range for the British regions was then £105, reflecting a startling growth of inequality. Rather than Northern Ireland 'catching up' with the richer British regions, Britain's poorer regions were falling to the level of Northern Ireland. By 1994–95, average household incomes in Northern Ireland were significantly greater than in either Wales of the North of England. At the same time, the income range within the British regions had risen to just over £150.

On this evidence, it would appear that a process of growing regional inequality was developing within the UK. Paradoxically, Northern Ireland did seem to improve its position. Rather than being a region which stood out in terms of low average household income, by the middle 1990s it looked like part of a group of weaker regions though, by no means, the poorest member. On this indicator, it would not appear that the region suffered dramatically in income terms because of the Troubles. Public expenditure grew steadily during the period supporting a high proportion of relatively well-paid jobs. Undoubtedly, this affected average household income. Over the period, average household income increased from 73 per cent to 75 per cent of that in the South East – in that respect, the relative gain was marginal.

The central thesis about the impact of the Troubles has been on output and job loss. Both Northern Ireland and the UK as a whole suffered a similar rate of decline in manufacturing output in the period 1979–81: –14.2 per cent in the case of Northern Ireland; and –14.3 per cent in the UK. While there appeared to be significant improvement thereafter in the UK as a whole, Northern Ireland did not experience a similar recovery. For example, between 1983 and 1986 production and construction output in the UK rose by 7.8 per cent whereas the figure for Northern Ireland was a mere 1 per cent. This disparity was mirrored in the patterns of employment change in the same period. While the UK experienced a growth of 2.6 per cent, Northern Ireland continued to endure a decline of 1.2 per cent. Only in the late 1980s did Northern Ireland show evidence of recovery.

While Northern Ireland's output showed some improvement, it remained behind the growth rate for the UK as a whole, particularly in the last two years. Output in UK manufacturing industries increased more than three times as fast as in Northern Ireland over the same period. Manufacturing continued to be the weakest segment of the regional economy. For much of the 1980s, the trends in the key economic indicators between Northern Ireland and the rest of the UK diverged. This was evident in the case of employment and unemployment. In the period 1979–86 when manufacturing faced a severe squeeze, employment in the sector dropped by a quarter in the UK but by one-third in Northern Ireland. Moreover, when employment started to rise in the UK after 1983, Northern Ireland continued to experience a jobs decline.

Table 3.7 Industrial Output, the UK and NI, 1983–89 (1985 = 100)

| | United Kingdom | | Northern Ireland | |
	Prod. Industry	Man. Industry	Prod. Industry	Man. Industry
1983	94.7	93.7	94	94
1984	94.9	97.6	97	97
1985	100.0	100.0	100	100
1986	102.2	101.0	100	100
1987	105.8	106.6	99	99
1988	109.5	114.0	102	102
1989	108.9	117.7	104	105

Source: Northern Ireland Economic Council (1989); PPRU (1989)

Table 3.8 Percentage Changes in Employees in Employment, Northern Ireland and the UK, 1979–88

	Northern Ireland	UK
All industries		
1979–83	−10.3	−9.1
1983–85	−0.6	+1.9
1985–86	−1.6	+0.4
1986–88	+0.7	+4.5
Manufacturing		
1979–85	−33.1	−25.0
1985–86	−4.0	−1.7
1986–88	−1.3	+0.1

Source: Coopers & Lybrand (1989); PPRU (1989)

It was not until 1986 that Northern Ireland's employment decline was arrested and began to switch to a modest reverse. Nevertheless, in the decade after 1979, over 40,000 manufacturing jobs were lost. In the period 1979–87, manufacturing employment in Northern Ireland slumped by over 45,000 (Coopers & Lybrand Deloitte, 1990). During the mid-1980s, there was a net loss of over 5000 manufacturing and 3000 construction jobs, a drain only partially compensated for by a consistent increase in service employment. Yet, jobs growth in the private services areas such as banking, insurance and business services was extremely modest – +0.7 per cent between 1982 and 1987 (see Table 3.8). These figures might be interpreted as the cumulative impact of the Troubles. At the same time, comparison with Britain can be misleading since other British regions suffered similar economic problems and diverged from the national average. Moreover, between June 1988 and June 1991 the number employed increased by over 8000 and those self-employed by over 3000. All of the increases took place in services, with manufacturing and construction shedding 6000 jobs, as can be seen in Table 3.9. Approximately 50 per cent of total employment in the manufacturing sector in Northern Ireland was still represented by 'traditional' sectors such as shipbuilding, textiles, clothing and tobacco industries.

Table 3.9 Employment Trends in Northern Ireland, 1981–91

Years (June)	Manufacture	Construction	Services	Total
1981	123,000	28,300	325,200	506,920
1982	111,550	28,750	328,900	499,760
1983	106,900	28,250	331,050	497,650
1984	107,230	26,970	333,310	498,040
1985	108,070	27,100	339,210	504,590
1986	104,810	24,550	343,800	502,510
1987	103,370	25,840	347,080	505,050
1988	105,550	26,360	357,640	518,050
1989	106,310	25,990	366,550	527,410
1990	104,890	25,940	371,140	530,330
1991	102,400	23,350	372,460	526,370

Source: Policy, Planning and Research Unit, Economics Division (1991), *Monthly Economic Report*, November, Table 3

By 1988, in terms of employment, Northern Ireland was a service economy. As the private sector declined, public sector jobs partly compensated. Between 1979 and 1988 manufacturing employment fell by 40 per cent. At that time, nearly 90 per cent of the remaining manufacturing jobs were directly or indirectly subsidised by the state. Public support for manufacturing jobs averaged about £39 per employee per week. Yet, despite the degree of public support, manufacturing jobs continued to haemorrhage.

The condition of the economy in the 1980s was summarised thus:

Northern Ireland's manufacturing sector, together with agriculture, is probably capable of supporting a regional income at only half to two-thirds of the current level. As a result of the contraction of manufacturing, without replacement by other sectors producing externally tradable goods, the Province has become dependent on the public sector, much of it externally financed to support current levels of employment and income. (Gudgin, 1989: p. 61)

Nevertheless, unemployment in the region steadily increased in the three decades before 1990. It moved from 31,980 in 1961, to 36,699 in 1971, 98,943 in 1981 to 100,400 in 1991.

Because of the changes in the unemployment count after 1982, the final figure is not comparable with the previous. Some estimates suggest that a comparable figure would be in the region of 140,000 (*Unemployment Unit Bulletin*, various issues). By 1991, unemployment was nearly three times higher than 1961. The problem has been more than just the Troubles. The region's demographic structure has also contributed. With a relatively high birth rate, the ratio of school leavers coming into the labour market compared to those retiring is about 12:8. This steady increase in the labour force imposes a severe burden on the region's capacity for job creation. (Gudgin and Roper, 1990: p. 61). At the same time, the participation rate for women is lower than in the rest of the UK, which partially offsets the trend for proportionately more young labour market entrants.

Reflecting the job shake-out in the 1980s, unemployment in Northern Ireland substantially increased. Between 1979 and 1981 unemployment rose by over 60 per cent and continued to increase until 1986, when the official unemployment rate reached 18.1 per cent (Northern Ireland Economic Council, Autumn 1989). This represented a total of 127,800 unemployed people, over 70 per cent of whom were men. Between 1978 and 1988 male unemployment as a share of the workforce more than doubled from 9.4 per cent to 20 per cent. Female unemployment nearly doubled from 6.1 per cent to 11 per cent in the same period. In 1989, official unemployment stood at 104,000, representing 15.1 per cent of the workforce, nearly two and a half times the UK rate of 6.3 per cent. As noted in an economic review:

> The gap between Northern Ireland and the next worst region, the North of England, remains a wide one. If Northern Ireland had the same rate as the North of England (9.8 per cent) total unemployment would be 68,000 – 36,000 less than it is at present. (Coopers & Lybrand, 1989: p. 37)

Despite changes in the unemployment count, and the expansion of government employment schemes (up by 30 per cent since 1979), the severity of Northern Ireland's jobless problem in the 1980s remained evident. Indeed, between 1979 and 1986 the percentage of the total unemployed in Northern Ireland in the long-term category doubled and for those out of work five years or more, it trebled – from 26 per cent to 55 per cent and 5 per cent to 15 per cent, respectively. Between then and 1990, unemployment fell by over 30,000. This apparent reduction in unemployment has to be seen in the context of the labour market effects of motivation programmes such as Restart, and availability for work tests on the number of unemployed claimants and in rule changes that disqualified under 18s from benefit. There were over 33,000 people in government employment and training schemes in 1990, a substantial increase since 1979 (Northern Ireland Economic Council, 1991: Table 5.3).

The severity of the unemployment problem is indicated by long-term unemployment figures shown in Table 3.10.

Table 3.10 Duration of Unemployment in Northern Ireland, 1981 and 1990

	1981		1990		% Change	
	Males	Females	Males	Females	Males	Females
Up to 6 months	30,122	18,671	21,583	12,208	−28	−43
6 months to 1 year	18,631	7667	10,364	4265	−45	−44
1 year to 2 years	13,625	4452	10,485	3360	−23	−25
2 years +	12,831	2090	31,330	5881	+144	+181
All	75,209	32,880	73,762	25,714	−2	−12

Source: Northern Ireland Annual Abstract of Statistics, 1982 and 1990

Between 1981 and 1990, unemployment fell for both men and women. The percentage declines were greatest for the groups with low unemployment duration. The very long-term unemployed category (two years +) saw very substantial increases. Thus, unemployment was recomposing over the decade with greater proportions falling into the longer-term category. Duration of unemployment is a crucial variable in determining the poverty of the unemployed. Moreover, prolonged absence from the labour market is associated with less job search activities and greater reluctance by employers to offer jobs. By 1990, 57 per cent of men and 37 per cent of women had been out of work for at least a year. Changes in the unemployment count in 1982 excluded some unemployed women from the register, so the 1990 figure undoubtedly under-represents their experience of long-term unemployment.

A comparison of the ratio of long-term unemployment to total unemployment between Northern Ireland and the UK reveals the relative severity of the problem. In 1979, the proportion of long-term unemployed in Northern Ireland was 27.9 per cent compared to 24.6 per cent in the UK. In 1982 the figures were 39.4 per cent as against 33.6 per cent, in 1987 51.1 and 42.6 per cent, and 51.3 and 31.6 per cent in 1990 (see Scott, 1993: p. 87).

The Northern Ireland ratio steadily diverged from the UK's between 1979 and 1990. Such figures reflect a substantial group of Northern Ireland's unemployed who remain untouched by periods of economic growth. Even when jobs are increasing, only one in three new jobs are taken by the unemployed. These go disproportionately to the short-term unemployed.

The uneven spatial distribution of unemployment in Northern Ireland was also exacerbated over the 1980s. The analysis of change in this respect is difficult because of the redesignation of 'travel to work' areas. Two such areas, Armagh and Downpatrick, which existed in 1981, had disappeared as 'travel to work areas' by 1990. The former was incorporated into Craigavon 'travel to work area' and the latter into Belfast. Moreover, Magherafelt did not exist in 1981 but appeared in the 1990 data. It appears that this was formerly part of the Derry Londonderry travel to work area (information from the Statistics Branch, Department of Economic Development, NI). Thus, to make a comparison over time, some data aggregation is required for each year. This exercise reveals that while unemployment fell by just over 5 per cent between September 1981 and July 1990, areas like Ballymena and Enniskillen enjoyed substantially greater falls – 70 per cent and 15 per cent, respectively. By contrast, Derry Londonderry and Newry saw significant increases in their numbers unemployed – 15 per cent and 11 per cent. Arguably, such spatial differentiation reflects a further unequal division in the distribution of employment and unemployment within the region.

In the 1990s, the picture changed again. First, Northern Ireland was spared the worst of the British recession generated by a collapse of the credit bubble following increases in interest rates. Having spent the 1980s lagging behind Britain, the region dramatically improved its performance between 1990 and 1995. In this period, manufacturing output and, for a shorter period, manufacturing productivity grew faster. Moreover, this was accompanied by employment growth. The consultancy Coopers & Lybrand, which conducts an annual review of the local economy, concluded that the region's performance in 1994 and 1995 (coinciding with the first IRA cease-fire) was particularly robust.

In short, it is not easy to separate out the effects of the Troubles from other processes impacting on the Northern Ireland economy. In general, two approaches to this problem have been developed:

- The first attempts to develop a statistical model for a Northern Ireland in a 'no Troubles' scenario and measures the difference with the real situation. While, estimates from these exercises suggest that about 20,000 jobs have been lost as a result of the Troubles, it is recognised that regional policy has created a similar number (Harris, 1991).

- The second looks at the additional burden of public expenditure created by the Troubles, particularly security expenditure in terms of the higher ratios of police, prison officers per head of population, the compensation for damage and the additional costs to other services. The costs of the Troubles are thus expressed in terms of public expenditure levels greater than they would otherwise be (Tomlinson, 1994).

Both approaches provide estimates of specific effects rather than a comprehensive assessment. The focus here has been on the human costs of the Troubles. Nevertheless, in analysing victims, it is important to recognise the importance of context. In this respect, a number of issues are pertinent:

- A strong sense of exclusion and inequality contributed to the political crisis that led to violence. A post-conflict society in Northern Ireland should thus seriously address these issues. This should be done without the illusion that such problems are easy to tackle or that infinite resources are available to do so.

- Despite 30 years of conflict, the regional economy continued to function. Indeed, it is difficult to see directly how the Troubles damaged the local economy – for example, the figures for GDP per head in Northern Ireland correlate highly with those for the North of England over the period 1969–94 (with a correlation coefficient of .93) suggesting that more general forces were affecting weak regions. Nevertheless, Northern Ireland benefited from high levels of public expenditure that helped sustain the economic and social fabric. Without substantial subsidy, the economic picture might have been very different. Those commenting on this have estimated that the Troubles have cost a large number of jobs and created a severe burden on the public purse.

- Finally, there does appear to be a relationship between the intensity of violence in an area and its level of deprivation. While the relation is not simple, it certainly implies that social and economic reconstruction is an irreducible component of a peace process.

THE HUMAN COST OF
THE TROUBLES

4 Profiling Those who Died in Northern Ireland's Troubles

It is both an appropriate time and an important task to examine the impact of almost 30 years of political violence on Northern Ireland in terms of the cost of human lives. The declaration of the second IRA cease-fire accompanied by the Good Friday Agreement, the Referendum and the establishment of the Assembly permit a cautious optimism that Northern Ireland's long war may be coming to an end. The situation remains volatile since difficulties on the decommissioning of weapons threaten to disrupt political progress, contentious marches threaten inter-community violence and Loyalist and Republican paramilitary fragments remain outside the peace process. Nevertheless, considerable efforts are being made on all sides to transform the conflict into a political process, and perhaps to reach a lasting settlement.

A crucial issue for building peace in Northern Ireland will be the recognition by all sides of where the primary costs of the conflict have fallen, the nature and extent of these costs and of the need to develop compensatory policies to assist those most affected. Northern Ireland's political conflict has endured for 30 years, caused almost 4000 deaths and over 40,000 injuries and has cost several billion pounds damage both directly and indirectly to the economy of Northern Ireland. Indeed, O'Leary and McGarry conclude that:

> it is legitimate to classify the Northern Ireland conflict as similar to those which have riven Lebanon, Sri Lanka, and Cyprus. The scale of the Northern Ireland conflict should therefore be seen as very intense ... given that it has taken place in the presence of moderately amicable relations between relevant neighbouring states and regional powers, and in the absence of superpower rivalries. (O'Leary and McGarry, 1993: p. 20)

They conducted an analysis of those killed in political violence in Ireland between 1886 and 1990 showing that the number killed in Northern Ireland in the last 20 years of this period was proportionately greater than in the whole of Ireland in each extended period of political violence in the first 60 years of the twentieth century. For example, as we pointed out earlier, they argue that the number killed in the current conflict was absolutely and proportionately greater than either the Irish War of Independence (1919–21) or the violence surrounding the formation of the Northern Ireland State (1920–22).

Carrying out research on political violence and its victims in Northern Ireland poses particular problems for researchers:

- In the conflict between Republican paramilitaries and the British State with the associated role of Loyalist paramilitaries, information has been a crucial commodity. Accordingly, those living in areas most affected by the violence are reluctant to impart information and are suspicious of those seeking it. A key problem is thus security.
- In addition, there are ethical questions about obtaining and using data on those who have been victims of the conflict itself. Such people have too frequently been the subject of academic research with only limited consent and with no control over the process or its results. How can research be conducted which obtains relevant, and robust, data while respecting the research subjects and, indeed, offering them a measure of control over the research process? Further, the trauma generated by violent incidents persists over time. Probing such issues can be intensely painful, reintroducing a high measure of stress into the person's life.
- Moreover, issues of the validity and reliability of data are acute. Individuals have very different views about the causes and nature of the conflict and these affect the information given. Respondents are being asked to record events which took place in the past (sometimes decades) which were, in any event, confusing to the participant. Events are interpreted through the lenses of differing (often opposing) ideologies which significantly colour the record of the event.
- Finally, there are issues about the combination and balance between the research methodologies involved – quantitative methodologies can present the scale of the damage but only qualitative methodologies can grasp the intensity of the trauma experienced by particular individuals.

THE RESEARCH APPROACH

The research associated with this book has been conducted in accordance with participatory action research principles, which have entailed a management structure involving a range of people with direct experience of the effects of the Troubles. The ethical considerations related to entering this field of research confirmed the desirability of this approach. One of the most devastating after-effects of trauma is the sense of disempowerment that it can bring. Working according to a principle of partnership is an attempt to avoid further disempowering those researched.

In order to enter a field of research such as this, where the research is concerned with the impact of violence on a population, the researchers must become involved in the most intimate and traumatic events in the lives of some of Northern Ireland's citizens. Yet these events – the deaths and injuries sustained as a result of violence – are also matters of public import and political consequence. The personal grief, anger, shock and fear of those directly affected by violence has often been subsumed into the collective sense of outrage, grievance, fear and victimhood.

The mechanism by which this incorporation occurs is the media coverage of the violent incident and its aftermath. Media coverage of violence in Northern Ireland has been the focus of substantial attention, much of which has been concerned with the manner in which the media manifestly or implicitly support one or other political position in Northern Ireland (Curtis, 1984; Rolston and Miller, 1996). The concern here with the function of news media coverage is more generic. It is the function of news media coverage of violent incidents to summarise the violent incident and its effects within a few hours of its occurrence. Such accounts and summaries may be repeated for a short period after the event, after which time the event often ceases to be considered newsworthy.

News coverage must also locate the violent incident within a larger political conflict, usually by specifying the socio-political identification of the victim and the perpetrator. Footage and sound-track collected at the time of the incident is archived, and treated as historical documentation. Similarly, the social researcher chooses the focus of the research, enters the field, makes contact with people, who become 'subjects', collects data, analyses them and publishes. Like media coverage, research is usually engaged in the collection of evidence to support or contradict pre-existing ideas about the subject of enquiry. In neither case does the interviewee nor the 'subject' exert much influence, if any, on the angle of the journalist or the analysis of the researcher. Furthermore, having given consent to being interviewed, filmed or otherwise being represented, usually the 'subject' exerts no further control over the manner in which the footage, sound-track or data are deployed. This material may be used again, usually without consultation with those portrayed in it, when documentary media material is being compiled, or in further research.

Value freedom and the professional distance which normally separates researchers from the details of people's lives (which become data) was also an area in which we decided to depart from the professional norm. There are a number of ethical concerns arising out of these practices which must concern researchers and others who propose to approach the process of interpreting and presenting violence. In particular, compiling a database of those killed by political violence involved us in the daily handling of the tragic and often heartbreaking details of people's deaths. We found that, even in the analysis phase, when we were scrolling through screen after screen of the list of deaths, we had to regularly confront the nature of the data we were handling, and had to deal with our own emotional responses. The discipline of remembering that this is a list of human beings that have died has meant a more real and complete connection with the data. We all know people on the list of those who have been killed, some of them are members of our extended families, some are close relatives of our management group. Contrary to the old models of scientific or professional distance, we have not denied this – rather, we have discussed our personal responses to the material, and made it part of our analysis.

Attempting to democratise the research process, by involving individuals from the researched population at a number of levels in the research process, is a research strategy used particularly in sensitive research fields. The term 'participatory action research' has been applied to such, often rather diverse, strategies that attempt to engage the researched population in this way. In Northern Ireland, this approach has been developed in previous work (Smyth, 1995, 1996a–1996f). Perhaps the best known proponent is William Foote Whyte (1991). Participative action research means different things to different researchers.[1] In the project which gave rise to this book, it entails, for example, democratising the management structure of the project management, the involvement of lay management in monitoring the ethical aspects of research practices; the involvement of lay people in analysis by discussion and by reading drafts of papers; a detailed process of providing transcripts to all interviewees; discussion and agreeing of transcripts; collaboration with interviewees on issues such as anonymity, and presentation of findings.

The Cost of the Troubles Study has assembled the first comprehensive independent database on deaths associated with Northern Ireland's conflict, together with extensive qualitative and survey data on the experiences and effects of the conflict on the population. It is the analysis of the database on deaths in the conflict, illustrated and informed by other data collected, that provides the core source for this book.

STATISTICAL SOURCES ON DEATHS IN NORTHERN IRELAND'S CONFLICT

We will now review the various sources of data on deaths in the Northern Ireland conflict. When we evaluated each source, we found variously that they excluded deaths outside Northern Ireland, or that they included no data on location, or that they were not comprehensive. All of these shortcomings were problematic for our project of producing a comprehensive analysis of deaths in the Northern Ireland conflict. A more detailed review of existing sources will now explain why we decided to compile a new database on deaths for the purposes of our analysis.

McKeown (1977) points out the problems of compiling lists of victims of the Troubles, and the discrepancies between existing lists of deaths. Problems arise, according to McKeown, because there has been a high number of deaths as an indirect consequence of the violence, but not directly attributable to the Troubles. This, he argues, is why no list fully reveals the true impact of the violence in terms of deaths, because deaths indirectly due to the Troubles are rarely included. Deaths outside Northern Ireland are a further issue, and McKeown points out that between 1969 and 1977 over 120 people were killed in Britain and in the Republic of Ireland as a direct result of the conflict in Northern Ireland, yet are not included in the official statistics. He argues that there are high numbers of accidental deaths involving members of the security forces, as well as a considerable number of road deaths due to military vehicles, none of which are included in official 'Troubles' statistics, but can be found under road traffic accidents in the official account. He points to deaths due to trauma and stress specific to the Troubles as a further issue in the under-representing of the impact of the Troubles in terms of deaths. Finally, McKeown discusses problems of attribution, responsibility and religious affiliation and concludes by arguing that death statistics should focus attention upon the enormity of the violence of the Troubles since 1969.

Given the delay between writing and publishing material, it is sometimes difficult to ascertain the period to which total figures refer. Perhaps for this reason, Rowthorn and Wayne's (1988) figure appears to fall below the official figure. They state that 2500 people had been killed at that time – presumably before the end of 1988 – whereas the official figure for the end of 1987 was 2631. Sutton (1994) finds 3285 deaths at the end of 1993, whereas the RUC figure (which excludes deaths outside Northern Ireland, whilst Sutton does not) for the same period is 3126. Estimates on the total number killed in Northern Ireland vary. Amnesty International's (1994) report, *Political Killings in Northern Ireland*, claims that 'about 3400 people have been killed' in Northern Ireland, whereas the official RUC figure at the end of 1994 was 3118. O'Duffy and O'Leary (1990) in 'Violence in Northern Ireland 1969–June 1989' review the available data sources available to them at that time – the RUC and the Irish Information Partnership (IIP). They regard these two sources as reliable, even though they 'differ very marginally in their aggregate figures on deaths'. They find the IIP data 'more exhaustive and illuminating in the categorisation of agents responsible for violent acts. The RUC data by contrast is less helpful, and in some cases less credible' (O'Duffy and O'Leary, 1990: p. 318).

Constructing the Deaths Database

In the initial stages of the project, it was overwhelming that the names, addresses, ages and other information held on over 3500 people were not merely data, but personal information about people who had died, often brutally, prematurely, and that for each death a number of other human lives had been inalterably affected. The authors hold the view that, even though some of the personal information on those killed is already in the public arena, they would not make available any personal details lest the information be used to invade the privacy of families, or worse, that revenge or other motivations be facilitated. Issues about personal information having been resolved however, there remain other ethical dilemmas.

The information presented, whilst as accurate as can be made, may lead others who read it to conclusions – or support them in actions – which are not in the long-term interests of establishing an end to the violence we study. The information we handle and present here is not objective or neutral. Behind the statistics we present here is the life-blood of our friends, enemies and those we cannot classify, who have lost their lives and the oceans of tears which have been shed as a result. Holding up to a community such hard facts and figures in such times as we are currently living is risky and fearful work. We worry that our work will lead parties to the conflict to entrench their positions, and more bloodshed and loss of life will indirectly result. We have tried to resist the 'publish and be damned' instinct which is both an occupational hazard and based on a naive assumption that more information is necessarily a good thing. Yet we must believe that clearer views of our situation, which we have endeavoured to provide, and evidence about the awful cost paid by this community will support, inspire and motivate some people to pursue new ways in which we can successfully address our situation.

We are hopeful that some of our work can be useful in shedding more light on the nature of the problem, particularly within some of the areas and sub-populations worst affected by the Troubles, and thereby illuminate the routes towards new and effective solutions.

The Northern Ireland conflict has produced several accounts of the numbers and characteristics of those killed as a result of the Troubles. There are a number of problems associated with the available list of deaths, which is manifest by the inconsistencies between the lists, and the various manners and criteria by which they have been compiled. For example, list lengths vary from around 3400 deaths to over 4000. Furthermore, we are unaware of any database on deaths which is publicly available and which enables the systematic examination of the geographic distribution of deaths. For the purposes of this study we have attempted to compile a comprehensive and reliable database, inclusive of all Troubles-related deaths both inside and outside Northern Ireland from 1969 to 1998.

Over a four-year period from 1990, Isobel Hylands, a cross-community volunteer from Lurgan in Northern Ireland, produced an exhibition called 'Violence: Count The Cost'. According to Hylands, the exhibition's aim was 'to put names to the numbers – to humanise, personalise and decategorise the statistics' (Hylands, 1996). The exhibition consists of lists which contained the date, name, age, of people killed in the Troubles, together with the location, cause of death and the perpetrators responsible for the death. Hylands' main sources were daily newspapers from 1969, contact with families of victims and research in graveyards. She used books and other literature written on conflict as secondary sources. On cross-checking, it was found that the database was incomplete, with a substantial number of entries which were entirely discrepant with several other sources. A number of the deaths included in Hylands' list were not Troubles-related, but were a result of domestic violence or other physical assaults unrelated to the Troubles.

At this point, we decided to compile a new list of deaths which we were confident could be made as accurate and reliable as possible. The criteria for including a death on the database were more inclusive than those used by Sutton (1994) (who excludes deaths indirectly due to the Troubles such as those caused by army vehicles) or the RUC statistics (which exclude deaths outside Northern Ireland). We included every death that could be proved to be Troubles related. Using the original incomplete Hyland database, RUC statistics and Sutton's index, a new list of deaths was created.

McGarry and O'Leary (1993) claim that both official and independent data collections on violence in Northern Ireland are generally reliable. We found that, whilst names of those killed and locations of the fatal incident were generally reliable, other data such as the date of death or the identity of the perpetrator varied quite substantially between lists. We used three main sources of data: RUC statistics; the Irish Information Partnership's published list; and Malcolm Sutton's (1994) *Index of Deaths*. In addition, we referred to Holland and McDonald's (1994) *INLA: Deadly Divisions*; Bruce (1992) *The Red Hand*; Flackes and Elliott's (1994), *Northern Ireland: A Political Directory*; de Baroid's (1989) *Ballymurphy and the Irish War* and Survivors of Trauma's list of deaths for the greater Ardoyne area.

RUC statistics are compiled according to more exclusive standards than those used by any other lists, and as a result their list is shorter. Where they do not hold a complete data set on a particular category of death – such as deaths due to trauma, heart attack and so on – that category is excluded, nor do they include deaths which took place outside of Northern Ireland. Another difficulty in using police data on deaths is that the geographical categories used are police sub-divisions. Sub-divisions are geographical categories used only in police data, and do not coincide with other spatial categories, postcodes or electoral wards for example. This means that RUC data cannot be directly correlated with other data such as indices of deprivation, which are almost invariably available by ward.

Our second main source of information was the Irish Information Partnership (IIP). This information service collected information in the period from 1982 to 1989, and provides extensive quantitative and qualitative data on deaths in the Troubles. Data and analyses are produced on the status of the victim, cause of death, place of death, religion, age and gender. Controversial deaths are particularly well covered in paragraphs which detail the victim's identity, cause of death, and information on the circumstances of death derived from the inquest and coroner's reports. The RUC and the Irish Information Partnership total death figures differ marginally. The IIP information is much more extensive and therefore more useful in clarifying the geographical distribution of victims. There were numerous inconsistencies between the Irish Information Partnership cited dates of death, and the dates given by Sutton, Hylands and the other minor sources.

Malcolm Sutton's *Index of Deaths*, published in 1994, is one of the most comprehensive published records on deaths in the Troubles in Northern Ireland. Sutton provides the personal details of the victims, information on the organisation responsible for the death and the circumstances in which the death occurred. His main sources are newspapers, coroners' reports and cemeteries. Sutton's list excludes certain types of incident such as accidental shootings, trauma-related deaths such as fatal heart attacks or suicides as a consequence of the Troubles. Accidents involving military vehicles are similarly omitted. As a published testament to those killed in the Troubles, there is no other record of its kind.

A number of cross-checks were carried out using further sources. Holland and McDonald's (1994) *INLA: Deadly Divisions* is an account of life inside the INLA and provides information on deaths caused by this paramilitary organisation. Since the INLA did not begin to claim responsibility for its actions until 1976, the earlier deaths at their hands – of which there were a number – are difficult to attribute. Furthermore, where Holland and McDonald cite the exact date of death, it is frequently inconsistent with other sources. Bruce's (1992) *The Red Hand* documents Loyalist paramilitary activity in Northern Ireland, and contains some limited data on names of victims and organisations responsible. Flackes and Elliott's (1994) *Northern Ireland: A Political Directory* is a useful reference for dates of more prominent deaths in the Troubles. De Baroid's (1989) *Ballymurphy and the Irish War* provides names and dates of death for victims from the Ballymurphy area. Similarly, a self-help group in Ardoyne, Survivors of Trauma, compiled a list of deaths for the greater Ardoyne area. These last two sources are potentially rather problematic since some of their information is based on the memories of local people, and, particularly on the issue of dates, memory can be an even less reliable source than newspapers.

Using these sources and cross-checks, we collected and cross-checked information on the date of the death, name of victim, age, gender, cause of death, town of incident, religious and political affiliation, occupation, organisation responsible for the death and, where possible, a complete address of where the death occurred. Our criteria for inclusion has meant that our list is longer than any of the other main sources: RUC; Hylands; or Sutton. We have collected data on a total of 3601 deaths (at the end of February 1998) due to the Troubles in Northern Ireland.

At that point, it was no longer viable to complete the gaps in the database. Certain variables had high levels of missing values (for example, occupational classification), causing difficulties in the analysis. For one variable, we were able to compensate for gaps in religious affiliation data. On closer examination, it was found that there was a high percentage of missing values in the religious affiliation of RUC members killed. Using data from the Fair Employment Agency, we established that the composition of the RUC was 92.2 per cent Protestant. For some analyses, we assigned 'Protestant' as the religious affiliation of 92.2 per cent of the RUC officers in the database, for whom we did not have religious affiliation.

The next task was to attach a postal code to each fatal incident address. Postal codes can be transformed into electoral ward. The purpose of attaching ward labels was to allow systematic examination of the geographical distribution of deaths and compare death data with other ward-based data. Difficulties arose with cases that did not have a full address of incident, but only the name of the town where the fatal incident happened, e.g. Lurgan or Enniskillen. It such cases, it was impossible to attach a postcode. For these, the incident was attributed to the centre of the town. For example, if we only had the address as 'Lurgan' we took the postal code for an address in the town centre, taking the postcode for a premises in the centre of High Street, Main Street, or Market Street. We followed this method consistently in cases where we did not have a full incident address.

Other problems arose where areas had been redeveloped and where street names changed. To find these addresses, we used early editions of postcode directories. There remain some outstanding postcodes that were recorded as missing values. The majority of these are in rural areas throughout Northern Ireland and neither the Yearbooks nor the Postal Address Book Inquiry Service contain the relevant codes. Addresses and postcodes of victims who lived outside Northern Ireland have been listed as 'GB' for Great Britain, 'ROI' for Republic of Ireland, 'GERM' for Germany and so on. When we completed the insertion of postal codes, we no longer used the names and addresses on the list, on the advice of the project

Board of Directors, in order to protect the privacy of families bereaved in the Troubles.

The final phase of work on the database was to find the home address of the victim and, as before with the incident address, attach a postcode. None of the available sources included the home address. For the purpose of our statistical analysis we considered it desirable to count both the postal code of the home address of the victim, and the postal code of the location of the fatal incident as 'fatal sites' in the Troubles. This allows calculation of a Troubles-related death risk using postal codes and wards for both addresses. Journalist David McKittrick and the Deramore group have been working for a considerable period compiling formidable and detailed files on the Troubles. We purchased a sub-set of their data providing 70 per cent of the home addresses of the victims. Searching documentary sources, local and national newspapers and reports found the majority of the missing 30 per cent in the deaths and obituaries. Postcodes were then attached using the same method as before.

A crucial issue is the criteria for inclusion of a death on our list. Sutton's and the RUC's list both exclude certain types of incidents such as army vehicle accidents, accidental shootings or deaths due to trauma, brought on by a conflict-related incident. The database includes such categories as fatal heart attacks, suicides and includes all trauma-related deaths that can be shown to be Troubles-related. For example, if there is evidence to support a fatal heart attack as being a direct consequence of a bomb explosion or a shooting or took place on hearing of a relative, friend or neighbour being injured or killed in the conflict, it was included. Deaths as a result of army vehicle accidents were also included, on the assumption that if there was no trouble or violence on our streets, there would be no need for the numbers or intensity of army vehicles patrolling the streets. The evidence on such deaths suggests that the large majority of these fatal accidents have also occurred in areas that have experienced the greatest concentration of violence. The RUC list excludes such deaths, on the principle that a complete list of such deaths is not available, and any inclusion will only be piecemeal. We considered that the missing data on such deaths was not sufficient reason to exclude those deaths on which we had data, and we fully accept that our data on such deaths are not complete.

Information and reports available informed decisions about inclusiveness on each death. One difficult decision has been to exclude the Mull of Kintyre crash in which 29 people were killed. All of the dead were security force personnel. On balance, the reason for excluding this incident is that there was no suggestion that the helicopter crash which killed these people was Troubles-related. The counter-argument for inclusiveness is that so many security personnel travelling together to a meeting outside Northern Ireland could be interpreted as a consequence of the Troubles. On balance, however, deaths due to this incident were excluded on the grounds that such an accident could conceivably have occurred had the Troubles not been happening.

There are a number of problems associated with the available list of deaths, which are manifest by the inconsistencies between the lists, and the various manners and criteria by which they have been compiled. For example, list lengths vary from around 3400 deaths to over 4000. The police database, which is one of the more consistent sources, is compiled according to police sub-division, making it impossible to compare with, for example, indices of deprivation or other data, which is almost invariably available by ward. Thus, part of our work has been to prepare a list which has been cross-checked with the existing data sources, and which is organised in a manner which allows comparisons with other ward-based data.

The database is as reliable and valid as the available sources will permit. We would emphasise that the magnitude of the task and the diversity of data available would indicate that any such database will inevitably contain data which are at variance with other available sources.

5 Patterns of Violence

Like many other phenomena, political violence in Northern Ireland has been distributed unevenly across space and time. Certain periods saw extreme concentrations of violence relating to particular events like the introduction of internment, Bloody Sunday or, more recently, the annual crisis associated with the determination of the Portadown Orange Lodges to march through the Catholic area of the Garvaghy Road following the church service at which they commemorate the battle of the Somme. Equally, over three decades of violence have been concentrated in particular places according to the different phases of the Troubles and the different types of conflict.

Indeed, the conflict itself has taken several forms:

- The war between Republican paramilitaries and the security forces has not merely exhibited different intensities over the years but has taken different manifestations in particular places. For example, the bombing campaign against 'economic targets' was primarily undertaken in cities and towns as was anti-security force rioting and, in the early period, attempts to establish 'no-go' areas. Such activities were associated a high rate of civilian casualties, particularly as the result of urban car bombs and the 'collateral' damage of the riot. In contrast, the 'rural' war was fought more directly between the protagonists themselves with ambushes carried out by both sides. This was a war whose success depended crucially on the intelligence each side possessed and the capacity for surgical strikes at precise targets. In this case, the profile of victims was remarkably different from that generated by urban confrontation.
- Moreover, different time cycles saw different strategies and tactics as each side developed the skills of insurgency and counterinsurgency. Crucially paramilitary actions depended on supplies of weaponry, the capacity to develop organisational structures that were difficult to penetrate and the ability to mobilise popular support. The overall strategic approach of the paramilitaries was to create the conditions under which

their own capacity for military action was maximised while those of the security forces were politically inhibited by international pressure and legal constraints. Conversely, the security forces sought to create a terrain of maximum manoeuvrability within these restraints. Hence, Northern Ireland has seen different legal strategies (e.g. Diplock Courts) and different security tactics ('supergrasses' or the endless debate over the existence of 'shoot-to-kill' policies). All these developments provided the framework within which the war was fought, influenced how it was conducted and determined the character and location of its victims.

- A wholly different category of violence was associated with inter-communal conflict, although this has also taken different forms. The territorial segregation of the two main religions in Northern Ireland has steadily increased over the period of the conflict. In certain cases, the degree of physical separation has been substantial – the River Foyle largely divides the Catholic and Protestant populations of Derry Londonderry – in Belfast, east of the River Lagan has only 12 per cent of the population Catholic, whereas west of the river has 55 per cent. In other instances, only a few streets, frequently intersected by 'peace walls', separate the different religions. North Belfast is the primary example, containing 14 out of Belfast's 17 peace walls. This proximity factor has often been associated with extreme inter-communal violence – segregation does not convey safety. Moreover, the necessity to move outside an area for work or leisure can carry high risk. Indeed, demographic change, particularly the increasing proportion of the Northern Ireland population who are Catholics, has had spatial implications – Catholics are now the majority in places where, previously, they were a tiny minority. Some such places have been associated with 'traditional' Loyalist marching routes and thus become contested spaces, flashpoints of confrontation and violence during the 'marching' season. During periods of tension, minority populations, predominantly Catholics, were frequently intimidated from where they lived or worked. Thus, patterns of contiguous territories give rise to particular forms of violence and specific categories of victims.

- Equally, the complex geography of religious segregation has also determined the terrain for sectarian assassination. Republicans legitimate their actions as 'anti-imperialist' struggle. The legitimate targets of this struggle are those involved in, or associated with, the British state. The definition of legitimate targets has been almost infinitely elastic – construction workers rebuilding police stations, those providing catering for the British Army or those long-time retired from the RUC reserve. The specific history of Northern Ireland has meant that those associated in some way with the state have been overwhelmingly Protestant. Accordingly, Protestants perceive Republican intentions as being directed primarily at them in an attempt to intimidate or evict from Northern Ireland altogether. Conversely, Loyalist paramilitaries had no 'obvious target' for their activities – the IRA, by definition, was a covert organisation. Nevertheless, they employed classic counterinsurgency tactics by terrorising the Catholic population which 'hid' the Republican guerrillas. Thus, particularly in the 1970s, all Catholics were regarded as 'legitimate' targets for Loyalist paramilitaries. The motivation was either revenge for the 'Republican terror campaign' or an effort to pressurise the IRA to desist or, in some cases, it was simply hate-crime. Belfast, and particularly North Belfast, was the cockpit for sectarian assassination. The fact that the two communities lived in such proximity facilitated the search for victims and ensured that escape from the scene could be quickly accomplished.

- Finally, there were internal struggles going on within both communities either as feuds amongst rival paramilitary groups or 'punishment' type activities. The former have tended to emerge out of ideological split within paramilitary organisations such as the early secession of key dissidents from the Official IRA to set up the Provisional IRA or the later conflict between Official Republicans and the Irish Republican Socialist Party. Paramilitary punishments have been viewed either as a necessary evil, a form of policing in areas where the writ of the RUC does not run and where petty criminals are 'turned' as informers or as a systematic strategy to maintain control and intimidate opposition to paramilitary power. A surprisingly high proportion of the deaths in each community has been perpetrated by organisations that claim to defend that community. Unlike the random violence associated with deprivation and urban crisis, the violence in Northern Ireland has tended for the most part to conform to certain rules, given that the protagonists keep a weather eye on the media and public opinion. Attempts are made to demonise people after they have been assassinated or attacked, in order to justify the violence, the warning codes surrounding bomb planting and the relatively few no-warning bombs that have been deployed are examples of how the violence has tended to been used according to certain codes.

This matrix of cycles, phases, types and locations of violence has created a complex pattern of violence not easily reducible to simple trends. The purpose of this chapter is to look at the patterns in terms of when and where. As indicated, the core analysis is derived from a comprehensive database of political deaths between 1969 and 1998. While this depicts the most extreme consequences of the conflict, it is also a good surrogate for violence in general. A comparison of the numbers of deaths each year and the number of injuries associated with political violence shows a correlation coefficient of .93. Injuries outnumber deaths by just over ten to one but have exactly the same cycle. The combination of deaths and injuries represents the primary human cost of the Troubles although these do not encompass the trauma of grief, imprisonment and intimidation. Nevertheless, the deaths have been taken as an appropriate reflection of the overall costs. Since Northern Ireland is made up of sets of different territories, some case studies – areas where violence was particularly significant – will also be highlighted. There has not been one uniform conflict in Northern Ireland, rather the Troubles are a mosaic of different types of conflict. Accordingly, the 'reality' of the Troubles is different for people in different locations and in different occupations. Thus, to grasp some of these different realities, comment is made on sub-populations living in specific areas. These have been chosen to illustrate either the intensity of the conflict or its particular character in certain locations.

WHEN DID THE DEATHS OCCUR?

The distribution of political deaths over time in Northern Ireland is described in Table 5.1.

Just over half of all deaths occurred in the period 1971–76. If the frequency of deaths can be regarded as a good indicator of the intensity of the conflict, then these five years stand out over the entire two and a half decades. The pivotal event was the introduction of internment in 1971. Only 32 deaths took place before 9 August. Thus, 154 people died in the remaining five months of the year – equivalent to a yearly figure of 370. The number killed in 1972 was even greater, as resentment against security policies (typified by the

Table 5.1 Distribution of Deaths (1969–98)

Year	Frequency of Deaths	% of Total★
1969	18	0.5
1970	26	0.7
1971	186	5.2
1972	497	13.8
1973	274	7.6
1974	307	8.5
1975	265	7.4
1976	314	8.7
1977	117	3.2
1978	83	2.3
1979	124	3.4
1980	86	2.4
1981	115	3.2
1982	112	3.1
1983	88	2.4
1984	74	2.1
1985	61	1.7
1986	64	1.8
1987	103	2.9
1988	105	2.9
1989	81	2.2
1990	84	2.3
1991	101	2.8
1992	93	2.6
1993	90	2.5
1994	68	1.9
1995	9	0.2
1996	21	0.6
1997	23	0.6
1998	12	0.3
Total	3601	100.0
Average no. of deaths per year	120	

★ to the nearest decimal point

Bloody Sunday deaths in Derry) increased. The proroguing of Stormont in 1972 fuelled Loyalist resentment and saw the growth of their paramilitary operations. A further high point was 1974, the year the Power Sharing Executive was dramatically brought down by the Ulster Workers' Council strike. After 1976, despite equally dramatic events such as the renewed Loyalist strike in 1977 and the hunger strike deaths of the early 1980s, the number killed in any one year never exceeded 125 and in only seven years was it greater than 100. Put another way, the average annual number of deaths for the whole period was 120, for 1969–70 it was 22, for 1971–76 it was 306 and for 1977–94 it was 91 – thus, the intensity of killing between 1971 and 1976 was more than twice that for the whole period and more than three times that for all of the subsequent years. This can be seen in Figure 5.1 which takes the average annual number of deaths (120) as 100 and scores each other year relative to that. As illustrated graphically, the first half of the 1970s stands out. Indeed, in 1972, the number of deaths was over three and a half times the yearly average for the entire period.

The data themselves cannot provide a comprehensive explanation for the trend. By cross-tabulating the years in which the deaths occurred by those organisations responsible, it is possible to say something about the roles of the various protagonists over time. Just over half of all those killed by the British Army (163 deaths or 51.6 per cent) died between 1971 and 1973 compared to 15.3 per cent of deaths (7 deaths) for which the RUC was responsible. It could be said that the most offensive security posture by the military occurred over the two and a half year period consisting of the last five months in 1971 and all of 1972–73. Although Republican and Loyalist paramilitaries killed very large numbers of people during these years (502 and 216), they constituted a lower share of their respective totals (25.4 per cent and 23 per cent). Thus, the overall distribution of deaths for which they were responsible is less concentrated in the short period characteristic of the British Army. Indeed, 40 per cent of deaths (452 deaths) perpetrated by Loyalist paramilitaries took place between 1974 and 1976.

There would thus appear to be different cycles amongst the organisations principally responsible for the killings that produced the massive concentration of deaths in the early 1970s. For the British Army, the most offensive period was 1971–73, for Loyalist para-

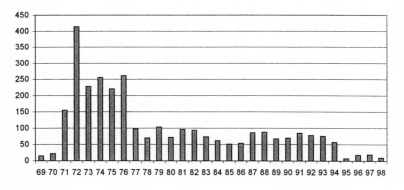

Deaths Ratio (Yearly Av. = 100)

Figure 5.1 Comparative Yearly Death Rates in the Troubles

militaries, it was 1974–76 and for Republican paramilitaries it was 1971–76 accounting for 47 per cent of all the deaths they have carried out in the entire period.

Explosions and shootings were the predominant causes of death. Almost 91 per cent of victims died from these causes. Deaths caused by explosions were more characteristic of the 1970s with shootings more evenly distributed across the period.

Given that violence has also been associated with regular annual events, for example, Loyalist marches or anniversaries of internment, it is also useful to examine the deaths in terms of a monthly cycle – i.e. the number of deaths occurring in particular months over the entire period. Table 5.2 gives the absolute number of deaths that occurred in each month and the percentage of the total. It also gives a ratio that is based on the fact that if the deaths had been evenly distributed across the months, then each would have contained 8.5 per cent of the total. The ratio column gives a figure for each month with its own score relative to 8.5 (treated as 100) so as to indicate clearly the months in which a disproportionate number of deaths occurred.

Table 5.2 Distribution of Deaths by Month (1969–98)

Month	Number of Deaths	% of Total	Ratio
Jan.	262	7.3	87
Feb.	308	8.6	103
Mar.	286	7.9	95
April	279	7.8	93
May	326	9.1	109
June	285	7.9	95
July	325	9.0	108
Aug.	345	9.6	115
Sept.	253	7.0	84
Oct.	342	9.5	114
Nov.	331	9.2	110
Dec.	256	7.1	85
Total	3598	100	

There is some indication of a cycle corresponding to periods of particular tension. The first four months had average or low ratios and the deaths begin to rise in May, with July and August also having high ratios. Months with equally high scores, however, were October and November, both outside the calendar of tension-associated events. It may have been that the years when deaths were most frequent have affected the general monthly cycle. Nevertheless, on this basis the notion of a systematic monthly cycle is not proved.

In summary, Northern Ireland's armed conflict began as a political struggle in the late 1960s that rapidly escalated into a violent struggle in the first half of the 1970s and which persisted at a lower intensity for the next 20 years. Interpretations vary about why an essentially political struggle about civil rights and modernisation so quickly moved into a violent phase:

- A traditional Unionist analysis contends that the initial civil rights campaign had at its core a Nationalist (and Republican) agenda designed to destabilise the state. The campaign's demands were 'transitional', designed to provoke conflict and, even when granted, fresh demands were raised to generate more friction. The Republican elements involved had a tradition of violence and were seeking a means of legitimating a new campaign against the Northern Ireland state.

- Nationalists argue that the absence of civil rights and indeed, the political centrality of organisations like the Orange Order within the state, were core elements of Northern Ireland. It had been established as structurally discriminatory and coercive. Thus, the state forces reacted violently to a programme of political protest because the state itself could not accommodate reform, thus catalysing three decades of ensuing conflict.

- It is possible, however, to interpret the situation by incorporating elements of both these approaches. The basis of Partition in Ireland lay in the uneven development of the island's economy. Given the industrialisation of the North East and the fact that its products depended crucially on British and Empire markets, the inhabitants of that area could not accept a 'home rule' (never mind independence) proposal because of the threat it posed to its economic infrastructure – Sinn Féin had openly talked of tariff barriers to protect infant industries in the South (Johnson, 1981). Had these been applied to Northern industries, with the probability that Britain would retaliate, the area would have deindustrialised even more rapidly than it did. The division of Ireland was not an 'imperialist conspiracy' (in any case, the industries were owned by local, rather than 'foreign' capital), but rather the result of the political and social implications of uneven economic development within the island. Nevertheless, the process of establishing the Northern Ireland state was sustained by an ideology of division and supremacy – sectarianism (O'Dowd et al., 1980). This outlived the economic conditions that determined Partition. Such economic variables almost guaranteed that the island would be politically divided, but sectarianism determined the form that Northern Ireland would take. While Protestants were faced with a Southern state which was predominantly Catholic in its institutions and culture, and while Catholic Nationalists persistently refused to accept the validity of Northern Ireland, the well-documented levels of social and economic exclusion experienced by Catholics were more than just a defensive reaction on the part of Protestants.[1] Given the history and character of the state, it was impossible to separate out the necessity to modernise, and thus eliminate all forms of discrimination, and challenges to its very existence. Such confusion created potent conditions for a rapid transition to violence. O'Leary and McGarry (1993) suggest that Northern Ireland was:

the territorial line of the retreat of the British state in Ireland, and was testament to the failure to build a British identity which would have enabled the descendants of Catholic natives and Protestant settlers to transcend their differences. It was also proof of an Irish failure: Nationalists lacked the coercive and ideological resources to achieve a popularly supported revolution throughout the whole island between 1916 and 1925. (p. 107)

As the conflict moved into the 1980s, the numbers dying dramatically reduced. It took on the form of a 'low intensity' conflict with around 100 deaths each year. The security forces could not subdue their Republican opponents nor could the latter militarily impose their will on the British government. Many within the Loyalist paramilitaries recognised that random sectarian assassination of Catholics only bolstered support for the IRA and, indeed, there was some effort to specifically target Sinn Féin members as surrogates for the IRA. Violence had settled nothing.

WHERE DID THE DEATHS OCCUR?

Table 5.3 describes the deaths that have taken place in each district council area in Northern Ireland comparing these figures with district populations in 1991.

The table records deaths in two ways: the first gives the number of violent incidents in which someone died (fatal incidents) occurring within the district; the second records the number of district residents who have been killed (victims). Neither covers the total number who were killed. This is because a number of deaths occurred outside Northern Ireland, a large number of non-Northern Ireland residents were victims and, in some cases, there are difficulties in assigning incomplete addresses to particular districts. The number of deaths in each category has been divided by the 1991 figure for the resident population to produce a comparable death rate per 1000 population and these have been ranked. Clearly, the death rates are exaggerated by the fact that the accumulated number of deaths is being compared with the population for a single year. True yearly death rates for each district would be considerably lower.

Table 5.3 Numbers and Death Rates with Northern Ireland District Council Areas

District Council	Pop. 1991 (000s)	Fatal Incidents	Rate 1000	Resident Victims	Rate 1000	Ratio In/HA
Belfast	294.3	1352	4.59	1216	4.13	0.90
Armagh	51.6	129	2.50	128	2.48	0.99
Dungannon	45	115	2.56	107	2.38	0.93
Cookstown	30.8	65	2.11	63	2.05	0.97
Strabane	35.4	58	1.64	67	1.89	1.16
Derry	97.5	244	2.50	170	1.74	0.70
Craigavon	75.1	110	1.46	121	1.61	1.10
Fermanagh	54.1	94	1.74	87	1.61	0.93
Newry and Mourne	82.7	325	3.93	131	1.58	0.40
Magherafelt	35.9	40	1.11	49	1.36	1.23
Castlereagh	61.6	32	0.52	65	1.06	2.03
Lisburn	101	77	0.76	106	1.05	1.38
Newtownabbey	75.9	39	0.51	75	0.99	1.92
Banbridge	33.4	8	0.24	27	0.81	3.38
Down	58.6	46	0.78	42	0.72	0.91
Limavady	29.6	27	0.91	21	0.71	0.78
Omagh	45.6	41	0.90	31	0.68	0.76
Ballymoney	24	13	0.54	14	0.58	1.08
Carrickfergus	33.2	8	0.24	17	0.51	2.13
Coleraine	52.9	22	0.42	24	0.45	1.09
North Down	72.5	12	0.17	32	0.44	2.67
Antrim	45.6	15	0.33	20	0.44	1.33
Ballymena	56.2	10	0.18	23	0.41	2.30
Larne	29.4	8	0.27	12	0.41	1.50
Ards	64.9	8	0.12	26	0.40	3.25
Moyle	14.6	4	0.27	4	0.27	1.00
Total		2902		2678		

In terms of absolute number of incidents, Belfast, Newry and Mourne, Derry, Armagh, Dungannon and Craigavon stand out. These constitute four areas worthy of greater attention, though the last three can be aggregated to constitute a 'Mid Ulster' (which is distinct from the electoral constituency of 'mid Ulster'). In both absolute and relative terms, Belfast has seen the greatest intensity of violent deaths. Indeed, the rates per 1000 population have been almost twice as high as the next district, Armagh. In some districts, the number of incidents and the number of resident deaths almost tally. As the last column of the table shows, the two lists were within plus or minus 10 per cent of each other in ten districts. In others, the number of incidents was substantially greater than the number of resident deaths, for example, Newry and Mourne. It may be hypothesised that this reflects the 'rural war' referred to earlier in which a high proportion of casualties were members of the security forces who did not live in the area. Equally, in still other areas, the number of residents who died was greater than the number of incidents, for example, Castlereagh and North Down. While such areas were relatively untouched by violence, their residents were less insulated reflecting either membership of the security forces or perhaps being victims of bombs in city centres.

A similar ranking of postal districts provides the next table (Table 5.4), which points to particular parts of Belfast, Derry, South Armagh and 'Mid Ulster' as locations for a high intensity of violence.

Table 5.4 Deaths by Location in Postal Districts

Home Postal District	Number	% of Total	Incident Postal District	Number	% of Total
14	248	8.75	12	326	9.88
12	242	8.54	14	272	8.24
13	180	6.35	35	268	8.12
15	164	5.78	13	223	6.76
11	146	5.15	48	197	5.97
48	113	3.99	15	191	5.79
35	91	3.21	11	129	3.91
5	87	3.07	7	104	3.15
71	86	3.03	1	98	2.97
7	79	2.79	71	89	2.70
47	74	2.61	70	78	2.36
60	70	2.47	60	77	2.33
36	66	2.33	5	74	2.24
70	59	2.08	47	71	2.15
6	48	1.69	61	64	1.94
61	46	1.62	34	59	1.79
34	45	1.59	92	54	1.64
66	44	1.55	9	45	1.36
62	43	1.52	66	44	1.33
45	42	1.48	62	43	1.30

With respect to local victims, postal districts BT14, BT12, BT13, BT15 and BT11 stand out. All are in Belfast and, indeed, define the North and West of the city. BT47 and BT48 define Derry. BT34 and BT35 cover Newry and South Armagh while BT60, BT61 and BT71 define 'Mid Ulster'. All these areas illustrate the spatial intensity of violence.

Belfast is the most extreme case. Here the impact of violence is revealed by the ward analysis in Table 5.5.

Table 5.5 The Number of Fatal Incidents and Resident Deaths in each Belfast Ward

Wards	Incidents	Victims	Location
Ballymacarrett	25	38	E
Island	16	7	E
The Mont	8	15	E
Ravenhill	7	12	E
Ballyhackamore	6	4	E
Sydenham	6	3	E
Woodstock	6	14	E
Bloomfield	4	3	E
Stormont	4	8	E
Knock	2	6	E
Orangefield	2	3	E
Belmont	1	3	E
Cherryvalley	0	1	E
Ward average	7	9	
St Annes	106	39	N
Ardoyne	71	67	N
New Lodge	58	62	N
Duncairn	56	24	N
Cliftonville	43	35	N
Waterworks	41	42	N
Crumlin	40	22	N
Highfield	35	30	N
Ligionel	35	26	N
Chicester Park	34	26	N
Ballysillan	26	29	N
Glencairn	24	24	N
Woodvale	24	23	N
Castelview	18	12	N
Fort William	6	12	N
Bellvue	4	4	N
Cavehill	3	14	N
Ward average	37	29	
Shaftesbury	55	30	S
Botanic	49	33	S
Blackstaff	25	11	S
Ballynafeigh	21	23	S
Windsor	11	11	S
Stranmillis	9	7	S
Rosetta	8	5	S

continued

Table 5.5 continued

Wards	Incidents	Victims	Location
Malone	5	11	S
Upper Malone	3	8	S
Ward average	21	15	
Falls	90	57	W
Clonard	70	56	W
Whiterock	50	55	W
Shankill	44	24	W
Upper Springfield	44	46	W
Falls Park	30	20	W
Andersontown	26	28	W
Beechmount	25	20	W
Glencolin	24	20	W
Glen Road	14	25	W
Ladybrook	10	19	W
Finaghy	4	8	W
Ward average	36	32	

The wards have been assembled under the headings of East, North, South and West of the city to provide an indication of the spatial concentration of deaths within it. The North and West of the city have the highest averages for both incidents and resident deaths. In East Belfast, only two wards had scores in double figures and only this area contained a ward in which there were no violent incidents resulting in death. It can be seen that some wards were virtually unaffected on this measure whereas some, like Falls, had more than the total for East Belfast. The number of incidents in St Anne's was even greater but this was a city centre ward affected by the violence taking place there. Accordingly, the number of resident deaths is considerably lower than the number of incidents.

These figures accord with everyday experience, i.e. there are parts of Northern Ireland which have only been marginally touched by the conflict. Within Belfast, the intensity of violence has been skewed towards the North and West of the city. One of these has the highest proportion of Catholics in its population and the other has the highest concentration of sectarianly segregated wards.

Another matter of debate has been the relationship between violence and deprivation – has deprivation been the breeding ground for violence? The Irish Congress of Trade Unions argued that 50,000 jobs would do more to end the conflict than 50,000 guns (Carlin, 1979). In the early 1990s an exercise in plotting spatial deprivation was undertaken by the Micro Statistics Centre at the University of Manchester (Robson et al., 1994). Thus it is possible to compare the death rates for particular places with their deprivation scores. Table 5.6 depicts the six district council areas that were ranked highest for fatal incident per 1000 population and gives the corresponding ranks for the rates of resident deaths and its deprivation score.

Table 5.6 A Comparison of Violence (1969–98) and Deprivation (1994) in Selected Districts

District Council	Rank (fatal incidents)	Rank (residents deaths)	Deprivation Rank
Belfast	1	1	2
Newry and Mourne	2	9	4
Dungannon	3	3	5
Derry	4	6	3
Armagh	5	2	13
Cookstown	6	4	8

Of the six districts ranked highest on fatal incidents, four were among the six worst deprived – the exceptions being Armagh and Cookstown. Strabane ranked highest on deprivation in the region and was ranked eighth on the rate of fatal incidents. There would appear to be some relationship between deprivation and violence, but it is not a simple one. The correlation coefficients of the two violence scores with the deprivation score across all 26 districts were .76 and .52, respectively. It would thus appear that there was a higher level of association between fatal incidents and deprivation than resident deaths and deprivation. The former is a better measure of the intensity of the violence that affected these areas. Many areas untouched by violence saw their residents die elsewhere. Thus, intensity of violence and deprivation do seem to be positively associated.

'HOT SPOTS'

Five areas have been chosen to illustrate the different reality of the Troubles in different parts of Northern Ireland. These were identified from the postcodes attached to the address of where the incident took place or the home address of the victim. They consisted of:

- West Belfast (BT10, BT11 and BT13) because of the intensity of violence there. This large area is predominantly Catholic but also includes the greater Shankill, a Protestant enclave whose population steadily fell between 1971 and 1991. In the last year, the population of its six wards was less than a quarter of the West Belfast total. The 'Shankill' and the 'Falls' run parallel, separated by only 200 yards. In 1969, this interface consisted mainly of dense housing across which the first serious upsurge of inter-communal violence took place. Both sides claimed that they were attacked first, although the Protestants were assisted by armed B-Specials, a paramilitary police force later disbanded following the recommendations of the Hunt Report. The Falls/Shankill interface has been a significant and symbolic site of the Troubles. The very first sectarian assassination of the present Troubles occurred on the Shankill in 1966 as did the penultimate bombing in which there were substantial civilian casualties;

- North Belfast (BT14 and BT15) a mosaic of ethnic territories, the site of some of the most sustained and intensive sectarian killing;
- Derry (BT47 and BT48), not merely because of the high levels of violence but because, arguably, violence started there when the police stopped and then attacked the first large-scale civil rights march. One of the most significant events of the Troubles, Bloody Sunday, occurred there;
- Newry and Mourne (including South Armagh) (BT34 and BT35) because this typified the rural war;
- 'Mid Ulster' (including the 'killing triangle' around the Moy) (BT61, BT62 and BT71) to exemplify a different form of rural war – the sectarian one.

This cannot be regarded as a comprehensive list; for example, some would argue that a process of 'ethnic cleansing' of Protestants from the border areas of Tyrone and Fermanagh has taken place over the years and this is not adequately reflected in death or injury data. Nevertheless, the areas chosen have been highly significant sites of conflict. Over the entire period, there were 2.26 political deaths per 1000 population (as measured by the 1991 Census) in Northern Ireland. The rate per 1,000 population for fatal incidents occurring within West Belfast was 8.29, North Belfast 5.88, Derry, 2.8 and Newry and Mourne 3.94. Since 'Mid Ulster' has been constructed artificially, a similar calculation is not possible. Nevertheless, the intensity of deaths in the other four all exceed the Northern Ireland average, in two very substantially. Such rates have to be treated cautiously. A significant number of those who have been killed in Northern Ireland were not residents of Northern

Ireland and the same is true for each locality. They are, nevertheless, an illustration of why the case studies were chosen.

These areas each exhibit differences in the distribution of deaths over time. Table 5.7 depicts the percentages of deaths of area residents in each year.

Table 5.7 The Distribution of Resident Deaths in Five Localities

Year	West Belfast %	North Belfast %	Derry %	Newry/ S. Armagh %	'Mid Ulster' %
1969	1	1	1	1	1
1970	2	1	3	1	0
1971	8	8	6	7	2
1972	19	14	23	10	3
1973	10	8	8	9	8
1974	5	7	8	7	7
1975	8	10	3	12	10
1976	9	14	8	13	13
1977	5	3	2	3	3
1978	1	4	2	5	3
1979	2	2	1	2	3
1980	3	2	1	2	2
1981	3	3	8	3	1
1982	2	0	3	2	3
1983	1	1	3	4	6
1984	1	1	2	2	3
1985	1	0	3	2	1
1986	1	2	3	1	3
1987	3	2	3	1	3
1988	3	1	1	2	4
1989	1	2	1	3	2
1990	1	1	1	2	2
1991	4	1	2	1	3
1992	2	3	2	1	8
1993	2	3	3	0	1
1994	2	1	1	1	1
1995	0	0	0	0	1
1996	0	1	1	0	1
1997	0	1	0	0	2
1998	1	0	0	1	0
Total	568	412	186	136	175
Av. Per Postal District	189	206	93	68	88

The first three areas exhibit the general tendency for an upsurge in violence in 1971 with a peak in 1972 thus conforming to the thesis that internment sparked off an almost instant reaction against the security forces. Almost a quarter of all the deaths of Derry residents happened in 1972, the year of Bloody Sunday. Both of the Belfast areas saw a second surge in 1975 and 1976 although the increase was greater in North Belfast, the site of the most concentrated bout of sectarian assassination. The same was true of Newry/South Armagh. For the 'Mid Ulster' area, these two years represented the peak of deaths rising from 1971. This does not suggest an anti-internment reaction, but, more likely, a growth of violence over a four-year period. With the exception of Newry/South Armagh, the other four areas also saw some small increases in the early 1990s, in the period before the 1994 IRA cease-fire. Of the two years of zero deaths in the early period ('Mid Ulster' 1970 and North Belfast 1982), the latter was a result of percentages being rounded down – there was actually one death in North Belfast. Only in the 1990s were there years in which no resident died. Indeed, 1995 was the most peaceful year since the Troubles began. The ending of the IRA cease-fire early the next year provoked a Loyalist response in the form of more sectarian killing in which 'Mid Ulster' figured.

A similar analysis of the fatal incidents in these areas demonstrated that this cycle was similar in each area to residents' deaths (see Table 5.8). There were, however, some important differences. First, the total numbers were different for each kind of event.

Table 5.8 A Comparison of Resident Deaths and Fatal Incidents in Selected Areas, 1969–98

	West Belfast	North Belfast	Derry	Newry/ S. Armagh	'Mid Ulster'
Resident deaths	568	412	187	136	175
Fatal incidents	678	463	268	327	196
Resident Deaths As % of Incidents	84%	89%	69%	42%	89%

In all five the number of fatal incidents exceeded the deaths of local residents – the surplus being largely explained by the deaths of members of the security forces. For the whole of Northern Ireland, just over 1700 victims lived within the postal district in which they were killed – almost half of the total. Accordingly, in four of the five areas, the proportion of residents' deaths was higher than for Northern Ireland as a whole (although less so for Derry than the other three) – emphasising a locality war. In Newry/South Armagh, many fewer local residents died than there were fatal incidents – the rural war against the security forces.

Such comparisons illustrate the different nature of the conflict within particular localities. Where the conflict consisted mainly of the Republican campaign against the security forces, fatalities were greater than resident deaths. When there was no dominant mode of violence (sectarian attack, intercommunal violence or attacks on the security forces) the numbers were within 10 per cent of each other. Such findings have implications for the differentiated character of the human costs of the Troubles. The experience of living in Republican areas, where there was a high level of support for the military campaign and where local casualties were relatively low (Newry/South Armagh), was very different from the interfaces of North Belfast where every trip to work or home after an evening out carried risk. In the latter, a very substantial proportion of the population lived through the deaths or injuries of relatives while, in certain periods, the fears for personal safety were constant. It is difficult to underestimate just how community life quality has been damaged. West Belfast has been a mixture of both – a terrain of great danger to the security forces and yet one where a very large number of residents died. In total, more than half of all fatal incidents took place in these five areas – 12 postcodes out of the 94 covering the region.

The monthly cycle of violence in these areas showed no consistent pattern (see Table 5.9).

Table 5.9 Monthly Cycle of Resident Deaths, 1969–98

	West Belfast	North Belfast	Derry	Newry/ S. Armagh	'Mid Ulster'
Jan.	6	6	11	10	5
Feb.	8	10	6	9	9
March	7	8	6	9	7
April	7	6	5	12	9
May	7	7	6	7	18
June	9	11	8	4	8
July	12	8	11	6	6
Aug.	13	8	9	13	9
Sept.	8	8	5	8	6
Oct.	10	11	11	7	10
Nov.	8	9	10	8	7
Dec.	5	9	11	7	6
Total	568	412	187	136	175

Certainly, in West Belfast, the highest shares of total deaths took place in July and August. Arguably, however, this area has been least affected by the marching season. In Derry, there were four peaks spread across the months, in Newry/South Armagh, April and August and in 'Mid Ulster', May and October. Moreover, the peaks were not substantially greater than the share in other months. This suggests that upsurges in violence may have been triggered by specific events, beginning with internment, but these were not part of regular cycles.

Although the numbers are insufficient to demonstrate a trend, more recent events do suggest a cycle of violence relating to particular months. In 1995, 1996, 1997 and 1998 there have been increases in the level of violence and deaths. This has been associated, in particular, with the conflict between the desire of the Portadown Orange Lodges to march a 'traditional' route from Drumcree church in early July and the wish of residents not to allow the march through an area inhabited mainly by Catholics. If the RUC force the march down this road, then Nationalists object violently and this spreads to other Nationalist areas. Conversely, when the march is prevented, Loyalists turn to violence. The latter has also involved the intimidation of Catholic families living in Loyalist areas – at its most extreme in 1998, petrol bombing a house in Ballymoney in which three young boys died. It should be recognised, however, that the horror of this action caused the majority of those engaged in protest to rethink their actions.

This is a situation in which both sides believe they have 'inalienable' rights – on one hand, the right to march the Queen's highway and on the other the right to live without being exposed to 'triumphalist' demonstrations. Both sides see themselves as victims. The Orange Order, believing that the British government has made a steady series of concessions to Nationalism, gradually backing the 'loyal' orders into a corner, has attributed a symbolic significance to this march. Nationalists, heavily outnumbered in Portadown which has a long history of sectarian violence, see the event as a test of whether the RUC can be truly impartial. The issue is complicated by the Orange Order's insistence that the local residents' group is a Sinn Féin front and will not engage in direct talks. Some residents' groups have no such links. While other residents' groups in Portadown and elsewhere are close to Sinn Féin, this organisation has to be recognised as a major component of Nationalism in Ireland to which many thousands give their allegiance. It is unsurprising, therefore, that, in Nationalist areas where the conflict is part of the way of life, it has substantial support. It remains to be seen whether this recent phase of violence is no more than an element of the difficult transition to peace in Northern Ireland or will be a running sore contaminating the whole process.

Where people live influences not only their level of exposure to Troubles-related violence, but also influences their perception of the overall pattern that Troubles-related violence takes. Based on local experience, a set of perceptions about the Troubles as a whole are developed and maintained– who has done the most killing, who has suffered most, and so on. When presented with the statistics on deaths in the Troubles for the whole of Northern Ireland, some people have concluded that the figures presented here 'must be wrong'. Data relating to Protestant to Catholic deaths and the levels of responsibility of each of the perpetrators have been particularly hard for some people to accept. When analysed, the explanation for this is not simply narrow-mindedness or bigotry – not to deny that bigotry can also exist – but rather, the figures presented here for the whole of Northern Ireland do not tally with people's experience. People do not live in 'Northern Ireland' but rather in sub-populations within Northern Ireland, in which the overall Northern Ireland pattern of deaths may well not pertain. When presented with a set of figures that do not reflect their local experience, it becomes impossible for them to accept their validity. These factors, in addition to the dynamic of the conflict – in which each side tends to perceive itself as the victim community and will therefore tend to resist information that suggests otherwise – can make it very difficult for some people to accept the overall statistical analysis of deaths.

The point was made earlier in this chapter that there has not been one uniform conflict in Northern Ireland, rather the Troubles are a mosaic of different types of conflict. It was also pointed out that North Belfast (BT14 and BT15) is a mosaic of ethnic territories. In order to illustrate the differences in local experiences of the Troubles, deaths in BT14 have been subjected to a further analysis.

BT14, in North Belfast, is a highly segregated area, in which many residents live in enclaves that are almost exclusively Catholic or Protestant. Deaths that touch the lives of residents in BT14 are likely to be deaths within their own community. Table 5.10 shows an analysis of BT14 residents' deaths – the overall figure, and then broken down by religion. The attribution of deaths to perpetrators for the whole of Northern Ireland is also shown. Within a relatively small geographical area, there is a substantial divergence of experience between those living in Catholic and Protestant enclaves. Over 12 per cent of Catholic deaths are due to Republican para-militaries, yet almost 61 per cent of deaths are due to Loyalist paramilitaries, and almost 25 per cent are due to the security forces. Neither the overall distribution of deaths between perpetrators for Northern Ireland, nor the distribution within Protestant communities will be recognisable or familiar to the Catholic resident, nor indeed will the Catholic picture be recognisable to the Protestant resident. In BT14, Republican paramilitaries have killed two and a half times the number of people in the Protestant community that they have killed in the Catholic community, and Loyalists have killed approximately three times as many Catholics as Protestants. Substantial differences exist between the experience of the security forces, who are responsible for almost 25 per cent of BT14 Catholic residents' deaths, yet just over 4 per cent of Protestant residents' deaths. Neither of these figures is consistent with the overall Northern Ireland figure, where the security forces are responsible for just over 10 per cent of all deaths in the Troubles.

Table 5.10 BT14 Residents Deaths by Perpetrator and Religion

	All BT14 deaths	All deaths %	Catholic deaths	Catholic deaths %	Protestant deaths	Protestant deaths %	All NI deaths
Loyalist	122	49.19	93	60.78	28	30.76	27.4
Republican	71	28.63	19	12.42	49	53.85	55.7
Security forces	42	16.94	38	24.84	4	4.40	10.7
Unknown	9	3.63	2	1.31	7	7.69	–
Other	4	1.61	1	.65	3	3.30	6.3
Total	248	100	153	100	91	100	100

Table 5.11 shows the equivalent breakdown for deaths that occurred within BT14, illustrating the other aspect of the experience of violence in BT14. Whilst there is a variation in the numbers and percentages between residents' deaths and deaths that occurred in BT14, in both cases there is a wide variation between the attribution of deaths to perpetrators within BT14 and the pattern for the whole of Northern Ireland.

Table 5.11 Fatal Incidents in BT14 by Perpetrator and Religion

	All deaths	% of all deaths	Catholic deaths	% of Catholic deaths	Protestant deaths	% of Protestant deaths*
Republican	98	36.03	14	10	45	51.14
Loyalist	121	44.49	91	65	29	32.85
Security Forces	41	15.07	34	24.29	6	6.82
Unknown	9	3.31	1	0.71	5	5.68
Other	3	1.10	0	0	3	3.42
Total	272	100	140	100	88	100

* to the nearest decimal point

Therefore, presented with statistics on the overall Northern Ireland situation, it is counterintuitive for a resident to accept the Northern Ireland figures as reflective of the true picture, since they do not reflect the experience of life within BT14. The same can also be said for other postal areas and sub-populations in Northern Ireland. The divided nature of the society, coupled with the fracturing and separating of experience by segregation makes it almost impossible to construct a consensus view on the consequences of Troubles-related violence in Northern Ireland.

In summary, political violence in Northern Ireland has exhibited two distinctive patterns:

- The most intensive violence was characteristic of the first half of the 1970s. This was a three-cornered fight: Republican paramilitaries engaged primarily against the security forces; Loyalist paramilitaries against Catholics; and the security forces simultaneously conducting a counter-insurgency campaign while having a general responsibility for law and order. With respect to the last, there have been persistent accusations that these dual responsibilities undermined an impartial law and order role. Even then, however, the forces unleashed were considerably more controlled than, for example, in Bosnia. Only for very short periods did there appear to be a threat to civil society itself – the mass movement of populations in 1969, the upsurge following internment, the 1974 Ulster Workers' Strike or the 1996 Drumcree crisis. After the 1970s, violence was more contained. For one thing, the IRA was convinced that 'spectaculars' outside Northern Ireland, typified by the Brighton bombing, an attempt to kill the entire British Cabinet, would be more productive than local violence. Loyalist paramilitaries did attempt to narrow the focus of their targeting although different factions behaved differently in this respect. Moreover, the security forces adopted strategies to contain or arrest rather than kill. For the most part, the Troubles in Northern Ireland have been distinguished by their duration rather than their intensity.

- Second, when the analysis focuses on localities, very different experiences of violence emerge. The areas chosen for case study each exhibited different patterns of violence and death, a reflection of very different experiences. This highlights one of the great difficulties in peace building in Northern Ireland – various sections of the population have experienced the situation as different and conflicting realities. When both sides feel they are victims, compromise is difficult to find. Furthermore, when we look closely at the experience of one area, Catholics and Protestants within that area may have widely differing experiences, none of which are reflective of the overall Northern Ireland situation. This illustrates the material basis for the widely various conclusions frequently arrived at by the two main traditions, and the consequent difficulty in achieving a common understanding of respective grievances and hurts.

6 Victims and Perpetrators

Because the Northern Ireland Troubles have consisted of a set of very different experiences for various sections of its population, perceptions of 'who has suffered the most' differ, as do opinions about the legitimacy of different kinds of violent action.

- Loyalists, viewing the conflict as the result of a violent Republican conspiracy, tend to see themselves as its primary victims. The religious composition of the local security forces only lends weight to this view since attacks are seen to be anti-Protestant. The Republican war has no ethical or political justification – it is a conspiracy conducted by a minority against the democratic wishes of a majority within a legitimate state. The actions of Republican paramilitaries are invariably murderous. Conversely, actions by the security forces designed to contain the Republican challenge are justifiable. If such actions are occasionally questioned by civil liberty organisations, like the Campaign for the Administration of Justice, they are accused of being soft on terrorism. Support for the activities of Loyalist paramilitaries has been more problematic. On one hand, these have been regarded as acting in the defence of Ulster and should thus be pursued with all ruthlessness. Kelley (1988) quotes from a letter printed in the UDA's monthly bulletin in February 1972:

  > I have reached the stage where I no longer have any compassion for any Nationalist, man, woman or child … Why have they (Loyalist paramilitaries) not started to hit back in the only way these Nationalist bastards understand? That is ruthless, indiscriminate killing. (Kelley, 1988: p. 169)

  On the other hand, the horrific killings carried out by, for example, the Shankill 'Butchers' have never sat easily with the majority of the Loyalist population and have been resolutely condemned by many. Nevertheless, Loyalists have no time for Republican insistence that its war is non-sectarian, merely designed to reunify Ireland. This is perceived as no more than a fiction to cover a campaign directed at the Protestant population.

• Nationalists have sympathy for the aims of Republicans though not necessarily for their methods. Republicans are seen to have some relationship with the iconographic figures of Irish history from Theobold Wolfe Tone to Padraig Pearce to James Connolly. After all, the Irish Republic honours those who struggled against Britain in the eighteenth, nineteenth and early twentieth centuries – liberation struggle has been the canon of the Southern state. Contemporary Republicans are perceived by some as simply 'completing the job'. As O'Doherty comments, the IRA 'has also claimed to be fighting a war of offence against a British occupation. This war is emphasised in its propagandist imagery and its press statements … soldiers of the IRA engaged in a battle with soldiers of the Crown' (O'Doherty, 1998: p. 93). The fact that the political dynamic of the Irish Republic is to fully integrate with Europe and to attract foreign direct investment to drive its growth rather than incorporate a region heavily dependent on public expenditure subsidy is perceived as irrelevant in that respect. Armed struggle has thus a certain legitimacy for some, so long as it is politically directed. The fact that Northern Ireland Protestants, who have a strong association with the security forces, are the front line targets of this struggle is perceived as no more than a reflection of their sectarian character. The object of the campaign remains the British State and its manifestation within Ireland – the Northern Ireland state. As Adams writes:

> this was an apartheid state in which a very substantial minority of the citizens were disenfranchised and denied social, economic, political and civil equality. It was a state fashioned by sectarian power and privilege, a state which practised wholesale suppression and discrimination. (Adams, 1986: p. 18)

The killing of Catholics by Loyalist paramilitaries is particularly hideous to Republicans – the random selection of victims based solely on their religion. This is seen as being outside the rules of confrontation even if counter-insurgency theory postulates the need to harass the civilian population in which the guerrilla 'swims'. Moreover, the security forces are expected to behave within the framework of law and the Geneva Convention even when their Republican opponents ignore both.

These are extreme caricatures of what people actually think, but they give a sense of why there is little consensus around the definition of victims. Neither Republicanism nor Loyalism is a completely undifferentiated entity. Patterson, for example, argues that Unionism has always contained a workerist faction, frequently at odds with its leadership. (Patterson, 1980). By extension, this analysis might help explain the growth of Loyalist paramilitaries, some of which were critical of mainstream Unionism not merely because of its 'inaction', but also because of its lack of a social programme. Similarly, Porter argues that Unionism can be interpreted as three broad strands, cultural, liberal and civic, each with very different characteristics (Porter, 1996). Similar factions can be identified within Republicanism. O'Connor talks of a 'synergy of Republicans and Marxists' as far back as the 1930s identifying a strand of Republicanism that wanted to embrace a broader philosophy than just Nationalism (O'Connor, 1992: p. 125). Divisions between the Official and Provisional IRAs or between the Official Republican movement and the Irish Republican Socialist Party were presented as being primarily ideological. Thus, the differences within Loyalism and Republicanism may be as significant as the gulf that divides them. All these divisions constitute the lenses through which various factions view the Troubles. As O'Brien argues:

> In many ways this refusal or inability to agree the 'truth' of what happened in those years lay at the root of the open sore of community division. Truth remained one of the casualties of the northern conflict. (O'Brien, 1993: p. 81)

The Cost of the Troubles database analysed here was constructed on the principle of inclusivity. All those who died were regarded as victims – civilians, security personnel and members of paramilitaries. The purpose of this chapter is to profile those victims in as much detail as is available and to examine which organisations were responsible for their deaths.

THE BIG PICTURE

Table 6.1 breaks down the deaths that happened between 1969 and 1994 (the year of the first IRA cease-fire) according to the status of the individuals involved.

Civilians (not members of the security forces or of Republican or Loyalist paramilitaries) account for more than half the total.

Moreover, while civilians accounted for almost 54 per cent of the total over the entire period, this share was less in the period 1972–73 which we have characterised as post-internment violence and greater in 1974/75/76, a period of intense bombing and sectarian attack. The share of civilian deaths rose again in the 1990s although the very low numbers of security personnel deaths influenced that.

Table 6.1 Deaths by Status, 1969–94

Year	Republicans	Loyalists	RUC	UDR/RIR	Army	Civilian	Civilian % of Total
1969	2	1	1			14	78
1970	5		2		1	18	69
1971	24		10	5	46	97	53
1972	77	11	16	24	108	258	52
1973	39	13	13	10	59	135	50
1974	24	6	15	7	45	204	68
1975	24	26	12	7	15	178	68
1976	25	12	25	15	15	217	70
1977	15	5	15	14	15	49	43
1978	9	1	9	7	15	40	49
1979	16	1	14	10	38	39	33
1980	5	2	9	9	12	42	53
1981	21	2	21	14	10	42	38
1982	9	5	12	8	32	39	37
1983	9	2	18	10	6	37	45
1984	16	1	9	10	10	24	34
1985	8	1	23	4	2	21	36
1986	6	2	12	8	4	31	49
1987	24	5	16	8	3	43	43
1988	17	4	6	12	23	38	38
1989	6	2	8	2	26	34	44
1990	8	1	12	8	10	41	51
1991	14	2	7	7	5	60	63
1992	14	2	4	3	4	64	70
1993	5	1	6	2	6	65	76
1994	17	2	3	2	1	38	60
Total	439	110	298	206	511	1868	
% of Grand Total	13%	3%	9%	6%	15%	54%	

The distribution of deaths among these categories is unusual for such conflicts. Paramilitary organisations account only for 16 per cent of the deaths and the combined security force total was 30 per cent. Guerrilla wars typically see a much higher proportion of fatalities amongst the insurgents and a lower proportion of state personnel. This was also true of previous struggles in Ireland. Referring to the Anglo–Irish War of Independence, Taylor comments: 'In the eighteen months during which the war raged, over 500 soldiers and policemen and over 700 IRA volunteers were killed. Over 700 civilians died' (Taylor, 1997: p. 12). In that period 37 per cent of the victims were civilians, a similar percentage members of the IRA and only 26 per cent were security personnel. The recent Northern Ireland conflict has thus taken a relatively greater toll on civilians and security force members while the fatalities amongst paramilitary organisations has been remarkably light. It is also probable that paramilitary organisations were responsible for a much higher proportion of civilian victims (see later) than in the earlier period.

Some figures have been provided by the RUC for the incidence of injuries resulting from the Troubles (see Table 6.2). The RUC total for injuries is likely to be low, for two reasons. First, the RUC collect data only on injuries that occurred within Northern Ireland, and second, they show only injuries that are known to the police. Furthermore, the time series is slightly different from above and there are no paramilitary categories. These are included as civilians.

Table 6.2 Injuries by Status, 1971–96

Year	RUC	Army	UDR/RIR	Civilian	Civilian %*
1971	315	381	9	1887	73
1972	485	542	36	3813	78
1973	291	525	23	1812	68
1974	235	453	30	1680	70
1975	263	151	16	2044	83
1976	303	242	22	2162	79
1977	183	172	15	1017	73
1978	302	127	8	548	56
1979	166	132	21	557	64
1980	194	53	24	530	66
1981	332	112	28	878	65
1982	99	80	18	328	62
1983	142	66	22	280	55
1984	267	64	22	513	59
1985	415	20	13	468	51
1986	622	45	10	773	53
1987	246	92	12	780	69
1988	218	211	18	600	57
1989	163	175	15	606	63
1990	214	190	24	478	53
1991	139	197	56	570	59
1992	148	302	18	598	56
1993	147	146	27	504	61
1994	170	120	6	529	64
1995	370	8	5	554	59
1996	459	53	1	896	64
Total	6888	4659	499	25,405	
% of Grand Total	18%	12%	1%	68%	

* to the nearest decimal point

The share of security force personnel amongst the injuries tallies closely with their share of total deaths (31 per cent). Even if members of paramilitary organisations are included in the civilian total, its very large size suggests that civilians represent a majority of those injured – there are simply not enough members of paramilitary organisations. Moreover, the injury table further reveals the concentration of violence in the 1970s. Almost a third of all injuries were suffered between 1972 and 1977.

VICTIM CHARACTERISTICS

By far, the victims of the conflict have been overwhelmingly male. As Table 6.3 demonstrates, more than nine out of ten of all those killed were men.

Table 6.3 Gender of Victims

	Number	%
Female	322	8.9
Male	3279	91.1
Total	3601	100

Men have been the most direct victims of the conflict in terms of the numbers killed. There have been too many images of women regularly visiting the prisons and standing at gravesides, or of children following coffins to suggest that only men have suffered. The indirect effects of these deaths are not revealed in the data – these are probably more visited on women. Men and women both died in substantially greater numbers in the most intensive period of 1971–76. This era accounted for 63.3 per cent of all female and 59.9 per cent of all male deaths.

Moreover, in terms of age, the victims were undoubtedly skewed towards the younger age groups.

More than a third of victims were in their 20s. More than half were in their 20s or 30s. Nor were the young spared – one in six victims were aged 19 or less. This can be plainly seen if death rates for each age group are calculated by comparing the ages of those in the database with the age distribution of the general population (see Figure 6.1 and Table 6.4). Since the Troubles lasted over 30 years, the population groups were constructed by taking the average figure for each age group from the 1971, 1981 and 1991 censuses. This is a constructed, rather than real, population but overcomes

the problem of calculating rates based on a single year from deaths
that happened over many years.

Table 6.4 The Age Distribution of Those Who Died

Age	Frequency	%
0–4	21	0.6
5–9	17	0.5
10–14	51	1.4
15–19	468	13.1
20–24	720	20.2
25–29	578	16.2
30–34	427	12.0
35–39	330	9.3
40–44	231	6.5
45–49	205	5.8
50–54	186	5.2
55–59	124	3.5
60–64	96	2.7
65–69	47	1.3
70–74	36	1.0
75+	23	0.6
Total	3560	100

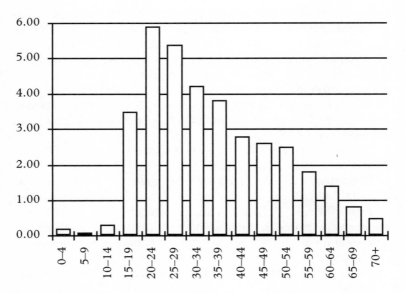

Figure 6.1 Death Rates for Age Groups per 1000 pop.

Even allowing for the differential numbers in the specified age groups among the population, the concentration of deaths remains in the younger age groups – 15–19, 20–24, 25–29, 30–34 and 35–39. Put another way, the death risk to the 20–24 age group was more than twice as high as any group over 40 and 40 per cent greater than for anyone over 30. The effect of the Troubles on children and young people is further examined in Chapter 7.

The concentration of deaths within particular age groups is further revealed by a reclassification of the age bands to highlight the impact on young people. Just under a quarter of all victims were 21 or younger. Almost another half were aged 22–39. Thus, nearly three-quarters of those who died did not reach their fortieth year. Young people are generally the modal victim group in all forms of civil conflict. The extraordinary concentration in the young age groups here points to the specific form the Northern Ireland conflict takes. Despite the territorial battles and population shifts, most obviously following the introduction of internment, the conflict has been primarily between individuals on the streets and in the countryside. Moreover, there has been virtually no use of heavy weaponry (with the exception of car bombs and anti-barrack mortars) on civilian areas as happened in Bosnia and Beirut. The more physically mobile and active sections of the population have thus figured prominently among the victims. This is particularly true for members of the security forces and of paramilitary organisations (more than two-thirds of the victims in all these categories were aged between 19 and 39), but is also the case with civilian victims (just over half were in the same age categories).

Table 6.5 A Different Age Distribution

Age	Frequency	Valid %*
0–15	119	3.3
16–18	272	7.6
19–21	483	13.6
22–39	1738	48.8
40–59	746	21.0
60–79	194	5.4
80+	8	0.2
Total	3560	100

* to the nearest decimal point

The 19–21 age group accounts for almost a seventh of all deaths and yet is a band spanning only three years. If the next large band (22–39) had suffered a proportional number of deaths, the figure there would be almost 3000. In terms of absolute numbers, deaths among the 16–18 age group is also high, although in this case no more significant than in the 22–39 band (see Table 6.5).

The religious breakdown of victims is described in Table 6.6. It was impossible to assign a religious affiliation to a high proportion of deaths among Northern Ireland security forces and these constitute the bulk of the 'not known' category. The same was true for victims from outside Northern Ireland (NNI) for whom, in any case, religion was less associated with the reasons they were killed.

Table 6.6 The Distribution of Deaths by Religion

Religion	Frequency	Valid %
Don't know	333	9.2
Protestant	1065	29.6
Catholic	1548	43.0
NNI	655	18.2
Total	3601	100

Desegregating the deaths by religion gets to the heart of the Troubles that have been fuelled by grievance and perceptions about what the 'other side' has done. The absolute numbers show that more Catholics than Protestants have died. The smaller proportion of Catholics in the general population suggests a significantly higher death risk for this religion. This tends to ignore the very high proportion of 'not known' religious affiliation among local security forces deaths. It is known that the local security forces are 92 per cent Protestant and this fraction can be used to distribute the 'not known' between the two religious groups. Redistributing the 'not known' and taking into account the time period involved produces the results shown in Table 6.7.

Table 6.7 Deaths Rates per 1000 between the main Religions

	Protestant	Catholic
Rate (91 base)	1.49	2.55
Weighted rate (91 base)	1.92	2.60
Weighted rate 69–76 (71 base)	0.69	1.88
Weighted rate 77–86 (81 base)	1.35	0.73
Weighted rate 87–98 (91 base)	0.42	0.61

The first row in Table 6.7 gives the number killed per thousand based solely on the number of victims for whom a religion could be identified and using the 1991 Census for the religious populations of Northern Ireland. The second row gives modified rates where the 'not known' have been redistributed according to the ratio of

Catholics in the local security forces (8 per cent). The next three rows contain rates where the 'not known' have been redistributed, are based on deaths between specific years and are calculated on census data relevant to those years. On the first rate, Catholics were about 70 per cent more at risk than Protestants and on the second 35 per cent. Thus, even when the deaths of local security forces are included almost totally within the Protestant category, Catholics were at greater risk in both absolute and relative terms.

That risk, however, varied substantially over the period. Between 1969 and 1976 (using 1971 Census figures) the Catholic death risk was more than twice that of Protestants. Between 1977 and 1986, it would appear as though the death risk for Protestants was considerably greater than for Catholics although, given that there was under-enumeration of Catholics in that census as part of the Hunger Strike protests, this figure should be treated with caution. In the final period, the risk for Catholics was again about 50 per cent greater. Other transformations of the data are possible. If the number of Catholics killed by Republican paramilitary organisations is subtracted from their total and likewise the number of Protestants killed by Loyalist organisations subtracted from theirs, the death rates become closer still – 1.9 and 1.6, respectively, based on the 1991 Census.

Such exercises are not arbitrary. They relate directly to perceptions of victimhood held by the two sections of the community in Northern Ireland. Each side believes not merely in the legitimacy of their objectives but also that the violence of the other side is directed at them. Each horrific incident can be counterposed by an even greater 'atrocity' committed by the other side. The presentation of dry statistics cannot move ideological conviction. In a period of transition to peace, each side has to reflect critically on its own actions while grievance about what the 'other side' has done should be based on the numbers actually killed by the other side even if this is ignored in popular perception. Moreover, as the calculations demonstrate, no side has a monopoly on grievance. State personnel, Republicans and Loyalists have all been killed in large numbers – violence has been a universal instrument. Nevertheless, all three groups of protagonists have killed civilians although, in this respect, the greater responsibility lies with paramilitary organisations.

Just over 60 per cent of Catholics were killed between 1971 and 1976 compared with 52 per cent of Protestants. As with the general population, both suffered the highest concentration of deaths in this five-year period.

For a majority of victims (61 per cent), details on their occupations were impossible to obtain. Therefore it was not possible to locate them within a standard occupational classification. Table 6.8 offers an 'ad hoc' occupational classification for those who had identifiable occupational status.

Table 6.8 Occupational Status of Victims

Occupational Status	Frequency	Percent
Not known	2198	61.07
British Army	486	13.50
Employee	346	9.61
Police officer	208	5.78
At school	80	2.22
Business people	48	1.33
Security related	35	0.97
Farmer	32	0.89
Pensioner	24	0.67
Prison officer	24	0.67
Taxi driver	24	0.67
Unemployed	19	0.53
Contractor to RUC/BA	15	0.42
Preschool	14	0.39
Civil Servant	11	0.31
Customs officer	8	0.22
Student	7	0.19
UDR	7	0.19
Politician	5	0.14
Prisoner	4	0.11
Housewife	2	0.06
Ex-paramilitary	2	0.06
Total	3599	100

Those employed by the security forces constitute the largest group – almost 20 per cent of the total or half of all those who could be assigned an occupational status. Employees constitute the only other large group. The number unemployed is extremely low suggesting that many of the unemployed were among the 'not known' occupational category. In general, there are too many in this category to draw substantial conclusions about the occupations of those who died. Outside of the security forces and general occupational categories, two specific occupations stand out – farmers and taxi drivers. Deaths of the former have been used to justify the charge that ethnic cleansing against Protestants was carried out along certain border areas. The latter stands out as the softest imaginable target for sectarian attack. Decades of interrupted public transport in Northern Ireland have made local taxis a popular way to travel. Some are organised to cover particular arterial routes in Belfast and Derry Londonderry. Others are summoned by phone. In general, the location of the firm determines the religious composition of the drivers. Thus, a favoured tactic has been to phone for a taxi in order to bring the victim within range. This has been more a characteristic of the most recent period.

By examining the 'political' status of those who died, it is possible to make some judgement about the degree to which those actively engaged in the conflict were its actual victims. While the political status categories in Tables 6.9 and 6.10 are idiosyncratic, they were constructed essentially for the purpose of separating non-involved from involved victims. Two classifications were developed: one to highlight the proportion of local security personnel (i.e. RUC, UDR and RIR) among the deaths (Table 6.9) and the other to highlights the distinction between the civil security force (RUC) and the military (British Army, UDR, RIR) which is described in Table 6.10.

In general, those actually engaged in pursuing the conflict (from whichever side) were a minority of victims. Thus civilians made up 53 per cent of all those who died.

Table 6.9 Affiliation of Victims

Political status	Frequency	Valid %*
Republic paramilitaries	359	10.0
Loyalist paramilitaries	117	3.2
Ex-Republican paramilitaries	4	0.1
Ex-Loyalist paramilitaries	2	0.1
Security (NI)	536	14.9
Security (NNI)	593	16.5
Civilian	1925	53.5
Others	65	1.8
Total	3601	100

* to the nearest decimal point

The next biggest group consisted of non-Northern Ireland security forces closely followed by local security personnel. Identifiable members of paramilitary organisations made up just 16 per cent of all deaths. Among the Northern Ireland security forces, the majority of victims were RUC members comprising 329 deaths, more than 50 per cent greater than UDR deaths. This particular classification reveals that the British Army suffered by far the greatest number of deaths amongst the various security forces (516).

The overall distribution of deaths amongst the three main groupings indicates the vulnerability of civilians within the conflict.

Among the protagonists, paramilitary organisations suffered fewer deaths than the security forces. Certainly, the active membership of paramilitary organisations has been relatively small. Accordingly, the risk of dying if a member of such an organisation can still be relatively high. Moreover, there are different operational procedures for these types of organisations. Activities by paramilitaries are designed to injure or kill. The security forces may also arrest their opponents. Thus, the differential deaths may not reflect a greater 'efficiency' on the part of paramilitaries It remains significant, however, that the combined total of deaths amongst the paramilitaries and security forces was less than the civilian total.

Table 6.10 Alternative Affiliation of Victims

Political Status	Frequency	Valid %
Republic paramilitaries	359	10.0
Loyalist paramilitaries	117	3.2
Ex-Republican paramilitaries	4	0.1
Ex-Loyalist paramilitaries	2	0.1
Police (RUC)	329	9.1
UDR	199	5.5
British Army	516	14.3
Other security forces	85	2.4
Civilian	1925	53.5
Others	65	1.8
Total	3601	100

PERPETRATORS

Paramilitary organisations accounted for just 80 per cent of the deaths and more than half were the responsibility of Republican paramilitaries. For each of their own members who died, Republican paramilitaries killed five and a half other individuals. On the same basis, Loyalist paramilitaries killed eight and a half people for each of their members' deaths. The figure for the British Army was just over half a person and for the RUC just less than a sixth of a person (see Table 6.11).

The categories of Republican and Loyalist paramilitaries each cover a number of different organisations. Within the Republican grouping, the IRA (formerly the Provisional IRA) was responsible for the greatest number of deaths (1684 or 85 per cent of those attributed to Republican paramilitaries). The numbers killed by other Republican organisations were substantially fewer. For example, the various factions and offshoots of the INLA accounted for 127 deaths. In the construction of the database, with its heavy reliance on newspaper archives, it was not possible to precisely distribute the deaths caused by Loyalist paramilitaries among the various organisations involved. Thus, 449 deaths were simply attributed to Loyalist organisations. Of those for which the organisation responsible was identifiable, 254 were attributed to the UVF and 177 to the UFF. In general, the IRA stands out as having made the most 'significant' contribution to the deaths' total.

Table 6.11 Organisations Responsible for Deaths

Organisation responsible	Frequency	Valid %*
Republican paramilitaries	2001	55.7
Loyalist paramilitaries	983	27.4
British Army	318	8.9
UDR	11	0.3
RUC	53	1.5
Civilian	11	0.3
Other	216	6.0
Total	3593	100

* to the nearest decimal point

Since the conflict in Northern Ireland involves religion, identity, and defence of and opposition to the presence of the British state, it is important to examine these variables as manifested in the distribution of deaths. Table 6.12 breaks down the deaths by religion and by those organisations responsible.

Table 6.12 Deaths by Religion by Organisation Responsible

Organisation responsible	Don't know	%*	Protestant	%*	Catholic	%*	NNI	%*
Republican paramilitaries	278	83.5	745	70.0	381	24.7	597	91.4
Loyalist paramilitaries	25	7.5	207	19.5	735	47.6	16	2.5
British Army	4	1.2	32	3.0	266	17.2	16	2.5
UDR			4	0.4	7	0.5		
RUC	1	0.3	7	0.7	43	2.8	2	0.3
Civilian			9	0.8	2	0.1		
Other	25	7.5	60	5.6	109	7.1	22	3.4
Total	333	100	1064	100	1543	100	653	100

* to the nearest decimal point

To some degree, the table confirms the 'common sense' fears of the Northern Ireland population built up during 25 years of conflict. The biggest source of deaths amongst Protestants has been Republican organisations, accounting for 70 per cent of the total.

If the 'not known' category is treated as before (namely that 92 per cent are regarded as Protestant), then Republican paramilitaries have killed over 80 per cent. Similarly, almost half of Catholic deaths can be attributed to Loyalist paramilitaries. At the same time, over a fifth of Catholic deaths can be attributed to security force activity, with the British Army having the most significant role.

Certain features of the table confound such common sense fears. Almost a fifth of Protestants have been killed by Loyalist paramilitaries and over a quarter of Catholics by Republican paramilitaries. The latter is partially explained by the Republican bombing campaign, particularly in city centres where casualties are more random than targeted. Analysis by individual year shows that Republican paramilitary organisations killed more Catholics in the 1971–76 period than any other, when the city-centre bombing campaign was at its height. Nevertheless, a significant source of deaths within each community has been the paramilitaries that claim to defend them.

Table 6.13 Political Status of Victims by Organisations Responsible for Deaths

Organisation responsible	Repub. paras	Loyal. paras	Ex Repub. paras	Ex Loyal. paras	Security (NI)	Security (NNI)	Civilian	Others
Republican paramilitaries	164	31			508	562	713	23
Loyalist paramilitaries	26	65	3	2	12	3	858	14
British Army	117	10			5	14	168	4
UDR	2						9	
RUC	16	3			1	2	31	
Civilian		1					9	1
Other	30	7	1		10	12	133	23
Total	355	117	4	2	536	593	1921	65

If the organisations responsible are cross-tabulated with the political status of victims (see Table 6.13), then it would appear that Republican paramilitaries have been a significant source of the deaths suffered by Republicans. Feuds and the punishment of informers would be obvious examples of such activities. Indeed, this seems to be the single biggest source of deaths among Republican paramilitaries. The British Army has been responsible for just over 30 per cent of deaths among these groups, although it should be noted that the process of cross-tabulation has eliminated a number of cases. At the same time, Republican paramilitaries have accounted for almost all the deaths of security forces (1070). For each of the organisations responsible, the biggest single category of victim has been civilians.

Earlier, some attention was paid to the age distribution of victims with emphasis on their relatively young age. Table 6.14 concentrates on the age groups prominent amongst victims and describes which organisation was responsible. Republican paramilitaries account for highest proportions of all three age groups, though more of the two older groups. In contrast, the highest share of deaths attributed to the British Army was in the youngest, as opposed to the other two. The pattern for Loyalist paramilitaries was more random.

Table 6.14 Selected Age Groups by Organisations Responsible

| Organisation responsible | Age Group | | | | | |
	16–18	%*	19–21	%*	22–39	%*
Republican paramilitaries	131	48.2	278	57.6	1008	58.2
Loyalist paramilitaries	69	25.4	97	20.1	459	26.5
British Army	49	18.0	62	12.8	140	8.1
UDR	3	1.1	4	0.8	3	0.2
RUC	7	2.6	13	2.7	23	1.3
Civilian	1	0.4	1	0.2	6	0.3
Other	12	4.4	28	5.8	92	5.3
Total	272	100	483	100	1731	100

* to the nearest decimal point

Given that Republican paramilitaries accounted for just over 55 per cent of all victims, their responsibility for deaths in the 16–18 age groups is somewhat lower than for the general population. Equally, Loyalist paramilitaries perpetrated 27 per cent of all deaths. Accordingly, they tended to account for a smaller proportion of these younger age groups. Conversely, the British Army was responsible for less than 9 per cent of all deaths. Thus, its shares with respect to the 16–18 and 19–21 age groups were greater than in general. The implication is that the British Army tended to kill more of those it confronted on the streets – the young – while paramilitary organisations concentrated on other targets. This must be qualified by the recognition that, while some security force victims have been very young, their general age profile is skewed towards the older age groups. In pursuit of their war, Republicans would thus attack those mainly aged over 21. This consideration does not apply to non-security force victims. This is discussed further in Chapter 7.

VICTIMS AND PERPETRATORS IN THE 'HOT SPOTS'

A central argument in the book is that violence has been a differentiated experience for various groups within the Northern Ireland population and that different places have had their own specific experience of it. To what extent is this thesis supported by evidence on the spatial patterning of victims? It should be recognised from the outset that the numbers involved in each of these areas were very different. There is thus the problem of not necessarily comparing like with like. Nevertheless, the figures do point to the varied character of the Troubles in specific localities. Table 6.15 looks at the religious composition of local victims and the gender of those involved in fatal incidents in the same areas selected previously.

Table 6.15 Deaths by Gender in Selected Areas

Gender	West Belfast	North Belfast	Derry	Newry/ S. Armagh	'Mid-Ulster'
			Local Victims		
Female	59	58	15	5	14
% of Total	10	14	8	4	8
Male	509	354	172	131	161
% of Total	90	86	92	96	92
Total	568	412	187	136	175
			Fatal Incidents		
Female	51	54	18	10	11
% of Total	8	12	7	3	6
Male	627	409	250	317	185
% of Total	92	88	93	97	94
Total	678	463	268	327	196

Just fewer than 9 per cent of all victims were female. With respect to local victims, West Belfast, Derry Londonderry and 'Mid-Ulster' exhibited patterns that were close to the regional figure. The two exceptions were North Belfast and Newry/South Armagh. It was previously argued that the former was the prime example of urban sectarian attacks and the latter, the rural war against the security forces. These findings tend to support both contentions. Moreover, in the early period, there was considerable Catholic population flight from North Belfast while, later, Protestants felt their population squeezed. This area has been a primary site for intimidation while housing close to interfaces has been progressively abandoned. In each of these areas, the proportion of female victims involved in fatal incidents was less than for local victims. Thus, the additional numbers in the second category were predominantly male – most likely members of the security forces. In absolute terms, the number of women dying in fatal incidents in West Belfast, North Belfast and 'Mid-Ulster' was actually less than for local victims. In each case, local women died elsewhere.

Something of the nature of local violence is revealed by examining the religious characteristics of those killed in the five areas (see Table 6.16).

Table 6.16 Deaths by Religion in Selected Areas (percentages)*

	West Belfast	North Belfast	Derry	Newry/S. Armagh	'Mid-Ulster'
Local deaths					
Not known	4	3	9	13	9
Protestant	25	33	27	39	39
Catholic	72	64	63	46	51
NNI	0	0	2	1	1
(Total)	(568)	(412)	(187)	(136)	(175)
Fatal incidents					
DK	4	6	8	16	11
Protestant	25	32	21	23	33
Catholic	54	54	44	25	46
NNI	16	9	27	36	10
(Total)	(678)	(463)	(268)	(327)	(196)

* to the nearest decimal point

In West and North Belfast and Derry Londonderry, the majority of local residents killed were Catholic. In the 1991 Census, the wards that made up West Belfast (including two Lisburn wards that are locally regarded as part of the area) were 84 per cent Catholic. This proportion has been increasing since 1971 so the figure of 72 per cent does not mean that Catholics were under-represented among the local dead in the area. Similarly, the Catholic population of Derry Londonderry in 1991 was 69 per cent of the total. Allowing for the growth of the Catholic share of the population since 1971, the Catholic share of local deaths would not appear disproportionate. Only 41 per cent of North Belfast's population was Catholic in 1991 so that the Catholic share of the area's deaths is disproportionately high. Conversely, the share in Newry/South Armagh is disproportionately low. Unfortunately, because the area 'Mid-Ulster' is an artificial construct covering a number of local government districts, it is not easy to assess whether Catholics suffered greater risk there. Even if the 'not known' is added largely to the 'Protestant' category in each area, only in Newry/South Armagh did Protestants constitute a majority.

The same set of figures for fatal incidents paints a different picture. In each case the Catholic share of deaths falls as the 'Non-Northern Ireland' category takes shape. In West Belfast, Derry Londonderry and Newry/South Armagh these constituted a sixth, a quarter and over a third of all fatal incidents. The last is particularly significant with 36 per cent of all fatal incidents referring, predominantly, to British Army personnel. Indeed, the Catholic share of fatal incidents was only a quarter in an area with a majority Catholic population. The small non-Northern Ireland share in North Belfast and, indeed, 'Mid-Ulster' supports the contention that the conflict was mainly an internal one. In general, only the Belfast areas continued having a majority of Catholic victims.

This has to be qualified by a recognition that Catholic populations are, in general, skewed towards the younger age groups – i.e. the average age of Catholics is lower than for Protestants. The very young (i.e. those aged 15 or under) were not a significant proportion of all deaths although the age categories immediately following this (16–29) were disproportionately at risk. It should also be remembered that the vast majority of victims were men although in each of these areas women were marginally in a majority.

This analysis can be further elaborated by looking at the political status of victims (see Table 6.17). Essentially the protagonists have been grouped under Republican paramilitaries, Loyalist paramilitaries, Northern Ireland security forces and non-Northern Ireland security forces.

Table 6.17 Deaths by Political Status (percentages)*

	West Belfast	North Belfast	Derry	Newry/S. Armagh	'Mid-Ulster'
Local deaths					
Republican					
paramilitaries	16	12	23	16	18
Loyalist					
paramilitaries	7	5	1	1	1
NI Security	3	3	18	23	28
NNI Security	0	0	1	1	1
Civilian	74	81	58	60	52
(Total)	(558)	(399)	(182)	(129)	(165)
Fatal incidents					
Reps	11	8	14	8	16
Loyal	5	5	0	1	1
NI Security	7	7	16	23	25
NNI Security	16	10	27	36	10
Civilian	62	70	43	31	48
Total	(665)	(447)	(262)	(318)	(186)

* to the nearest decimal point

By far the lowest share of deaths in both parts of the table were those belonging to Loyalist paramilitaries accounting for just 1 per cent of local deaths in Derry Londonderry, Newry/South Armagh and 'Mid-Ulster'. Republican paramilitaries accounted for a greater share of local deaths in Derry Londonderry amounting to almost a quarter of the total. In West and North Belfast, the share of civilians among local deaths was extraordinarily high, particularly when compared to the 54 per cent within the population generally. Equally, these areas had very low shares of security deaths whether from Northern Ireland or elsewhere – members of the security forces tend not to live there. This is in contrast to the percentages of Northern Ireland security force members among local deaths in the other three areas, particularly in 'Mid-Ulster'. This table suggests a war in 'Mid-Ulster' that was internal but not necessarily sectarian in the narrow sense of the word. The proportion of civilian victims was lower than for Northern Ireland as a whole. Indeed, Republican paramilitary and Northern Ireland security force deaths account for almost as many deaths as civilians.

The relative 'efficiency' of the Republican campaign in Newry/South Armagh is well demonstrated here since Republican paramilitaries accounted for just 8 per cent of all fatalities in the area. In contrast, the security forces' share was almost 60 per cent. The next highest was Derry Londonderry at 43 per cent. North Belfast had the lowest proportion of deaths among members of security forces. Given, also, the relatively low share of paramilitary deaths, the intercommunal nature of the struggle is emphasised. Moreover, the respective shares of deaths among Republican and Loyalist paramilitaries in this area were closer than in any other.

Table 6.18 describes which organisations were responsible for the deaths in each locality.

Table 6.18 Those Responsible for the Deaths in Selected Areas (percentages)*

	West Belfast	North Belfast	Derry	Newry/S.Armagh	'Mid-Ulster'
Local deaths					
Republican paramilitaries	40	31	57	78	54
Loyalist paramilitaries	38	55	13	11	28
BA	18	12	28	10	15
UDR	1	0	0	0	3
RUC	4	1	1	1	0
Civilian	0	1	1	0	0
(Total)	(520)	(380)	(176)	(125)	(167)
Fatal incidents					
Republican paramilitaries	52	36	70	88	56
Loyalist paramilitaries	28	50	8	6	26
BA	15	12	21	5	15
UDR	0	0	0	0	1
RUC	3	1	1	0	2
Civilian	0	1	0	0	0
(Total)	(633)	(433)	(259)	(314)	(189)

* to the nearest decimal point

Even in West Belfast, Republican paramilitaries were responsible for the largest single proportion of local deaths. Their share of total fatalities was greater still suggesting that they were the primary organisations responsible for security force deaths (although some fatal incidents will have involved civilians from other areas). In contrast, Loyalist paramilitaries accounted for a higher share of local deaths than general fatalities (again it should be noted that cross-tabulation tends to eliminate cases and it may do so unevenly across categories). Republicans were thus engaged both in an external and an internal war. For Loyalists, it was essentially internal. This is reinforced by an examination of their role in North Belfast where they accounted for more than half of all local victims. Indeed, Republican organisations in North Belfast were responsible for a lower share of deaths than anywhere else. In Newry/South Armagh, the Republican paramilitaries had an almost exclusive role, being responsible for 78 per cent and 88 per cent of the deaths, respectively. Here the role of Loyalist paramilitaries was very small. Republican paramilitaries and the security forces accounted for 93 per cent of all fatalities with the latter's responsibility, by far, the minor one. Derry Londonderry also saw a dominant role for Republican paramilitaries, responsible for 70 per cent of all fatalities. In 'Mid-Ulster', the deaths caused by Loyalist paramilitaries were proportionately less than in West and North Belfast, but greater than in the other two areas.

The situation is even more complicated. As a result of feuds, paramilitary organisations killed members of other paramilitaries even when ostensibly on the 'same' side. Such feuds have taken place between the Official IRA and the IRSP, the Official and Provisional IRAs and, notoriously, within the INLA. Take, for example, West and North Belfast, where, by comparing who was responsible for the deaths with the political status of victims, it is possible to see something of the complicated pattern of killing (see Table 6.19).

This level of detail is available only via three-way cross-tabulation with an increase in missing cases and cell numbers falling dramatically. Accordingly, the exercise was attempted only in the areas where the numbers involved were highest. Republican paramilitaries accounted for 198 deaths of those who lived in West Belfast. Yet over a fifth of those were also members of Republican paramilitary organisations. In contrast, a tenth of the victims of Loyalist paramilitaries were also members of Loyalist organisations. Over 80 per cent of the victims of Loyalist organisations were civilians. In a similar vein almost two-thirds of those killed by

Republican paramilitaries and the British Army were civilians. In North Belfast, the two sets of paramilitary organisations were responsible for six-sevenths of all residents' deaths. Yet, Republican paramilitaries killed more of their own members than did Loyalist paramilitaries. This pattern is repeated elsewhere. A fifth of Republican victims in Derry Londonderry and a seventh in Newry/South Armagh were killed by other Republicans.

Table 6.19 Organisations Responsible for Deaths by the Political Status of Resident Victims

| | Political Status | Organisations Responsible | | | | |
		Republican paras	Loyalist paras	BA	UDR	RUC
West Belfast	Republican paras	42	6	29		6
	Loyalist paras	13	19	3		
	NI Security	16	1	1		
	NNI Security	1				
	Civilians	126	169	62	4	13
	Total	198	195	95	4	19
North Belfast	Republican paras	16	7	18		1
	Loyalist paras	6	10			
	NI Security	11				
	NNI Security					
	Civilians	79	189	27		3
	Total	112	206	45		4

Equally, 116 Catholic residents of West Belfast were killed by Republican paramilitaries. Loyalists killed 43 Protestant residents. In North Belfast, Loyalists killed 168 Catholics but also 39 Protestants. Republicans were responsible for the deaths of 35 Catholic residents. In Newry/South Armagh, Republican, rather than Loyalist, paramilitaries killed more Catholic residents. This complicated picture suggests that crude attempts to blame one side or the other or to believe that one grievance holds greater weight than another are futile. The evidence suggests that all the protagonists killed many more than intended victims, that all have a shared responsibility and that every death involved a victim.

CONCLUSIONS

The purpose of this chapter was to:

• explore the characteristics of those who died in the Troubles both in Northern Ireland and specifically within the five key localities;

- look at who was responsible; and
- assess whether the proposition that the Troubles consisted of a collection of smaller 'wars' with their own distinctive features was valid.

Victims were predominantly men in younger age groups while, on any measure, Catholics had a significantly greater risk of dying than Protestants. Moreover, while the primary protagonists were the paramilitaries and security forces, civilians were the primary victims accounting for just over 60 per cent of the dead. Among the security forces, the British Army suffered most casualties despite the 'Ulsterisation' of the security agenda in the latter part of the period. The intensity of violence in the 1970s meant that the British Army bore the brunt.

Paramilitary organisations were responsible for the greater part of the deaths. Among these, the Provisional IRA/IRA stands out accounting for over 50 per cent of all deaths. Moreover, those killed by the IRA were spread across all categories, other Republicans, Loyalist paramilitaries, the security forces and civilians. Its share of all deaths was a result not just of its primary role as the largest, most active Republican organisation but also that it operated at all levels – attacks on the security forces, bombing campaigns, internal feuds/'policing' and engagement with Loyalist paramilitaries. Essentially, it has been an offensive rather than defensive organisation, with little evidence that it was able to protect the Nationalist population from either the security forces or sectarian attack. Loyalist paramilitaries were more narrowly focused for much of the period acting against the Catholic population. This, more than any other factor, accounts for the higher Catholic death risk. From this evidence, it would appear that the security forces carried out an aggressive counter-insurgency campaign from the early to the mid-1970s, but thereafter were more engaged in containment. Accordingly, they accounted for a substantially smaller proportion of victims from the 1980s onwards – over two-thirds of those killed by the British Army died between 1969 and 1976 compared to just less than half of all victims.

The patterns of deaths did suggest that the experience of the Troubles was radically different in different places. West Belfast not only had most victims but also saw every element of the conflict. North Belfast was primarily the terrain of sectarian attack with its Catholic population most exposed. Derry Londonderry was more like West Belfast but with a significantly less pronounced sectarian war. Republicans had their 'best' war in Newry/South Armagh inflicting the highest number of deaths on the security forces with relatively low numbers of local deaths. It is understandable that the area has entered Republican (and security forces) mythology – a straight fight between the freedom fighters and the forces of the Crown – a terrain in which the countryside itself was constantly dangerous for the security forces. In 'Mid-Ulster', it was also largely an internal war. While the deaths of non-Northern Ireland security members outnumbered local personnel in Newry/South Armagh, the reverse was true in 'Mid-Ulster'. Moreover, while 51 per cent of the victims were Catholic, 39 per cent were Protestant. Indeed, adjusting for the 'not known' would suggest that 47 per cent were Protestant. This is a very different picture from North Belfast.

Finally, this review of such suffering and death suggests two things:

- first, that as policies are developed to help and compensate those still living, there should be extreme sensitivity to the different nature of the violence in different locations. This implies a strong local participation in the development and delivery of such programmes;
- second, that peace building in Northern Ireland requires that all accept a responsibility for what happened and that all recognise the vocabulary of hate (Fenians, Brits, Orangies) cannot hide the humanity of the victims.

7 Half the Battle: The Impact of the Troubles on Children

In Chapter 6, evidence was presented that young people, of any age group in the population, had a very high risk of being killed, with almost 26 per cent of all victims aged 21 or less and the 19–20 age group having the highest death rate for any age group in Northern Ireland. This chapter is most concerned with presenting a statistical picture of the deaths of children and young people. The issues facing that minority of children and young people who have had the most difficult and traumatic experiences in the Troubles have been dealt with at greater length and depth elsewhere (Smyth, 1998; Cost of the Troubles Study, 1998). It is this minority of children and young people who are likely to require the most urgent attention, and for whom the need for policy development is most keenly felt. The severity and long-term nature of effects of the Troubles have not always been directly apparent. Even within the communities and groups who saw at close quarters the death and destruction of the last decades, we must now ask if we, as adults, have had sufficient imagination to realise the impact on children and young people within those communities that have been worst affected.

From the outset it is important to state that it is not possible to 'average out' the experiences of the Troubles that children and young people have had. Some children and young people growing up in Northern Ireland have been relatively unaffected by the conflict. Here, however, we will begin by considering what is now known about those who lost their lives.

This chapter is based on an extrapolation from the database on deaths of those deaths under the age of 25 and those under the age of 18 years. Qualitative data was also collected, in a series of individual and group interviews with young people in some of the areas with high Troubles-related death rates in Belfast, conducted between January and May 1998. These interviews were transcribed and analysed and have informed this chapter, even if they are not directly cited.

The term 'child' here is used to refer to the United Nations definition, namely those under the age of 18. The term 'young person' is used more loosely, to refer to adolescents and young adults. Occasionally data are presented on those over the age of 18 for comparative purposes, and where this occurs, ages are specified.

Chapter 3 also sets out the other factors defining the distribution of deaths, namely gender, location, religion, and political affiliation. Specifically how these factors have structured deaths among children will be the subject of the first part of this chapter.

DEATHS OF CHILDREN AND YOUNG PEOPLE IN THE TROUBLES

An examination of those killed in the conflict since 1969 illustrates the particularly vulnerable situation of children and young people. An age breakdown of deaths in the Troubles as shown in Table 7.1 reveals that of all age groupings examined, the 18–23 age group contains the highest number of deaths – 898. This age group alone accounts for 25 per cent of all deaths in the Troubles. People of 29 years and under account for over half the deaths in the Troubles to date.

Table 7.1 Deaths from 1969 to 1.3.1998 in the Northern Ireland Troubles by Age Grouping

Age group	Number of deaths	As % of total deaths	Cumulative total number	Cumulative %
0–5	23	0.64	23	0.64
6–11	24	0.67	47	1.31
12–17	210	5.84	257	7.15
18–23	898	24.96	1155	32.11
24–29	697	19.37	1852	51.48
30–35	509	14.15	2361	65.63
36–41	344	9.56	2705	75.19
42–47	261	7.25	2966	82.44
48–53	227	6.31	3193	88.75
54–59	156	4.34	3349	93.09
60–65	112	3.11	3461	96.20
66–71	42	1.17	3503	97.37
72–77	31	0.86	3534	98.23
78–80	8	0.22	3542	98.45
81+	8	0.22	3550	98.67
Age unknown	48	1.33		
Total	3598	100	3598	100

When we reorganised the age categories so that we could compare them with census categories the following picture emerged. Table 7.2 shows the numbers killed in each age group up to the age of

24, with a death rate for the age group which can be compared to the overall death rate of 2.23 per thousand for the total population. Both the 15–19 and the 20–24 age groups show a death rate that is higher than that for the total population.

Table 7.2 Children and Young People Killed in the Troubles 1969 to 1.3.1998 by Age Grouping, Total Population in Age Group and Death Rate for Age Group

Age group	Total pop. in age group	Number killed	Those killed as percentage of total	Death rate per thousand for age group
0–4	128,253	21	0.58	0.16
5–9	129,153	17	0.47	0.13
10–14	127,869	51	1.4	0.40
15–19	127,581	468	13.0	3.66
20–24	126,120	719	20.0	5.70
All	638,976	1276	35.5	2.00
Total	1,610,300	3598	100	2.23

Table 7.3 shows in more detail how the death rate rises from around age 12 onwards, peaking around 19 or 20. Clearly adolescence is a high-risk period, and only in early adulthood does the death risk begin to diminish. The risk remains relatively high for young adults, and one only sees substantial diminution after the age of 40. The risk for those in their late teens and early 20s is unmatched by any other age group. If we see death as a surrogate for the effect of the Troubles as a whole, we can surmise that similar patterns will occur amongst the population of those injured in the Troubles. High levels of participation by young people in rioting and other street activities ensures that in relation to injury, young people are also the highest risk group.

Age is clearly only one factor in death rates in the Troubles. Table 7.3 shows a breakdown of deaths by gender and age at death up to age 24. This table also shows a cumulative total percentage of deaths up to age 24.

GENDER

As in the overall population, the risk of death in the Troubles for young males is much greater than for young females. Whilst the risk for female children of childhood sexual abuse is much greater than for males, in the case of death in the Troubles, this is reversed.

In both genders, death rate is related to age. The highest number of deaths is at the age of 19 and 20, with declining death rates for all age groups thereafter. Twenty-year-old males are 13.48 per cent of all males under 24 killed, while 19-year-old females are 15 per cent of all females under 24 killed. Deaths of people aged 24 and under account for 35.46 per cent of all deaths in the Troubles, whilst people of age 24 and under account for roughly 40 per cent of the total population. The data on age demonstrate how Northern Ireland's Troubles have been a killer of young people, particularly young men. Again, one can see the death rate steadily rise as age increases from birth onwards, and beginning to rise substantially at around the age of 12 to 14 years old. Gender, as a factor in the social context, particularly in relation to the culture of violence, will be discussed below.

Table 7.3 Death Rates at Each Age 0–24, 1969 to 1.3.1998

Age	Males	Females	Total	Total in age as % of total killed	Cumulative total	Cumulative % of all killed
unborn	0	1	1	.03	1	.03
<1	3	3	6	0.16	7	0.19
1	1	2	3	0.08	10	0.28
2	2	1	3	0.08	13	0.36
3	4	0	4	0.11	17	0.47
4	1	3	4	0.11	21	0.58
5	1	1	2	0.06	23	0.64
6	2	2	4	0.11	27	0.75
7	1	1	2	0.06	29	0.81
8	0	2	2	0.06	31	0.86
9	4	3	7	0.19	38	1.06
10	4	1	5	0.14	43	1.20
11	4	0	4	0.11	47	1.31
12	5	4	9	0.25	56	1.56
13	10	5	15	0.42	71	1.97
14	11	7	18	0.5	89	2.47
15	26	4	30	0.83	119	3.30
16	45	4	49	1.36	168	4.67
17	77	12	89	2.47	257	7.14
18	125	9	134	3.72	391	10.87
19	147	19	166	4.61	557	15.48
20	155	12	167	4.64	724	20.12
21	137	13	150	4.17	874	24.29
22	140	7	147	4.08	1021	28.38
23	131	3	134	3.72	1155	32.10
24	113	8	121	3.36	1276	35.46
Total ages 0–24	1149	127	1276	35.46		

GEOGRAPHICAL DISTRIBUTION

Table 7.4 shows the distribution of death of those under the age of 25 and those under the age of 18 by the home postal area of the victim. For Northern Ireland deaths, the postal area is given, and for deaths outside Northern Ireland, the region is given. Since British soldiers could serve in Northern Ireland in the early 1970s from the age of 16, some of the deaths under 18 shown with home addresses in Great Britain are British soldiers. The age for serving in Northern Ireland was subsequently raised to 18, yet still, a substantial number of the 353 people killed in England, Scotland and Wales under the age of 25 were members of the British Army.

What emerges from the Table 7.4 is that the Northern Ireland deaths are concentrated in a relatively small area in Northern Ireland. The six Northern Ireland postal areas BT11–15 and BT48 account for 33.5 per cent of all deaths under the age of 25 and an astounding 58 per cent of all deaths under the age of 18. What emerges from this is that certain sub-groups of children and young people are identified as being particularly at risk of becoming victims (or perpetrators) of violent acts, namely young males, resident in these areas where the overall death rates are particularly high.

Table 7.4 Troubles-Related Deaths of Children and Young People under the ages of 25 and 18 by Postal Area in Northern Ireland and by other Locations: 1969–1.3.1998

Location	Postal Area	Number of residents under 25 killed	Number of residents under 18 killed
England, Scotland & Wales	GB	353	13
Ballymurphy/Falls/Antrim Rd/ Sandy Row/Donegall Road	BT12	106	37
Ardoyne/Ballysillan/Silverstream	BT14	88	32
Andersonstown/Turf Lodge	BT11	66	23
Derry City/Ballymagroarty/Galliagh	BT48	63	24
Antrim Rd/New Lodge/Shore Rd	BT15	53	19
Shankill Glencairn/Highfield/ Crumlin Road	BT13	51	14
Dungannon/Stewartstown	BT71	32	4
Republic of Ireland	Republic of Ireland	32	5
Newry/Bessbrook/Newtownhamilton/ Silverbridge/Carnlough/Crossmaglen	BT35	31	6
Braniel/Castlereagh Road, Belfast	BT5	25	5
Newtownabbey/Monkstown/ Greencastle/Glengormley	BT36	23	8
South Belfast/University Rd/ Ormeau Rd	BT7	22	6
Waterside, Derry/Dungiven/ Strathfoyle/New Buildings/Greysteel	BT47	19	3
Strabane/Victoria Bridge/Sion Mills	BT82	17	4
Ravenhill Road, Belfast	BT6	16	5

continued

Table 7.4 continued

Location	Postal Area	Number of residents under 25 killed	Number of residents under 18 killed
Armagh/Keady/Darkley/Killyleagh	BT60	16	7
Dungannon, Co Tyrone	BT70	15	2
South Belfast/Upper Malone	BT9	12	1
Markets Area/Donegall Pass, Belfast	BT17	10	3
Rosstrevor/Rathfriland/Warrenpoint/ Kilkeel	BT34	10	0
Craigavon/Portadown/Tandragee	BT62	10	4
Armagh/Richill/Loughgall/Kilmore	BT61	9	1
Craigavon/Scarva/Gilford/Portadown	BT63	9	1
Craigavon/Waringstown	BT66	9	0
Newtownards/Scrabo/West Winds/ Comber	BT23	8	0
Coagh/Monkstown/Rathcoole/ Whiteabbey	BT37	8	2
Magherafelt/Knockloughrim/ Moneymore/Castledawson/Bellaghy	BT45	8	0
Eden/Carrickfergus/Greenisland	BT38	7	0
Omagh/Dromore/Fintona/Trillick	BT78	7	0
Postal area unknown within NI	DK	7	4
Finaghy/Derriaghy	BT10	6	1
Lisburn/Ballinderry/The Maze	BT28	6	1
Newtownards Road, Belfast	BT4	6	1
Moira/Magheralin/Aghalee/Craigavon	BT67	6	1
Castlereagh/Killeter/Killen, Co Tyrone	BT81	6	0
Newtownbutler/Lisnaskea/Rosslea, Co Fermanagh	BT92	6	1
Markets Area, Belfast	BT16	5	0
Downpatrick/Crossgar/Killyleagh/ Killough/Ardglass, Co Down	BT30	5	1
Maghera/Upperlands/Swatragh	BT46	5	1
Enniskillen/Letterbreen/Lesky, Co Fermanagh	BT74	5	2
Cookstown	BT80	5	0
Central Belfast	BT2	4	0
Bangor	BT20	4	2
Castlewellan	BT31	4	1
Larne/Kilwaughter/Glynn/Islandmagee	BT40	4	0
Camlough/Cushendun/Portglenone/ Rasharkin/Dunloy	BT44	4	1
Ballymoney	BT53	4	2
Shaw'sBridge/Carryduff/South Belfast	BT8	4	1
Ballymena/Tannaghmore	BT43	3	0
Limavady/Ballykelly/Drumsurn/ Aghanaloo	BT49	3	2
Coleraine Town	BT52	3	1
Craigavon/Legahory	BT65	3	1
Beleek/Kesh/Garrison	BT93	3	0
Australia	Australia	2	0

continued

Table 7.4 continued

Location	Postal Area	Number of residents under 25 killed	Number of residents under 18 killed
Holywood, Co Down	BT18	2	0
Dromore, Ballynahinch	BT24	2	1
Lisburn/Lambeg	BT27	2	0
Dundrum/Newcastle	BT33	2	0
Toome/Templepatrick	BT41	2	0
Augher/Aughnacloy/Glassdrumond, Co Tyrone	BT69	2	0
Omagh/Carrickmore/Gortin/Mountfield, Co Tyrone	BT79	2	0
Holland	Holland	2	0
Bangor	BT19	1	0
Dromara/Dromore, Co Down	BT25	1	0
Hillsborough	BT26	1	1
Banbridge, Co Down	BT32	1	1
Templepatrick/Ballyclare	BT39	1	1
Ahoghill/Ballymena	BT42	1	0
Garvagh/Ballycastle	BT54	1	0
Portstewart	BT55	1	0
Portrush	BT56	1	0
Tempo/Maguiresbridge/Lisbellaw, Co Fermanagh	BT94	1	0
Germany	Germany	1	0
Unknown	–	1	
	Total	1276	257

SPATIAL DISTRIBUTION THROUGHOUT NORTHERN IRELAND

The gender disparity in death risk is coterminous with a highly localised distribution of violent deaths, with the highest risk areas being the urban areas – North and West Belfast and Derry Londonderry. Generally it is these same areas that experience the highest levels of deprivation and family poverty. Not only do children live with this poverty, but they also live with the effects of militarisation, and the interplay between violence and deprivation. The relationship between deprivation and the spatial distribution of Troubles-related deaths is dealt with more fully elsewhere.

The implications for Northern Ireland's children are that some children in the worst affected areas are likely to have a great deal of experience of the violence of the Troubles, whilst others have very little experience. This has had major ramifications for our understanding of the situation of children in Northern Ireland. Because of the localisation of conflict, research that takes a representative sample of young people in Northern Ireland will tend to overestimate the experiences of children in low violence areas like Bangor, whilst underestimating the experience of children in high violence areas such as North or West Belfast. To speak of the 'average Northern Irish child's' experience is somewhat misleading, since children's experience is widely diverse, with a substantial number of children having little experience of the Troubles, and a relatively small number of children having very intense and concentrated and prolonged experiences of life-threatening Troubles-related events.

THOSE RESPONSIBLE FOR THE DEATHS

Table 7.5 shows an analysis of the deaths of those under 25 and under 18 years by perpetrator. Suicides, where there is an indication that the suicide was related to the Troubles, are included among the unattributable deaths. Similarly, road accidents where the Troubles were a causative factor in the accident leading to the death are included. This means that these figures are somewhat higher than the official figures, which exclude these deaths. We have also included a number of deaths in cross-fire where it has not been possible to attribute the death to any one perpetrator and we have included deaths of children killed by Army vehicles.

The same pattern emerges in both age groups – the under-25s and the under-18s. Republican paramilitaries are responsible for the largest share of the deaths, followed by Loyalist paramilitaries, with the security forces accounting for the third largest share.

Table 7.5 also shows individual organisations' death toll. Here a difference between the two age groupings emerges. In both age groups the Republican paramilitaries, in particular the IRA, are responsible for the largest number of deaths, followed in both age groups by the security forces, particularly the British Army, and in the under-25 age group by unspecified Loyalist paramilitaries.

Table 7.5 Who Killed Those Under 25 and Under 18? (1969–1.3.1998)

	Numbers of under-25s killed	Numbers under 18
Unattributable to one perpetrator		
Accident	1	1
Suicide related to Troubles	5	
Road accident	1	
Crash	2	
Cross-fire	1	

continued

Table 7.5 continued

	Numbers of under-25s killed	Numbers under 18
Don't know	51	14
Hunger strike	2	
Accidental shooting	16	11
Total unattributable	79	26
Security forces		
RUC	29	6
RUC/Civ	3	–
British Army	182	58
UDR	8	2
Army vehicle	2	1
Total security forces	224	67
Republican groups		
Republican Action Force	6	1
IPLO	2	1
Unspecified Republican paramilitaries	24	3
Official IRA	17	2
INLA	42	9
IRA	610	73
IRA Fianna	1	1
Total Republicans	702	90
Loyalist groups		
LVF	2	1
UDA	3	1
UFF	40	10
UVF	74	19
Red Hand Commandos	2	1
Protestant Action Force	10	2
Protestant Action Group	1	
Unspecified Loyalist paramilitary	140	40
Total Loyalists	272	74
Overall total	1276	257

Perpetrators of killings of those under 18

In the case of the under-18s, the IRA again are responsible for the largest number of deaths, followed by the British Army, but the variation in the scale of difference in the two age groups is not quite as marked. In the under-25 age group, the IRA were responsible for by far the largest number of killings and the difference between them and the next largest – the British Army – was quite marked (610 to 182) – whilst the difference in the under-18 age group is not as great (73 to 58). A large number of under-25s (771) were killed by shooting (see Table 7.8) and shooting is used by both security forces and paramilitary organisations alike. A substantial number of under-25s were killed in explosions (415), which are most likely to be the responsibility of the IRA. Furthermore, whilst the British Army have concentrated their efforts in combating the IRA and other paramilitary organisations, making their focus of attack outward towards the communities which house paramilitaries, the IRA has also dealt with the threat of informers and performed a controversial role in policing. The increase in the number of killings by the IRA in the under-25 compared to the under-18 age group may reflect these factors.

RELIGIOUS AFFILIATION OF CHILDREN AND YOUNG PEOPLE KILLED

Table 7.6 shows the numbers of those under 25 and those under 18 who have been killed, according to the community they have been identified with.

Table 7.6 Religious Affiliation of Those Under 25 and Those Under 18 Killed 1969–1.3.1998

| | Under 25 | | Under 18 | |
	No.	as % of total*	No.	as % of total*
Catholic	615	48.1	190	73.9
Non Northern Ireland†	362	28.3	12	4.7
Protestant	231	18.1	50	19.5
Unknown	68	5.3	5	1.9
Total	1276	100	257	100

* to the nearest decimal point

† Non Northern Ireland refers to those who are not residents of Northern Ireland

It demonstrates that in both age groups Catholics are the largest group. The startling difference between them is that whilst Catholics are just over 48 per cent of those under 25 killed, they are almost 74 per cent of those killed under the age of 18.

In the total death figures for all age groups Catholic deaths outnumber Protestant deaths both in relative and absolute terms, but the scale of the difference is much less than it is for the under-18 age group. The higher number of Catholics killed, together with the information in Table 7.5 on perpetrators, would suggest that a substantial number of Catholic deaths are due to Republican para-militaries. Republican paramilitaries are responsible for the largest percentage of deaths of any group in both the under-25 age group (55 per cent) and the under-18 age group (34.6 per cent). Republican paramilitaries are responsible for 58.8 per cent of all deaths, compared to 55 per cent of those under the age of 25 and 34.6 per cent of those under the age of 18. Loyalist paramilitaries are responsible for 27.9 per cent of all deaths, compared to 21.3 per cent of deaths under the age of 25 and 28.8 per cent of deaths under the age of 18. Security forces are responsible for 11.25 per cent of all deaths, 17.5 per cent of deaths under the age of 25 and 26.1 per cent of deaths under the age of 18. Although Republican paramilitaries remain the most responsible for deaths at all ages, there is a marked increase in the share of total deaths of young people due to the security forces, and this is particularly striking in deaths under the age of 18.

POLITICAL AFFILIATION

Table 7.7 examines the political affiliation of those killed in the two age groups. Civilians were 45.6 per cent of those under the age of 25 killed, and 79 per cent of those under 18 killed. Security forces were 34.2 per cent of those under 25 killed, and only 1.95 per cent of those under 18 killed. Republican paramilitaries composed 15.7 per cent of those under 25 killed, and 18.68 per cent of those under 18 killed. Finally, Loyalist paramilitaries were 3.3 per cent of those under 25 killed, and 2.72 per cent of those under 18 killed.

Clearly, most children and young people killed in the Troubles were civilians, and this is particularly true of the under-18 age group. Children and young people have also been combatants. If we are to judge by the death figures, the grouping within whose ranks children and young people are most likely to die as combatants are the Republican paramilitaries, the IRA (21 deaths) and their junior wing, Na Fianna (14 deaths), with the Official IRA having three combatants under 18 killed, and two in the Fianna branch of their organisation. Both other categories of combatants – Loyalist paramilitaries (the UDA with four deaths and the UVF with three) and the security forces (British Army with five deaths, three of whom died in England) – have also recruited and armed persons legally defined as children. Deaths of combatants under 18 peaked in 1972, with 18 combatants under the age of 18 dying that year. Deaths of combatants under 18 subsequently declined, with the British Army no longer sending soldiers under 18 to serve in Northern Ireland – although they continue to be recruited into the Army – and an obvious change of strategy on the their part.

Table7.7 Political Affiliation of Those Under 25 and Under 18 Killed 1969–1.3.1998

	Under 25		Under 18	
	Number	% of total*	Number	% of total*
Civilians				
NI civilian	531		191	
GB civilian	29		7	
Civilian in Irish Republic	14		4	
Civilian political activists (NI)	8		1	
Total civilians	582	45.6	203	79.0
Security forces				
British Army	316		5	
Ex-RAF	1			
Ex-RUC	1			
Ex-British Army	2			
Ex-UDR	2			
UDR	46			
Garda	3			
Prison officer	2			
British police	2			
Royal Air Force	3			
RIR	2			
RUC	56			
RUCR	1			
Total security forces	437	34.2	5	1.95
Republican paramilitaries				
INLA	9			
IRA	157		21	
IRA (Fianna)	17		14	
Official IRA	10		3	
Official IRA Fianna	2		2	
PLA	1			
Unspecified Republican group	1			
IPLO	3			
Total Republicans	200	15.70	40	15.56
Loyalist paramilitaries				
Unspecified Loyalist group	1			
UDA	28		4	
UVF	13		3	
Total Loyalists	42	3.30	7	2.72
Affiliation unknown	15	1.10	2	0.78
Overall total	1276	100	257	100.00

* to the nearest decimal point

CAUSE OF DEATH

The most frequent cause of death in the Troubles in both children under the age of 18 and those under the age of 25 is shooting, followed by explosions, as is shown in Table 7.8. Together these account for 224 or 87 per cent of all deaths of children under the age of 18. In those under 25, shooting and explosion have killed 1186 people, 93 per cent of all those killed under the age of 25. The use of armoured vehicles, where the driver's vision of small objects is restricted, and where vehicles come under attack by stones and other missiles, requiring them to move fast in restricted spaces constitutes a hazard to children in heavily militarised areas. There are no reliable figures for the numbers of children and young people who have been killed and injured in this manner, but the cases that are verifiable are included here. A number of deaths due to rubber and plastic bullets are also shown.

Table 7.8 Cause of Death 1969–1.3.1998

Cause of death	Under 25 Number killed	Under 18 Number killed
Accident	6	6
Accident armoured personnel carrier/ army vehicle	11	4
Accident riot	1	0
Assault	24	6
Beating/brain haemorrhage	1	1
Burned/shot	1	0
Burns	9	6
Crash	7	0
Civilian vehicle in riot	2	2
Explosion	415	87
Prison/hanged	2	0
Hunger strike	4	0
Rubber/plastic bullet	13	8
Poisoned	1	0
Shot	771	137
Stabbed	6	0
Stillborn	1	1
Suicide	2	0
Total	1277	258

Plastic bullets

Policing policy in Northern Ireland has developed in a context where street violence and rioting is a frequent occurrence. Successive security strategies have variously deployed CS gas, water cannon and, most consistently, rubber and plastic bullets. Rubber bullets were used initially, and these were later replaced by plastic bullets, in response to complaints about the severity of injury caused by the earlier rubber bullet.

Table 7.9 shows a further analysis of these deaths, which have particular relevance to children and young people.

Table 7.9 Deaths from Plastic Bullets by Age of Victim at 13.11.1991

Age	Male	Female	Total
10	1	0	1
11	2	0	2
12	0	1	1
13	1	0	1
14	0	1	1
15	2	0	2
16	1	0	1
18	1	0	1
21	2	0	2
22	1	0	1
33	0	1	1
40	1	0	1
41	1	0	1
45	1	0	1
Total	14	3	17

Since these bullets, also referred to as baton rounds, are used in riot situations against unarmed combatants, they are frequently deployed in situations involving young people and children. The purpose of such weapons is to temporarily disable people, and thereby control the situation.

By 1991, the use of plastic bullets in Northern Ireland had led to the deaths of an estimated 17 people, 10 of whom were aged 18 or under. RUC officers fired four of the fatal bullets, and members of the British Army fired the remainder. Numbers of others have been injured, some very seriously and permanently, by plastic and rubber bullets. Arguably, children are more vulnerable because of the size of the bullet relative to the size of a child's body. There has been a campaign to ban the use of plastic bullets in crowd control and riot situations because of the danger to children. To date they remain in use.

Punishment beatings and shootings

In situations where civil conflict arises, the breakdown or erosion of normal law enforcement is commonplace. Children can grow up with mixed and confusing messages about the law and where it intersects with what has come to be called in Northern Ireland antisocial behaviour. The real erosion of law enforcement, and the crisis in the acceptability of the security forces, particularly but not exclusively in Catholic areas, has meant the growth of 'community policing' by paramilitary organisations. Much of this activity is in the areas that have seen the worst of the Troubles-related violence, and much of the punishment is ostensibly directed at curbing antisocial behaviour including drug-related behaviour. The issue of drugs and substance abuse is discussed in greater depth later.

In general, official figures would suggest that Northern Ireland is a more law-abiding society in general, than for example the rest of the United Kingdom. The reluctance, particularly though not exclusively in Catholic areas, to report crime to the police, or to call on the police to intervene would indicate that the true extent of the law and order problem may be underestimated in official figures. Local communities are divided on the issue of policing of their communities, with some advocating paramilitary policing in the absence of an acceptable state police force, and others horrified at the brutality of the punishments meted out, and the summary nature of the attribution of guilt. These kinds of dilemmas and the practice of summary punishment at the hands of local people can be seen in other societies that have experienced conflict, and can be seen as a by-product of such conflict. Lynching and beatings as punishments for petty crime are administered in, for example, Guatemala and South Africa in local communities. In Northern Ireland, this kind of punishment can range from attacks with sticks and iron bars, to extremely brutal beatings, and in one case the impaling of the victim's arms and legs. Tables 7.10–7.12 show the totals for such attacks and the numbers of young people attacked.

Table 7.10 Casualties Under 20 as a Result of Paramilitary Punishments

Year	Loyalist	Republican	Total
1988	5	14	19
1989	12	32	44
1990	13	18	31
1991	8	10	18
1992	11	20	31
1993	13	7	20
1994	13	15	28
1995	0	0	0
1996	6	0	6
1997	10	7	17
Total	91	123	214

Source: Central Statistical Unit, Northern Ireland Office

Beatings in some areas operate on a tariff system, where repeated offences can lead to the victim being ordered to leave the country within a specified number of hours. At least one voluntary organisation facilitates the flight of young people in order to help them avoid the ultimate sanction – the death penalty. The victims of such beatings are almost invariably male, working class and in their teens or early 20s. Two recent cases concern young men with mild learning difficulties, who were involved in petty crime, and who 'defied' the local IRA. In one case, the victim's family took to sleeping in one room, in anticipation of the regular paramilitary raids on the house (which broke the door down) to look for the offender.

Table 7.11 All Casualties of Paramilitary Attacks

	Loyalist		Republican		Total	
	All	Under 20	All	Under 20	All	Under 20
Assaults 1982–97	528	104	755	183	1283	287
Shootings 1973–97	868	91	1228	123	2096	214

Source: Central Statistical Unit, Northern Ireland Office

According to Northern Ireland Office statistics, in the period 1973–97, a total of 2096 people were victims of 'punishment shootings', 214 of whom were under the age of 20. A further 1283 people were casualties of 'punishment beatings' in the period 1982–97, and of those 287 were under the age of 20.

Table 7.12 shows the figures for casualties under 20 years old. In terms of shootings, Loyalists shoot four times the number of young people under 17 years of age compared with Republicans, whilst Republicans shoot slightly more than the Loyalist in the 17–19 years age category. In the case of punishment beatings, the Republican figure was substantially higher for both age groups.

Yet undoubtedly, a proportion of the local community look to paramilitary groups to 'police' the area in an attempt to control the level of local crime against the community. In the absence of acceptable and effective policing, there is a demand for some form of summary justice. Whilst some members of the local community are undoubtedly horrified at the brutality of the punishments meted out, others take a hard line, particularly around the issue of drugs and violence against vulnerable members of the community. Therefore those who offend, very often young people already marginalised from the education system and other systems, can end up fugitives within their own communities, and their families fearful and resentful.

Table 7.12 Age Breakdown of Punishment Shootings and Assaults 1991–97

Punishment shootings	Loyalist	Republican	Total
Under 17 years	8	2	10
17–19 years	53	57	110
Total	61	59	120
Punishment assaults			
Under 17 years	25	36	61
17–19 years	64	109	173
Total	89	145	234

Source: Central Statistical Unit, Northern Ireland Office

The issues of punishment beatings and shootings have been a focus of concern in recent years, and are likely to remain so whilst the social fabric of communities remains damaged by the attritional effects of militarisation. Such practices also fill a gap created by the absence of consensus on policing within local communities. Should peace become established, part of the task of reconstruction would be the replacement of violent 'policing' practices with non-violent methods.

THE WIDER CONTEXT OF CHILDREN'S LIVES

Children and young people do not experience violence in a vacuum, nor is it the only problem they are faced with. Violence and conflict are experienced by children and young people in the context of the assets, resources, impediments and handicaps in the child or young person's wider social context. In Northern Ireland, this wider social context is characterised by a number of features that help construct and mediate the experience of violence. These cannot be presented here, but are discussed in detail elsewhere (Smyth, 1998). It is worth noting that children in Northern Ireland are not immune from deprivation, residential and educational segregation, together with low educational attainment in deprived areas, alongside the common childhood risks of physical and sexual abuse. Children in Northern Ireland experience the violence of the Troubles in addition to the ordinary risk of childhood, and we have reason to conclude that it is those children who already suffer from deprivation and marginalisation that are most at risk from the violence of the Troubles. The militarisation of communities, the acculturation of young people to violence, in the absence of proper leisure and creative opportunities is, and has been, a grave risk for children and young people. In such circumstances, substance abuse as a method of 'coping' is already prevalent amongst young people in the most marginalised communities, with alcohol abuse being particularly common. McAuley and Kremer's (1990) study found that in an area badly affected by the Troubles over 90 per cent of 9- to 11-year-old children had observed a hijacked vehicle burning, over 50 per cent had seen 'people shooting guns', and approximately 37 per cent had 'witnessed a bomb explosion'. Within such communities, often the only 'exciting' activity for adolescents is involvement in street violence, or watching or participating in joy-riding. The relationships of some children and young people to adults in general, and to parents and those in authority in particular, require major adjustments. The relationship between adolescents and the security forces in particular is often one of mutual distrust. The security forces often view young people as potential rioters, look-outs for paramilitary groups or as some other form of threat, whilst the young people complain of harassment at the hands of the security forces.

Within families, children and young people have often had to cope with responsibilities beyond that which is normally expected of a child, because of the particular circumstances of the Troubles. Yet children have also sustained their own losses; they have lost parents to death and imprisonment, they have lost friends, freedom of movement, security and often hope. In some cases children and young people have coped alone with these losses, fearful of upsetting adults if they speak of their feelings or experiences. The children who are most vulnerable are those children who have been separated from parents, and who are most dependent on parents or guardians. Age, personality, family and school support are likely to be important factors in helping children to cope in such circumstances. Yet the culture of silence that has surrounded the Troubles has often left children and adolescents isolated with their experiences. Services available to young people who develop mental health difficulties as a result have been acknowledged to be totally inadequate and often ill prepared to deal with Troubles-related issues.

PUBLIC POLICY AND THE POLICY GAP

The silence on the part of public agencies and professionals, whilst understandable, has meant that not only is there no professional or policy culture of openly addressing these issues, but the very language to do so is not in existence. This lack of language, and the culture of silence and denial within which it resides, and the honest fear of naming the unnamable has left the children of Northern Ireland who live in the worst affected areas in a limbo of isolation and violent vicious circles.

In June 1994, the General Assembly of the United Nations appointed Grac'a Machel as expert to coordinate a study on the impact of armed conflict on children. Her (1996) report to the United Nations concludes:

> The impact of armed conflict on children must be everyone's concern and is everyone's responsibility; governments, international organisations and every element of civil society. Each one of us, each individual, each institution, each country, must initiate and support global action to protect children ... Children present us with a uniquely compelling motivation for mobilisation. Universal concern for children presents us with new opportunities to confront problems that cause their suffering. By focussing on children, politicians, Governments, the military and mono-state entities will begin to recognise how much they destroy through armed conflict and therefore how little they gain. Let us take this opportunity to recapture our instinct to nourish and protect children. Let us transform our moral outrage into concrete action. Our children have a right to peace. Peace is every child's right. (Machel, 1996: pp. 88–9)

On the issue of reconstruction and reconciliation, Machel argues that children, particularly those who have been most affected and involved in conflict, are crucial to the process of reconstruction.

> Children are rarely mentioned in reconstruction plans or peace agreements, yet children must be at the centre of rebuilding. Part of putting children at the centre means using youth as a resource. Young people must not be seen as problems or victims, but as key contributors in the planning and implementation of long-term solutions. (Machel, 1996: p. 68)

In the Good Friday Agreement, reached in multi-party talks in Northern Ireland in 1998, the issue of victims of violence is raised in Strand Three, under 'Rights, Safeguards and Equality of Opportunity'. Paragraph 12 of the Agreement states:

> The participants particularly recognise that young people from areas affected by the Troubles face particular difficulties, and will support the development of community-based initiatives based on international best practice. The provision of services that are supportive and sensitive to the needs of victims will also be a critical element and that support

will need to be channelled through both statutory and community based voluntary organisations facilitating locally based self-help and support networks.

The report of the Northern Ireland Victims' Commission further recommends that 'consideration should be given to the creation of a fund to assist in particular children and young people affected by the death or injury of a parent' (para 6.5). So thanks to lobbying of politicians by interested groups, Northern Ireland has at least managed to ensure that children and young people are mentioned in the preliminary declarations of intent at the outset of peace building. Much depends on the ability to sustain the end of the armed conflict, but a great deal also depends on the imagination and energy that goes into designing and carrying forward the work of reconstruction. It is clear that international experience will be invaluable in stimulating and informing such work.

The position of children in Northern Ireland is not as extreme as that of children from many other countries that have experienced armed conflict. Our civilian casualty rates are around 50 per cent rather than the 90 per cent mentioned. Our children are rarely forced to flee as unaccompanied refugees. Generally, whilst health and nutrition may be problems for poorer children in Northern Ireland, with the possible exception of traveller children, children in Northern Ireland can have access to clean water and basic food and shelter.

A number of the issues faced by children and young people in other situations of armed conflict happily do not have great relevance in Northern Ireland, namely, unexploded landmines, prostitution of children, displaced unaccompanied children. The individual child does not experience the trauma of armed conflict in isolation. The contexts of family, school, community and culture either support or undermine the child's capacity to manage difficult experiences and develop effective coping strategies. Therefore, the families, schools and communities are crucial in any period of reconstruction and this understanding is crucial for the work of designing policy and intervention. The task of healing and recon-struction in societies coming out of armed conflict is not only a matter of offering support to individual children and their families, but is also about addressing the community, educational, political, cultural and other aspects of the child's environment. Much of this work will be concerned with creating a new context in which individuals and families can begin to rebuild their lives. Trust in authority and in each other must be re-established, people need to develop a new sense of their own power and responsibility, and explore new ways of dealing with difference and conflict.

In order to achieve such change in Northern Ireland, it will be necessary to transform the aura of stigmatisation and blame attached to many marginalised communities. Furthermore, sensitivity and imagination will be required in order to build capacity within families and communities in a way that does not blame or further marginalise them. Nor indeed should intervention be solely targeted at communities and families worst affected. The dominant ideology, the schools, churches and other institutions that influence family and community life in Northern Ireland contain many ideas and practices that might usefully be revised in the interests of achieving positive social change and supporting reconstruction in families and communities.

8 Conclusions and Next Steps

Since 1969, 3601 people have been killed in Northern Ireland. Given average household size, this means that at least 6800 people have had the experience of one of their immediate family – parent or sibling – being killed in a Troubles-related incident. According to the official figures, over 40,000 people have been injured in the Troubles, although this is likely to be a conservative figure. There is no readily available data on how many of this 40,000 suffer from major disability as a result of the Troubles.

The analysis described here has confirmed many of the findings and trends identified by others, if not in the numbers of deaths, then certainly in the high levels of death in the first half of the 1970s. The suggestion that deaths peak in the summer months has not been supported but rather October and November have emerged as the months with the highest death rates. Furthermore, different cycles have been identified among the organisations principally responsible for killings, with peaks of activity occurring at different points in the period 1969–94.

The findings point to the gender and age characteristics of those who have been killed, and therefore those who would appear to be at highest risk in the Troubles. The overwhelming majority of those killed in the Troubles have been male, with the death risk greatest in the younger age groups, the 20–24 age group being highest, and almost 26 per cent of all victims aged 21 or under. The absolute number of Catholics killed is greater than Protestants killed, and the death rate for Catholics is greater than that for Protestants, as other researchers have found. If security forces deaths are included in the analysis of death by religion, and Catholics killed by Republican paramilitaries and Protestants killed by Loyalist paramilitaries are excluded, the death rates for Protestants and Catholics become much closer – 1.9 per 1000 for Catholics and 1.6 per 1000 for Protestants. Civilians are the largest category killed, and make up 53 per cent of the total killed, with the British Army as the second largest category making almost 15 per cent, Republican paramilitaries accounting for almost 13 per cent, the RUC accounting for 8 per cent and the other groups each accounting for less than 6 per cent.

The findings concur with those elsewhere in terms of responsibility for deaths – the predominance of Republican paramilitaries followed by Loyalist paramilitaries, then the British Army and the RUC with other groups accounting each for less than 1 per cent. Republican paramilitaries have killed 74 per cent of all Protestants killed, over 25 per cent of all Catholics and almost 96 per cent of those who were classified as 'non Northern Ireland'. Loyalist paramilitaries killed 19 per cent of all Protestants killed, almost 50 per cent of all Catholics and just 2 per cent of the 'non Northern Ireland' category. Our findings on the distribution of deaths, calculated a death rate by ward and found a concentration of deaths in Belfast with only 15 of the 57 highest ranking wards outside the Belfast area. Derry Londonderry and Armagh account for most of the remaining wards.

The distribution of deaths in the Troubles was correlated with the Robson deprivation indicator, and it is clear that wards with high deprivation scores predominate amongst those with the largest number of deaths.

The analysis of death rates from other conflicts internationally suggests that Northern Ireland is not in the 'first league' of intensive killing. It might be argued that this region is part of a major European power that is generally at peace and is therefore unique. That contention must confront the mass killing that accompanied the break-up of Yugoslavia for which detailed figures are not yet available and which happened on the immediate periphery of the European Union, indeed a significant holiday destination for many European citizens. Nevertheless, primarily because of its small population size, Northern Ireland's Troubles remain significant at the international level with death rates roughly equivalent to the annual homicide rate for the United States and greater than, for example, Turkey.

APPROACHES TO THE TROUBLES

All discussions about 'victims' of the Troubles run the risk of becoming politicised in the following ways. Acknowledgement of the damage done to a particular grouping or community can seem to some as an admission of defeat, which will gladden their enemies, and so is to be avoided. Conversely, acknowledgement of such damage can be a way of highlighting the wickedness of those who are responsible for the attacks, and so can become a political weapon. All of this runs the risk of compounding the damage done to those who have been hurt. It is of crucial importance that all discussion about 'victims' or people affected is shifted on to a humanitarian basis, based on an inclusive concern about the human needs and the resources required to meet them.

The importance of timing, especially in relation to the risk of the recurrence of violence, is difficult to exaggerate. It only became possible for some people affected by the Troubles to begin to address what has happened to them when the cease-fires were announced. Maintaining a relative absence of violence is crucial to the task of addressing the situation of those affected by the Troubles. Should there be a return to violence, it will not be possible to take this work forward in the same way. People who have been drastically affected by the Troubles often live with high levels of fear. It is only when this fear is reduced, and when an atmosphere of increased safety is in place that it is possible to work constructively with the issues of coming out of violence. This is not to say that people do not have needs when violence is ongoing, but rather to point out that substantial progress can be made only in the absence of violence. Therefore the peace process and progress therein is at the heart of creating services and measures to address the needs of those affected by the Troubles.

THE LEVEL OF NEED

The assumption that people 'get over' such things in time is not true. In the case of physical disablement, this is visibly not the case. One study showed that roughly 50 per cent of people still had symptoms of emotional distress and sleep disturbance over 20 years after they had been bereaved in the Troubles. This means that the scale of the problem may be very large. Counting only immediate family members, there could be over 41,400 people in the population whose immediate family death or injury in the Troubles has directly affected them, and who suffer distress or emotional disturbance as a result. This figure does not include all the eye witnesses, neighbours, friends, extended family, co-workers and so on who have been affected by deaths and injuries in the Troubles. Not all of this 41,400 need or require, for example, counselling. The public acknowledgement of their suffering, and the provision of supportive networks or services for those who need them is an important part of Northern Ireland's recovery as a society.

The converse of this is that some people who have been affected by the Troubles have developed their own way of coping with their situation, and have found ways that work for them. Some of these ways involve not talking about what has happened, or distancing themselves from anything which might require them to think too deeply about what has happened, or to look at the issues from another angle. This must be recognised, and people's right not to participate must be recognised and supported.

Many of those affected by the Troubles complain about their lack of control over the use of television or still photography of the circumstances of their loss or injury. The reprinting or broadcasting of such material can be very distressing for families and those close to such incidents, and currently little recognition is given to the distress caused by their use without consultation with those closely involved. Journalism has made extensive use of such material, yet has rarely considered it necessary to seek consent or views from those whose lives have been represented. Media representation has also concentrated on certain aspects of victims' experience, such as the period immediately after the loss, at the expense of more considered coverage. This narrow coverage has contributed in no small way to a rather low level of public awareness of the long-term effects of the Troubles on people's lives. Most worryingly, few working in the media recognise any of this as problematic.

Many of those who have been disabled in the Troubles have often been made dependent on benefit, and removed from the job-market. Services for the disabled are often inadequate to their needs, and can leave them bitter about their circumstances. Poverty is also another by-product for many that have suffered in the Troubles. A common fantasy is that the financial compensation system has ensured that people have at least been provided for financially. The 1998 announcement by the government of a comprehensive review of the compensation system is an indicator that this has not been the case.

There is a particular need for the provision of an effective pain management service to cater for those in chronic pain as a result of gunshot and shrapnel wounds. There is also a need to support those who care for those with disabilities acquired as a result of the Troubles. Such support could take the form of respite care, social networks and practical services such as help with transportation. We estimate that around 100,000 people in Northern Ireland live in households where someone has been injured in a Troubles-related incident. Some of these injuries were relatively minor, but some have been severely disabling.

Certain groups of people have specific and different needs. For example, members of the security forces who have been injured may suffer more from isolation as a result of being unable to use civilian services, or join, for example, voluntary groups for disabled people. Families whose members have disappeared have a need for information about the bodies of their relatives. Those living in areas where levels of Troubles-related violence have been high often have their lives made more difficult by repeated experiences of Troubles-related violence.

Many individuals and groups have a sense of injustice and grievance against the paramilitaries, the authorities, the media, politicians or the human service organisations. The lack of acknowledgement or denial of their needs, questioning of their rights to be considered sympathetically or the lack of support for them after their bereavement, injury or loss has often exacerbated this.

Often the needs and wishes of one group are directly opposite to the needs of another group. There are understandably strong feelings among those injured by a particular grouping about, for example, that grouping receiving attention, services or sympathy. This means that the provision of services according to need or the creation of, for example, a monument including all names is unconscionable to some, while others consider such a step as important to their own coming to terms with what has happened to them.

There has been an assumption that counselling is the appropriate and sometimes only form of service required by those affected by the Troubles. This assumption is questionable. Many people are not in need of counselling, but rather of some other service. Even some of those who could benefit from counselling are reluctant to use counselling because of the stigma attached and the implication that there is 'something wrong' with the person being counselled.

A small number of people only will need psychiatric, psychological or counselling help. It is erroneous to assume that because so few require or want psychiatric help that the general level of needs of those affected by the Troubles is low. Those who do not need or wish to use psychological or psychiatric help often have other needs, such as needs for befriending, social support, relief for carers, physiotherapy, pain relief, public recognition, legal or financial advice, control over old footage or photographs of the incident involving them or at least advance consultation about their use by the media, or further information about the circumstances of the incident which caused their suffering.

SERVICES TO THOSE AFFECTED BY THE TROUBLES

Statutory Services

Many, including those providing services to vulnerable people, have operated during the Troubles by not mentioning the Troubles, not identifying themselves or their true responses to certain situations, and being cautious or silent when Troubles-related issues were raised. This has meant that there can be a 'conspiracy of silence' in organisations about the effects of the Troubles. People are often fearful that if the issues are discussed, it will be divisive and lead to conflict, so they are ignored.

Currently there is no specialist training available for psychiatrists, psychologists, social workers, health visitors, general practitioners, teachers and other professionals to prepare them for the kinds of effects the Troubles may have on their clients and patients, nor is there specific training or information on the range of appropriate services or approaches to use.

At present, there is one trauma team based in Belfast, which caters for the needs of people immediately after a major incident. This does not address the long-term needs of people, and does not cater for individuals injured, bereaved or traumatised in incidents where small numbers are involved.

There is an acute shortage of psychiatric help for all adolescents, so adolescents who require such help as a result of the Troubles are unlikely to receive it. There are only six beds available in Northern Ireland for adolescents requiring in-patient psychiatric care. In 1994, 242 young people were held in adult psychiatric wards, hardly the place for distressed adolescents. Levels of outpatient support can be similarly inadequate.

Voluntary Services

Currently, the major service providers providing dedicated services for those affected by the Troubles are in the voluntary sector: WAVE, whose main service is befriending and home visiting throughout Northern Ireland and who also provide a counselling service and facilities for children; Survivors of Trauma, who are a locally based self-help group in North Belfast; An Crann/ The Tree who listen and collect people's accounts of the Troubles; Cunamh, a locally based project in Derry Londonderry; CALMS a project which offers training in stress management for local groups. Other voluntary organisations, such as CRUSE and Victim Support, which have experience of working in allied areas such as bereavement or the effects of crime, began to become more involved in working with those affected by the Troubles after the cease-fires.

The system of financial compensation for those who have been bereaved, injured or have had property damaged as a result of the Troubles has also caused some disquiet and distress. There are wide disparities between amounts paid to those with apparently similar injuries. Compensation in the case of injury or bereavement is based not on need but on loss sustained, and is partly calculated according to loss of earnings. This means that some have received little or no compensation where the victim was unemployed, whereas others receive relatively large amounts. This is perceived as some lives being regarded as more valuable than others. There are strong feelings amongst some that the system is unjust and insensitive.

Those suing for criminal damage to property have also found the system of compensation unsatisfactory. Long delays in processing and paying claims, together with interest payment incurred on loans taken to rebuild or repair business premises, have caused financial difficulty to claimants, and in some cases the collapse of businesses.

NEXT STEPS

Any initiative in this area carries a heavy emotional charge, and those injured and bereaved have often been used to further political agendas, sometimes at the expense of their own welfare. It is imperative that any new initiatives on so-called victims of the Troubles avoid further misuse of people's suffering and loss. Provision that has been made elsewhere has fallen into the trap of raising unrealistic expectations on the part of those who have suffered, only to have their disappointment added to their suffering.

As we finish writing this book, the prospects of peace and political settlement in Northern Ireland seem to be changeable. The work of counting the costs of violence in a society whilst violence has continued has been a heart-breaking one, and can seem like an endless – and perhaps pointless – task. We conclude this book in the belief that the cost of violence matters, irrespective of the identity of the victim or the perpetrator. Careful auditing of the effects of violence will, we hope, contribute towards building a sense of urgency and an understanding of the need to find peaceful means of change.

Finally, there should be some recognition of the limitations of this exercise. As we indicated earlier, the Troubles in Northern Ireland are driven by ideologies that variously justify killing according to particular versions of reality. On the one hand, Republicans believe they are in legitimate conflict with the British state as part of an unfinished revolution to free Ireland. From that perspective, Unionists are either deluded about their essential interests or are occasionally the shock troops of imperialism in the form of the RUC and UDR. The latter are thus legitimate targets along with British military personnel. On the other hand, Protestants see the IRA as engaged in illegitimate and therefore criminal insurrection against the majority of the Northern Ireland population which is, in effect, sectarian. The presentation of data of this kind will not substantially affect such perceptions. It will, however, confront such perceptions, particularly with the fact that no one side has a monopoly on suffering. In that sense, it may make some small contribution to reconciliation.

As the search for peace and reconciliation begins in Northern Ireland there are certain difficult issues which must be addressed. In any discussion of the Troubles, there must be an acknowledgement of the hierarchies of pain and responsibility. Some individuals, families and communities have suffered more than others. Some individuals, groups and institutions have harmed and killed people more than others, and some people have had more power to change things than others.

Moving towards a peaceful society also means dealing with the past and addressing key questions. What will we remember? If truth is the first casualty of war, then complexity is its second casualty. The nature of war itself means that complexity is masked by polarised, black and white accounting of the rights and wrongs of the conflict. Unless we strive to overcome this dynamic, our own hurts will blind us to the hurts we have inflicted on others. In order to rebuild a society in which the past can be understood and not repeated, we must remember not only what has been done to us, but also what has been done to others in our name. The danger is, however, that if we remain caught in that polarising centrifugal force that is violence and its aftermath, we will rewrite our past to hide our own shame and display that of our former enemies.

As Northern Ireland apparently emerges from almost 30 years of conflict, discussion has already begun about how will we remember the last 30 years, and how we will commemorate those who have lost their lives. If we are to achieve the goal of an inclusive society, then commemoration, too, must be an inclusive process. We must remember the harms we have done as well as the pain we have suffered; we must look at and learn to be compassionate towards the pains of our former enemies as well as those of our allies. Early in such processes, anger and rage about the past can prevent us from hearing and acknowledging the wrongs suffered by the other side, yet in order to complete our understanding of what has happened, we need to remember what has been forgotten, covered up from us, denied and silenced. Some of that information must come from our former enemies. In order to build a complete collective account of the last period, we must communalise our memories, so that things can be seen in the round. We must also witness the experience of those who have suffered most: some have too many memories of loss due to the Troubles and others have not enough.

The purpose of remembering is threefold: to reconcile our accounts of what happened, so that we understand each other's experiences; to publicly acknowledge and end the isolation of those who have suffered most within a culture of silence; to come to terms with the irreconcilable nature of the losses that have been sustained. None of us can retrieve what was lost. We may only learn from it.

Notes

INTRODUCTION

1. NUD.IST is a software package, which provides a facility and a system for conducting qualitative analysis of text-based data for qualitative analysis.

4 PROFILING THOSE WHO DIED IN NORTHERN IRELAND'S TROUBLES

1. See for example Benson, L. (1996) 'Communal Participatory Action Research as a Strategy for Improving Universities and the Social Sciences', *Educational Policy*, Vol. 10, June, pp. 202–22; Small, S.A. (1995) 'Action Orientated Research: Models and Methods', *Journal of Marriage and the Family*, Vol. 57, No. 4, November, pp. 941–55; Bartunek, J.M. (1993) 'Scholarly Dialogues and Participatory Action Research', *Human Relations*, Vol. 46, No. 10, October, pp. 1221–333; Greenwood, D.J. (1993) 'Participatory Action Research as a Process and as a Goal', *Human Relations*, Vol. 46, No. 2, February, pp. 175–92; Chelser, M.A. (1991), 'Participatory Action Research with Self-Help Groups', *American Journal of Community Psychology*, Vol. 9, No. 5, October, pp. 757–68; Kennedy, G.E. (1989) 'Family Life Education: Involving Students in Participatory Action Research on Fatherhood: a Case Study', *Family Relations*, Vol. 38, No. 4, October, pp. 363–70; O'Connor, P. (1987) 'Hospital Records as a Tool for Staff Education: a Participatory Research Project in Guatemala', *The Journal of Community Health*, Vol. 12, No. 2, pp. 92–107; Oliver, M. (1992) 'Changing the Social Relations of Research Production', *Disability, Handicap and Society*, Vol. 7, No. 2, pp. 101–14; Argyris, C. (1989) 'Participatory Action Research and Action Science Compared', *American Behavioural Scientist*, Vol. 32, No. 5, May, pp. 612–23; Whyte, W.F. (ed.) (1991) *Participatory Action Research*. Newbury Park, CA: Sage.

5 PATTERNS OF VIOLENCE

1. For a balanced account of labour market and social disadvantage of Catholics, see Cormack, R.J. and Osborne, R.D. (1983) *Religion, Education and Employment: Aspects of Equal Opportunity in Northern Ireland*, Belfast: Appletree.

References

Adams, G. (1986). *The Politics of Irish Freedom*. Dingle: Brandon Books.

Adams, G. (1988). *A Pathway to Peace*. Cork: Mercier.

Amnesty International (1994). *Political Killings in Northern Ireland*. London: Amnesty International.

Arthur, P. (1997). 'Reading Violence: Ireland', in Apter, D. (ed). *The Legitimization of Violence*. London: Macmillan.

Bew, P., Gibbon, P. and Patterson, H. (1979). *The State in Northern Ireland, 1921–1979, Political Forces and Social Classes*. Manchester: Manchester University Press.

Bew, P., Gibbon, P. and Patterson, H. (1995). *Northern Ireland 1921–1994: Political Forces and Social Classes*. London: Serif.

Bishop, P. and Mallie, E. (1987). *The Provisional IRA*. London: Corgi Books.

Borooah, V. et al. (1993). 'Catholic–Protestant Income Differences in Northern Ireland'. Unpublished Paper, University of Ulster.

Boyd. A. (1985). *Have the Trade Unions Failed the North?* Dublin: Mercier Press.

Boyle, K. and Hadden, T. (1985). *Ireland: A Positive Proposal*. Harmondsworth: Penguin.

Boyne, S. (1998). 'The Real IRA: After Omagh What Now?', in *Jane's Intelligence Review*, October.

Bradley, J. (1996). 'Exploring Long-Term Economic and Social Consequences of Peace and reconciliation in the Island of Ireland', paper to the Forum for Peace and Reconciliation. Dublin: Forum for Peace and Reconciliation.

Browne, V. (1982). 'In the Shadow of a Gunman', *Magill*, April.

Bruce, S. (1986). *God Save Ulster! The Religion and Politics of Paisleyism*. Oxford: Oxford University Press.

Bruce, S. (1992). *The Red Hand*. Oxford: Oxford University Press.

Bruce, S. (1994). *The Edge of the Union*. Oxford: Oxford University Press.

Buckland, P. (1979). *The Factory of Grievances: Devolved Government in Northern Ireland 1921–1939*. Dublin: Gill and Macmillan.

Buckland, P. (1981). *A History of Northern Ireland*. Dublin: Gill and Macmillan.

Burton, F. (1978). *The Politics of Legitimacy: Struggles in a Belfast Community*. London: Routledge.

Byrne, D. (1978). 'The De-industrialisation of Northern Ireland', paper to the Social Administration Annual Conference, Bristol.

Canning, D., Moore, B. and Rhodes, J. (1987). 'Economic Growth in Northern Ireland: Problems and Prospects', in Teague, P. (ed.) *Beyond the Rhetoric: Politics the Economy and Social Policy in Northern Ireland*. London: Lawrence and Wishart.

Carlin, T. (1979). Speech at the launch of the NICTU. Belfast: 'Better Life for All' campaign.

Collins, M. (ed.) (1985). *Ireland after Britain*. London: Pluto Press.

Compton, P. (ed.) (1981). 'The Contemporary Population of Northern Ireland and Population Related Issues.' Belfast: The Queen's University.

Coogan, T.P. (1995). *The Troubles: Ireland's Ordeal 1966–1995 and the Search for Peace*. London: Hutchinson.

Coopers & Lybrand (1989). *The Northern Ireland Economy: Mid Year Review*. Belfast: Coopers & Lybrand.

Coopers & Lybrand Deloitte (1990). *The Northern Ireland Economy: Review and Prospects*, Belfast: Coopers & Lybrand.

Cormack, R.J. and Osborne, R.D. (1983). *Religion, Education and Employment: Aspects of Equal Opportunity in Northern Ireland*. Belfast: Appletree.

Cost of the Troubles Study (1998). *Do You See What I See? Young People's Experiences of the Troubles in their own Words and Photographs*. Derry Londonderry: INCORE/United Nations University/University of Ulster.

Cox, W.H. (1985). 'Who Wants A United Ireland?', *Government and Opposition*, 22(3) Summer: 336–51.

Cradden, (1993). *Trade Unionism, Socialism and Partition*. Belfast: December Publications.

Curtis, L. (1984). *Ireland, the Propaganda War*. London: Pluto Press.

Cusack, J. and McDonald, H. (1997). *The UVF*. Dublin: Poolbeg.

Darby, J. (1976). *Conflict in Northern Ireland: The Development of a Polarised Community*. Dublin: Gill and Macmillan.

Darby, J. and Williamson, A. (1978). *Violence and Social Services in Northern Ireland*. London: Heinemann.

de Baroid, C. (1989). *Ballymurphy and the Irish War*. Dublin: Aisling Publishers.

Deutsch, R. and McGowan, V. (1975). *Northern Ireland 1968–1974: a Chronology of Events*. Belfast: Blackstaff.

Dillon, M. (1994). *The Enemy Within: The IRA's War Against the British*. London: Doubleday.

Eversley, D. (1989). *Religion and Employment in Northern Ireland.* London: Sage.

Fair Employment Agency (1983). *Report of an Investigation by the Fair Employment Agency into the Non-Industrial Northern Ireland Civil Service.* Belfast.

Farrell, M. (1976). *Northern Ireland; The Orange State.* London: Pluto Press.

Farrell, M. (1983). *Arming the Protestants: The Formation of the Ulster Special Constabulary and the Royal Ulster Constabulary.* London: Pluto Press.

Fay, M.T., Morrissey, M. and Smyth, M. (1997). *Mapping Troubles-related Deaths in Northern Ireland.* Derry Londonderry: INCORE (University of Ulster and the United Nations University).

Fitzgerald, G. (1972). *Towards a New Ireland.* London: Charles Knight.

Flackes, W.D. and Elliott, S. (1994). *Northern Ireland: A Political Directory 1968–1988.* Belfast: Blackstaff.

Foster, R. (1988). *Modern Ireland 1600–1972.* London: Penguin Press.

Freeman, J., Gaffikin, F. and Morrissey, M. (1987). *Making the Economy Work.* Belfast: Transport and General Workers Union.

Gaffikin, F. and Morrissey, M. (1990). *Northern Ireland: The Thatcher Years.* London: Zed Books.

Gallagher, F. (1957). *The Indivisible Island: The History of the Partition of Ireland.* London: Gollancz.

Garvin, T. (1988). 'The North and the Rest: The Politics of the Republic of Ireland', in Townshend, C. (ed.), *Consensus in Ireland: Approaches and Recessions.* Oxford: Clarendon Press.

Gibbon, P. (1975). *The Origins of Ulster Unionism: The Formation of Popular Protestant Politics and Ideology in Nineteenth Century Ireland.* Manchester: Manchester University Press.

Gillespie, N. (1997). 'Employment, Unemployment and Equality of Opportunity: an Introduction', in McLaughlin, E. and Quirk, P. (eds), *Policy Aspects of Employment Equality in Northern Ireland.* Belfast: The Standing Advisory Commission on Human Rights.

Greaves, D. (1972). *The Irish Crisis.* London: Lawrence and Wishart.

Gudgin, G. (1989). *Job Generation in Manufacturing Industry.* Belfast: Northern Ireland Economic Research Centre.

Gudgin, G. and Roper S. (1990). *The N.I. Economy: Review and Forecasts to 1995.* Belfast: Northern Ireland Economic Research Centre.

Guelke, A. (1988). *Northern Ireland: The International Perspective.* Dublin: Gill and Macmillan.

Gwynn, D. (1950). *The History of Partition (1912–1925).* Dublin: Brown and Nolan.

Hall Report (1962). 'Report of the Joint Working Party on the Economy of Northern Ireland', Cmnd 446. Belfast: HMSO.

Harris, R.I.D. (1991). *Regional Economic Policy in Northern Ireland 1945–1988.* Aldershot: Avebury.

Hartwig, F. and Dearing, B.E. (1979) *Exploratory Data Analysis.* London: Sage.

Haughton, J. (1987). 'The Historical Background', in O'Hagan, J.W. (ed.) *The Economy of Ireland.* Dublin: Irish Management Institute.

Heslinga, M.W. (1962). *The Irish Border as a Cultural Divide* (reprinted 1971). Assen: van Gorcum.

Hewitt, C. (1993). *The Consequences of Political Violence.* Aldershot: Dartmouth.

Hillyard, P. (1983). 'Law and Order', in Darby, J. (ed.) *Northern Ireland: The Background to the Conflict.* Belfast: Appletree Press.

Holland, J. and McDonald, H. (1994). *INLA: Deadly Divisions.* Dublin: TORC.

Hylands, I. (1996). Leaflet accompanying her exhibition, 'Violence: Count the Cost'.

Irish Information Partnership (1987). *Information Service on Northern Ireland Conflict and Anglo–Irish Affairs. Agenda.* London: Irish Information Partnership.

Isles, I. and Cuthbert, N. (1957). *An Economic Survey of Northern Ireland.* Belfast: HMSO.

Johnson, D.S. (1981). 'Partition and Cross-Border Trade in the 1920s', in Roebuck, P. (ed.) *Plantation to Partition.* Belfast: Blackstaff Press.

Kelley, K. (1988). *The Longest War: Northern Ireland and the IRA.* London: Zed Press.

Kennedy, L. (1989). *Two Ulsters: A Case for Repartition.* Belfast: the author.

Kenny, A. (1986). *The Road to Hillsborough: The Shaping of the Anglo–Irish Agreement.* Oxford: Pergamon.

Kilbrandon, Lord (1984). *Northern Ireland: Report of an Independent Inquiry, Chairman Lord Kilbrandon* (the Kilbrandon Report). London: Independent Inquiry.

Labour Force Survey (1990). Department of Economic Development, Statistics Board, Belfast.

Lyons, F.S.L. (1971). *Ireland Since the Famine*. London: Weidenfeld & Nicolson.

McAuley, P. and Kremer, J.M.D. (1990). 'On the Fringes of Society: Adults and Children in a West Belfast Community', *New Community* 16(2): 247–59.

McCann, E. (1974). *War and an Irish Town*. Harmondsworth: Penguin.

McCartney, R., Hall, S., Somers, B., Smyth, G., McCracken, H.L. and Smith, P. (1981). 'The Unionist Case'. Belfast: Unpublished Typescript.

McGarry, J. and O'Leary, B. (1993a). *The Politics of Ethnic Conflict Regulation*. London: Routledge.

McGarry, J. and O'Leary, B. (1993b). *The Politics of Antagonism*. London: Athlone Press.

McGarry, J. and O'Leary, B. (1995). *Explaining Northern Ireland*. Oxford: Blackwell.

Machel, Grac'a (1996). *Impact of Armed Conflict on Children*. United Nations Department for Policy Co-ordination and Sustainable Development (DPCSD), August, Geneva.

McKeown, M. (1977). 'Considerations on the Statistics of Violence', *Fortnight*, 5: 4–5.

McKeown, M. (1989). *Two Six Seven Three: An Analysis of Fatalities Attributable to Civil Disturbances in Northern Ireland in the Twenty Years between July 13, 1969 and July 12, 1989*. Lucan: Murlough.

McKittrick, D. (1989). *Dispatches from Belfast*. Belfast: Blackstaff.

Martin, J. (1982). 'The Conflict in Northern Ireland; Marxist Interpretations', *Capital and Class*, 18 (Winter): 56–71.

Miller, D. (1978). *Queen's Rebels: Ulster Loyalism in Historical Perspective*. Dublin: Gill and Macmillan.

Mitchell, J.K. (1979). 'Social Violence in Northern Ireland'. *Geographical Review* (April): 179–200.

Moloney, E. and Pollack, A. (1986). *Paisley*. Swords: Poolbeg.

Morrissey, H.. (1982). 'Unemployment in the Inter-War Years', in Morrissey, M. (ed.) *The Other Crisis: Unemployment in Northern Ireland*. Belfast: PIRC.

Murphy, D. (1978). *A Place Apart*. London: John Murray.

Murray, R. (1982). 'Political Violence in Northern Ireland 1969–1977', in Boal, F.W. and Douglas, J.N.H. (eds) *Integration and Division: Geographical Perspectives on the Northern Ireland Problem*, pp. 309–22. London: Academic Press.

New Ireland Forum (1983–84). *Report of Proceedings*, Nos 1–13. Dublin: Stationery Office.

Northern Ireland Economic Council (April 1989). *Economic Assessment*. Belfast.

Northern Ireland Economic Council (1989). *Autumn Economic Review*. Belfast.

Northern Ireland Economic Council (1991). *Autumn Economic Review*. Belfast.

Northern Ireland Economic Council (1998). *A Framework for Economic Development: the Implications for Northern Ireland of the 1998 UK and EU Budgets and the Chancellor's Economic Strategy for Northern Ireland*, Report 127. Belfast.

Northern Ireland Victims' Commission (1988). 'We Will Remember Them: The Report of the Northern Ireland Victims' Commissioner, Sir Kenneth Bloomfield KCB'. Belfast: The Stationery Office.

O'Brien, B. (1993). *The Long War: The IRA and Sinn Fein from 1985 to Today*. Dublin: O'Brien Press.

O'Brien, C.C. (1972). *States of Ireland*. London: Hutchinson.

O'Connor, E. (1992). *A Labour History of Ireland, 1824–1960*. Dublin: Gill and Macmillan.

O'Connor, F. (1993). *In Search of a State: Catholics in Northern Ireland*. Belfast: Blackstaff Press.

O'Doherty, M. (1998). *The Trouble with Guns*. Belfast: Blackstaff Press.

O'Dowd, L., Rolston, B. and Tomlinson, M. (1981). *Northern Ireland: From Civil Rights to Civil War*. London: CSE Books.

O'Duffy, B. (1993). 'Containment or Regulation? The British Approach to Ethnic Conflict in Northern Ireland', in McGarry, J. and O'Leary, B. (eds) *The Politics of Ethnic Conflict Regulation*. London: Routledge.

O'Duffy, R. and O'Leary, B. (1990). 'Violence in Northern Ireland 1969–June 1989', in McGarry, J. and O'Leary, B. (eds) *The Future of Northern Ireland*. Oxford: Clarendon Press.

O'Halloran, C. (1987). *Partition and the Limits of Irish Nationalism: An Ideology Under Stress*. Dublin: Gill and Macmillan.

O'Hegarty, P.S. (1952). *A History of Ireland under the Union 1801–1922*. London: Methuen.

O'Leary, B. (1985). 'Explaining Northern Ireland: A Brief Study Guide', *Politics*, 5(1) (April): 69–74.

O'Leary, B. and McGarry, J. (1993). *The Politics of Antagonism: Understanding Northern Ireland*. London: Athlone Press.

O'Malley, P. (1983). *The Uncivil Wars: Ireland Today*. Belfast: Blackstaff.

O'Neill, T. (1972). *The Autobiography of Terence O'Neill.* London: Ruper Hart-Davies.

Paisley, I., Robinson, P. and Taylor, J. (1982). *Ulster: The Facts.* Belfast: Crown Publications.

Patterson, H. (1980). *Class Conflict and Sectarianism: The Protestant Working Class and the Belfast Labour Movement 1868–1920.* Belfast: Ulster Polytechnic.

Policy, Planning and Research Unit, Economics Division (1991). *Monthly Economic Report,* November. Belfast.

Policy, Planning and Research Unit, Department of Finance and Personnel (1993). *1992 Labour Force Survey: Religion Report.* Belfast.

Poole, M. (1983). 'The Demography of Violence' in Darby, J. (ed.) *Northern Ireland: the Background to the Conflict.* Belfast: Appletree Press.

Poole, M. (1993). 'The Spatial Distribution of Political Violence in Northern Ireland: An Update to 1993', in O'Day, A. (ed.) *Terrorism's Laboratory: The Case of Northern Ireland.* Aldershot: Dartmouth.

Porter, N. (1996). *Rethinking Unionism.* Belfast: Blackstaff Press.

PPRU (1989) Department of Finance, Northern Ireland.

PPRU Monitor (Feb. 1993). Department of Finance, Northern Ireland Office, Belfast.

Probert, B. (1978). *Beyond Orange and Green.* London: Zed Press.

Punamaki, P.L. (1988). 'Political Violence and Mental Health', *International Journal of Mental Health,* 17(4): 3–15.

The Quigley Report (1976). Belfast: Department of Finance and Personnel.

'Regional Trends' (1976, 1981, 1989, 1996) Central Statistical Office, London.

Robson, B. et al. (1994). *Relative Deprivation in Northern Ireland.* Belfast: PPRU.

Rolston, B. and Miller, D. (1996). *War and Words: the Northern Ireland Media Reader.* Belfast: Beyond the Pale Publications.

Rolston, B. and Tomlinson, M. (1989). *Winding Up West Belfast.* Belfast: Obair.

Rose, R. (1971). *Governing Without Consensus: An Irish Perspective.* London: Faber and Faber.

Rowan, B. (1995). *Behind the Lines: the Story of the IRA and Loyalist Cease-fires.* Belfast: Blackstaff.

Rowthorn, B. and Wayne, N. (1984). *Northern Ireland: The Political Economy of Conflict.* Cambridge: Polity Press.

RUC (1990–97). *Statistical Information.* Belfast.

Schellenberg, J.A. (1977). 'Area Variations of Violence in Northern Ireland', *Sociological Focus*, 10: 69–78.

Scott, R. (1993). 'Long-Term Unemployment and Policy Response in Northern Ireland', in Northern Ireland Economic Research Centre, *Unemployment Forever?* Belfast.

Shearman, H. (1942). *Not an Inch: A Study of Northern Ireland and Lord Craigavon.* London: Faber and Faber.

Smith, M.R.L. (1995). *Fighting for Ireland: the Military Strategy of the IRA.* London: Routledge.

Smyth, J. (1995). 'Poking at the Entrails', *Fortnight*, November.

Smyth, M. (1995). *Sectarian Division and Area Planning: a Commentary on the Derry Area Plan 2011.* Derry Londonderry: Templegrove Action Research.

Smyth, M. (1996a). *Hemmed In and Hacking It: Life in Two Enclave Areas in Northern Ireland: Words and Images from The Fountain and Gobnascale.* Derry Londonderry: Guildhall Press.

Smyth, M. (1996b). *A Report of a Public Hearing on the Experiences of Minorities in Derry Londonderry.* Derry Londonderry: Templegrove Action Research.

Smyth, M. (1996c). *A Report of a Series of Public Discussions on Aspects of Sectarian Division in Derry Londonderry, held in the period December 1994–June 1995.* Derry Londonderry: Templegrove Action Research.

Smyth, M. (1996d). *Two Policy Papers: Policing and Sectarian Division* (with Ruth Moore) and *Urban Regeneration and Sectarian Division.* Derry Londonderry: Templegrove Action Research.

Smyth, M. (1996e). *Three Conference Papers on Aspects of Sectarian Division: Researching Sectarianism: Borders within Border: Material and Ideological Aspects of Sectarian Division;* and *Limitations on the Capacity for Citizenship in Post-cease-fires Northern Ireland.* Derry Londonderry: Templegrove Action Research.

Smyth, M. (1996f). *Life in Two Enclave Areas in Northern Ireland. A Field Survey in Derry Londonderry after the Cease-fires.* Derry Londonderry: Templegrove Action Research.

Smyth, M. (1998). *Half the Battle: Understanding the Impact of the Troubles on Children and Young People.* Derry Londonderry: INCORE (University of Ulster/United Nations University).

Smyth, M. and Hayes, P. (1994) 'Post Traumatic Stress Disorder and Victims of Violence in Northern Ireland. The Case of the Families of Bloody Sunday Victims', paper to the European Regional Conference of the World Federation for Mental Health, Belfast.

Stewart, A.T.Q. (1977). *The Narrow Ground: Aspects of Ulster 1609–1969*. London: Faber and Faber.

Sutton, M. (1994). *An Index of Deaths from the Conflict in Ireland 1969–1993*. Belfast: Beyond the Pale.

Taylor, C.L. and Jodice, D.A. (1983). *World Handbook of Political and Social Indicators, Volume III, 1948–1977*. Ann Arbor.

Taylor, P. (1997). PROVOS: *The IRA and Sinn Fein*. London: Bloomsbury.

Tomlinson, M. (1994). *25 Years On: the Costs of War and the Dividends of Peace*. Belfast: West Belfast Economic Forum.

Trewsdale, J. (1980). *Unemployment in Northern Ireland, 1974–79*. Belfast: Northern Ireland Economic Council.

Unemployment Unit (various years) *Unemployment Unit Bulletin*. London.

Whyte, J. (1991). *Interpreting Northern Ireland*. Oxford: Clarendon Press.

Whyte, W.F. (ed.) (1991). *Participatory Action Research*. Newbury Park, CA: Sage.

Wilson, D. (1985). *An End to Silence*. Cork: Mercier.

Wilson, R. (1994). 'In a Trench or a Hole', *Fortnight*, March.

Wright, F. (1987). *Northern Ireland: A Comparative Analysis*. Dublin: Gill and Macmillan.

Index

Note: The Chronology of Key Events (pages 25 to 50) has not been indexed. **Bold** page numbers refer to Tables and Figures.